I0889756

Race Relations in the Bahamas, 1784–1834

BLACK COMMUNITY STUDIES

Willard B. Gatewood, General Editor

WHITTINGTON B. JOHNSON

Race Relations in the Bahamas, 1784–1834

The Nonviolent Transformation from a Slave to a Free Society

THE UNIVERSITY OF ARKANSAS PRESS

Fayetteville 2000

Copyright © 2000 by Whittington B. Johnson

All rights reserved
Manufactured in the United States of America

04 03 02 01 00 5 4 3 2 1

Designer: Sheila Hart

⊗ The paper used in this publication meets the minimum requirements of the American National Standard for Permanence of Paper for Printed Library Materials Z39.48-1984.

Library of Congress Cataloging-in-Publication Data

Johnson, Whittington Bernard, 1931–
Race relations in the Bahamas, 1784–1834 : the nonviolent transformation from a slave to a free society / Whittington B. Johnson.
p. cm. — (Black community studies)
Includes bibliographical references (p. -) and index.
ISBN 1-55728-570-5 (cloth : alk. paper)
1. Free Blacks—Bahamas—History. 2. Bahamas—Race relations. 3. Bahamas—History. I. Title. II. Series.
F1660.B55J64 2000
972.96'00496—dc21 99-41379
CIP

To Thomas Pearson Johnson, 1899–
My uncle and Johnson family patriarch

Acknowledgments

I am among a minority of fortunate Americanists who have had an opportunity to conduct research in Nassau, Bahamas, and London, England. In fact, my colleagues in the History Department at the University of Miami questioned whether I really made summer research trips to the Bahamas and England, or were these merely junkets. Publication of this volume should answer the question for them. Speaking of Nassau, Bahamas, I am indebted to the staff of the Department of Archives for its courteous assistance during my visits to the research room of the archives. Lulamae Gray, Prudence Morris, and Anna Christie were especially helpful. Sherriley Strachan, Jolton Johnson, David Wood, and other staff personnel helped when called upon. Similarly, I am indebted to the staffs of the Public Record Office (Kew), the British Library and Museum, the British Library Newspaper Library (Colindale), and Rhodes House Library, Oxford University, for their help in securing requested sources. Moreover, I thank the library staff of the Richter Library, University of Miami, for ordering books and microfilm through interlibrary loan and locating materials that my tired eyes could not find in the library.

The University of Miami generously provided research funds to underwrite my trips to the Bahamas and England. Throughout the research, indeed, throughout their years at the university, the provost, dean, and department chairman have been very supportive. I am especially grateful to

Paul Blaney, interim dean of the College of Arts and Sciences (1996–97), for providing research funds in the summer of 1997. The staff of the History Department, Jesus Sanchez, Lenny del Granado, and Kathryn Harrison, never tired of answering my telephone calls, assembling my mail, typing letters, and acceding to a host of other requests when I was on sabbatical leave the school year of 1996–97, when most of the work on this volume was completed. My university family have been just great. I am also indebted to my church family, especially the vestry and chalice bearers/lay readers of the Episcopal Church of the Incarnation (Miami, Florida) who substituted for me for the long periods I was away on research trips, and to my priest, the Reverend J. Kenneth Major, for tolerating a part-time senior warden of the parish for much of the past three years.

It is delightful to have friends like Donald Spivey (former chairman of the History Department), Timothy S. Huebner, Vincent Thompson, and Kathy Gordon, who all graciously agreed to read the manuscript with a discerning eye. D. Gail Saunders, director of the Department of Archives, Nassau, Bahamas, always welcomed me when I used the archives reading room. Howard Johnson graciously agreed to read the manuscript of a total stranger. I thank all these persons for their opinions, but assume total responsibility for any shortcomings in the work.

Finally, I thank my family: Toni Lyn Johnson-Thomas, who has left the nest, Traci-liegh, and Todd Lennard continue to make *father* a cherished word for me. My wife, Gene, besides being an excellent cook and a full-time high school counselor, acted as my research assistant during a trip to Nassau, Bahamas, and on trips to England, in addition to keeping me well fed. She is the indispensable person in my life.

This was indeed a labor of love because of the many fine people who helped with it and because the work concerns a place that is special to me: the Bahama Islands, the birthplace of my deceased parents. My mother was born in Matthew Town, Inagua Island, and my father in Hatchet Bay, Eleuthera Island. Since I was born in Miami, I cannot claim to be Bahamian, but I am a "descendant," as my aunts and uncles constantly reminded me during my childhood.

Contents

Illustrations and Tables

Introduction

The Islands comprised under the general name of Bahama Islands are so numerous . . . all of them have Not hitherto obtained names.
—Governor Thomas Shirley, 1768
—C.O. 23/22/59

Although free blacks and persons of color comprised a smaller percentage of the population than either slaves or Europeans, this group was far more active on the islands in effecting changes in race relations than were the slaves. Moreover, free blacks and persons of color were in the vanguard of the movement to build churches and schools for blacks and coloreds, and they worked to carve a niche in the economy. Similarly, they were forceful and articulate allies of colonial governors in the fight to win concessions from stubborn white leaders who were reluctant participants in the movement to end slavery and remove civil disabilities; and, together with liberated Africans, they constituted a significant part of the land-based military defense of the Bahama Islands. In short, free blacks and persons of color were the major players, among nonwhites, in pushing for humanitarian reforms, carving a niche for free nonwhite labor in the economy, and institutionalizing a mixture of African-British-American customs in Bahamian society. While the group's small size is dwarfed by that of the slave population, free blacks and persons of color loom large in their contributions to race relations during the period.

The Bahama Islands is different from its sister islands in the British West Indies in that it is composed of many islands rather than a single landmass. Gail Saunders, in *Slavery in the Bahamas, 1648–1848,* groups the islands into three occupational categories—agricultural, salt, and other—and she includes twice as many islands in the agricultural category as in the other two categories combined.[1] B. W. Higman's *Slave Populations of the British Caribbean, 1807–1834* places the Bahamas in a category that he calls marginal colonies, because they did not produce major agricultural export staples.[2] Which is the true Bahamas, Saunders' or Higman's? Both historians have accurately depicted the economic status of the Bahamas, where the inhabitants continued to farm—but mainly for domestic consumption—long after the cotton kingdom collapsed. The Bahamas' inability to grow exportable produce placed it in the bottom tier of colonies and resulted in the grant of only a small share of the funds awarded to colonies as compensation for manumitting their slaves; it received a mere £128,296 out of the allocated £20,000,000.[3] Similarly, the Bahamas receives a small share of attention from historians in general accounts of the British West Indies, accounts which tend to focus on large colonies such as Jamaica, Barbados, Trinidad, and a few others. In spite of this, the history of the colony has not been neglected over the years. Michael Craton and Gail Saunders' *Islanders in the Stream: A History of the Bahamian People* is the best general history of the islands. Other notable general accounts are A. Deans Peggs's *A Short History of the Bahamas,* Michael Craton's *A History of the Bahamas,* Paul Albury's *A Story of the Bahamas*, and Howard Johnson's *The Bahamas from Slavery to Servitude,* 1783–1933.[4] Saunders' work on slavery is the best on that subject. However, none of the works devote much attention to free blacks and persons of color; neither do they address the issue of race relations from 1784 to 1834, the half century between the advent of the Loyalists and the enactment of the Manumission Act. This study aims at addressing that void in the literature.

Free blacks and persons of color is the expression generally used throughout the study when referring to free nonwhites because this is the characterization that is usually found in the documents. Free blacks and persons of color probably did not interact socially as a general practice, seldom intermarried, and formed separate militia units. On the other hand, they attended the same churches and schools, worked in the same occupations, lived in the same neighborhoods, labored under the same legal encumbrances, and collaborated on petitions to end discriminatory legislation against them. Nevertheless, the constant appearance of "free blacks and persons of color" in the documents and the identifying of nonwhites by color in church documents suggest that a mind-set was present that perceived blacks and persons of color as separate groups. Moreover, this is probably the way nonwhites of that day referred to themselves, if text of their wills is indicative of the vernacular, because the expressions *free black* and *free person of color*, along with the gender of the departed, often appear in the title and text of wills.

There were times, however, when the term *free persons of color* may have been used to include both blacks and coloreds. Thus, using the terms *free blacks and persons of color* does not imply that the Bahamas had a mulatto aristocracy; recognition of color differences among nonwhites really amounted to a distinction without a difference. Nevertheless, this study departs from the usual practice and identifies nonwhites by color: black and colored.

The Loyalists arrived in the Bahamas at a time when the abolitionists were in the ascendancy in Great Britain and the Colonial Office came under their influence. This resulted in the abolition of the slave trade from Africa (1807), followed by the amelioration period (1823–1833), and ultimately the Manumission Act, which both the English Parliament (1833) and the Bahamas legislature (1834) passed. This succession of events caused tensions between the Assembly of the Bahamas and Britain. Although the assembly did not lodge loud protests against the abolition of the slave trade, mainly because by the time it was implemented the islands had more slaves than duties for them to perform, in the wake of the debacle in cotton production, that body did protest loudly against a result of that act: the capturing of Africans off slave ships. These Africans were then brought into the Bahamas and freed. These "liberated Africans," as they have been called, were subsequently apprenticed for a period, supposedly to acclimate them prior to restoring their lost freedom. The outcry over stationing units from the West India Regiments, all black troops, most of whom were African born, in New Providence was much louder and more anguished than the outcry over the issue of liberated Africans. The British adopted this policy because of the high mortality rate among the European troops sent to the West Indies, but the assembly was oblivious to Britain's concerns about the immense losses among its European troops at a time when France posed a serious threat to English sovereignty. White settlers were concerned about the threat posed by armed black troops in their midst. The assembly did not protest as vehemently over the mandated amelioration reforms, except for the ban on flogging female slaves, but it did harp on the point that the reforms infringed upon the property rights of slaveholders. Therefore, throughout the period encompassed in this study, Britain and the Bahamas were on opposite sides of the race relations issue, with Britain proposing progressive reforms and the assembly protesting against these.

Prior to 1784, however, the situation was different. A cursory look at the early history of the Bahama Islands reveals few bumps along the pathway of its first century and a half, which began in 1629 when the British first occupied the islands.[5] Settlement occurred almost a decade after the Pilgrims landed in Provincetown, along the New England coast, and a few years before Lord Baltimore established his colony in Maryland. The first Africans in the Bahamas were brought to Eleuthera from Bermuda when authorities there banished all free blacks and some unruly slaves to that island.[6] Captain William Sayle, one-time governor of Bermuda, gave the name Eleuthera, taken from a Greek word meaning freedom, to the island as a tribute to the Puritans who settled there in the hope of enjoying liberty of conscience.[7] Sayle also named the main island of the Bahamas Providence when he was forced to land there on his way to the Carolinas.[8] Later "New" was added to the name of the island to distinguish it from the little island of Old Providence, which is located to the west of the Mosquito shore.[9] Andros Island, located twenty miles west of New Providence, was so named by the Carolina proprietors, who, in honor of Sir Edmund Andros, a person with close ties to two of the Carolina proprietors (the Earl of Craven and Sir George Carteret), received a charter in 1670 for the Bahama Islands from Charles II.[10] For more than a century, therefore, the Bahamas had close political ties with the Carolinas, especially with South Carolina; and the economic ties established then continued well beyond the American Revolution.

Although the Bahamas was established concomitantly with the British North American colonies and it had close political ties to the well-connected Carolina proprietors, the islands did not grow at the same rate as those colonies. This is evident in population figures of a 1723 report that Captain George Phenney, governor of the Bahamas, submitted to his superiors in response to queries from the Colonial Office: "There are about five hundred whites and two hundred negroes on this Island of Providence; about two hundred whites and forty Negroes on Elathera [Eleuthera]; and about one hundred and thirty whites and twenty negroes on Harbour Island."[11] Providence (the name change had not then occurred) had emerged as the largest and principal island by this time. Few islands had settlers, and whites were in a majority on all the inhabited islands. The relatively small ratio of blacks to whites suggests that economic activities were not of the labor intensive kind that required large numbers of slaves.

Complaints of Governor Phenney that economic growth and the emergence of a landowning class were retarded because the settlers did not have security of tenure on the land they occupied resulted in action to correct the situation.[12] Accordingly, in 1728 the Privy Council authorized the creation of a general assembly; and on September 29, 1729, that body met for the first time.[13] So, almost a century after the first settlers planted their roots in the Bahamas representative government was introduced. This is much longer than the process took in the North American colonies, where it took New York longer, almost twenty years after the Dutch were defeated, than any other colony. In most of the other colonies representative assemblies were established almost immediately, once the precedent was set in Jameston, Virginia, on an uncomfortably hot August day in 1619.

The population of the Bahamas and inhabited islands expanded over time. Governor Thomas Shirley, one of the two Shirleys to occupy the position, reported in 1772 that New Providence had 1,024 whites and 1,800 "reputed" blacks, Harbour Island had 410 whites and 90 blacks, Eleuthera had 509 whites and 237 blacks, Exuma Island had 6 whites and 24 blacks, Cat Island had 3 whites and about 40 blacks, and Turks Islands had about 150 whites and blacks.[14] By this time blacks constituted a small majority of the population, but New Providence was the only large island, so to speak, with a black majority; blacks were in a decided minority on Harbour Island, and whites outnumbered blacks by two to one on Eleuthera Island. So, New Providence was really an aberration. It had rural and urban areas similar to the situation in Chatham County (Savannah), Georgia, and Charleston County (Charleston), South Carolina. Moreover, New Providence had a black majority like Charleston County, South Carolina.

Marine occupations were the main means of livelihood, with seafaring leading the way. Ships were built in the Bahamas and conducted trade between North America, mainly South Carolina, and the Bahamas since the Bahamian fruits did not find a market in either Britain or the Continent. In fact, the Bahamas engaged in relatively little trade with the mother country, as the trade figures of 1771 and 1772 indicate. In the former year the value of goods exported to Britain was $2,650, and in the latter it was $1,750.15 Governor Montforte Browne, who arrived in the colony in October 1774, praised shipbuilders for their constuction of a beautiful twenty-gun ship that compared favorably with frigates built in Great Britain. He nevertheless blamed Bahamians, whom he called lazy, for the economic underdevelopment of the colony. The governor said, for instance, Bahamians failed to capitalize on opportunities to establish a whaling industry in the colony, leaving it to New England whalers to profit from this resource. The governor cited one example of a small New England sloop that made nearly three hundred casks of spermaceti oil and sold them in New England (Boston and Rhode Island) for about one dollar a gallon.[16]

Governor Browne was even more critical of the manner in which the soil was butchered and forests were destroyed. Speaking of this destructive practice, he said: "These people now range from island to island, and so soon as the land in one place refuse to yield its increase agreeable to their expectations, or the timber by the distance from the place of cutting becomes troublesome, they immediately change to a situation more convenient and more profitable, which they first strip of all its valuable timber for exportation, to the French and Dutch Island and then burn the land to such a degree, that after yielding two or three crops it becomes impoverished, and vegetation so completely destroyed, that it can scarcely recover itself in ten years."[17]

Soil butchery was not unique to the Bahamas. Their North American counterparts engaged in it also, but without the same consequences because the soil was richer and more plentiful. In the Bahamas, however, soil butchery exacerbated an existing unpromising situation occasioned by very poor soil. Although the soil yielded a small crop of corn and an abundance of fruits, the future of the colony lay in growing cotton, according to the governor: "The only commodity that may be considered a staple is most certainly cotton, which with a trifling encouragement from home, may be raised in the most flattering abundance, and of a superior quality to any I have seen."[18] This suggests that a small quantity of cotton was probably grown in the Bahamas before the Loyalists arrived. As events later show, however, the governor's notion about cotton production was misguided. He doubtless associated cotton growing with long summers and short winters, without giving due attention to other factors, such as soil and climatic conditions. As a consequence, Governor Browne was wrong on that score. The Bahamas was not suited to become a cotton kingdom.

The large slave population in New Providence alluded to earlier may have resulted from early efforts to grow cotton on the island. The increase in the slave population did not lead to a rush to pass stringent legislation controlling the behavior of slaves, free blacks, and free persons of color. As a matter of fact, instead of regimenting the lives of blacks the assembly concluded that free blacks and persons of color had the same obligation to defend the colony as the whites. Hence all whites, free blacks, and free persons of color between the ages of sixteen and sixty were required to serve in the militia. During Governor William Shirley's administration, the colonial militia consisted of 300 men who were divided into two companies, one of which probably consisted of free blacks and persons of color. Later the same number of men was divided into three companies.[19] The presence of the militia did not dissuade an American force of eight vessels and 550 men from invading New Providence in March 1776, defeating the outnumbered and outgunned defenders, taking the governor and several others prisoner, and returning with them to America. The signal to assemble in Fort Nassau and repel the invaders was the drumbeat.[20] Was this the usual manner of sounding the alarm, or was the drumbeat used to summon blacks, perhaps even slaves?

When the governor was released, he returned to New Providence and immediately became embroiled in a dispute with the legislature, which he accused of cowardice in the face of the American invaders. The council responded with an attack on its own, accusing Governor Browne of tolerating many irregularities in his administration.[21] This bickering between the two branches of government continued in subsequent administrations, degenerating into intense hostility on a few occasions after the Loyalists arrived, with the nadir being reached during the administration of Governor James Carmichael Smyth in the early 1830s over amelioration of the slaves' conditions. Over time, the assembly gained a well-deserved reputation for being obstreperous.

Shortly after fighting stopped in the American Revolution, the Bahamas came under two attacks. The first came from the Spaniards, who had fought on the side of the Americans, not out of sympathy for the cause but because France, the Americans' ally, dangled the prospect of regaining Gibraltar, which Spain was forced to cede to Britain in 1713. The Spaniards attacked New Providence in May 1782 and took control of the Bahamas.[22] A year later, the Americans returned, this time led by the Loyalist major Andrew Deveaux of South Carolina, who defeated the Spaniards only to learn later that the military operation was unnecessary because Britain and Spain had signed an agreement switching islands—East Florida for the Bahama Islands.[23] This set the stage for the arrival of the Loyalists in 1784.

Once they learned that East Florida was no longer a possession of Great Britian, the Loyalists, the eighteenth-century version of the seventeenth-century Plymouth Pilgrims, but with political baggage rather than religious convictions as their identifying mark, probably began to wonder whether they had used good judgment in casting their lot with the Crown. They had nothing to show for it but grief. On the other hand, the so-called "bad guys," the Patriots, instead of spending time in the Tower of London waiting to join Mary Queen of Scots, another so-called traitor, were now the proud leaders of a new nation, and they would later be called, in reverence, the Founding Fathers. For some Loyalists, the move to the Bahamas would be their second in less than three years. Moving their families and personal property, including slaves, was demanding; leaving behind the soil that they had tilled and the homes that they had built was demoralizing. From all appearances, the Loyalists kept coming up short.

British leaders were sensitive to the Loyalists' situation and they tried hard to ease the transition by providing generous land grants and underwriting the travel expenses to the Bahamas.[24] This eased the disappointment, but did not eradicate it. There were still many unanswered questions. The land grants seemed generous, but what kind of land were they getting? In an attempt to answer this question, Lewis Johnson, former member of the Georgia Council, visited New Providence, and he was not impressed with it: "I think it very doubtful, whether more than 8, or so negroes could be profitably employed on any one plantation I have seen," he said.[25] The report of Lieutenant John Wilson, a British engineer stationed in St. Augustine who was ordered to the Bahamas by Sir General Guy Carleton, British commander in charge, to evaluate the situation, was not as disheartening as Johnson's, but neither was it a ringing endorsement. Wilson said Indian corn, other vegetables, and fruits held great promise for skillful planters. This was a dig at Bahamians, whom he believed were lazy and did not till the soil properly.[26] It is significant that Wilson did not say the soil was conducive for planting cotton, the crop Loyalists were bent upon planting.

Diverse groups of Loyalists converged on the Bahamas from many parts of the United States: New York, Virginia, North Carolina, South Carolina, and Georgia. From the port of New York came 1,458, at least half of whom were British soldiers and some of whom were free African Americans.[27] Moreover, they came from East Florida. At the time of the scheduled departure, there were four classes of blacks in East Florida: (1) those absolutely free, (2) those deserving their freedom under British proclamation, (3) those belonging to British subjects known to be their owners, and (4) those strolling about without known masters.[28] Free blacks from East Florida signed on to move to the Bahamas, even though it was a slave society; but many free blacks in other regions refused to settle in an area "where traffick in slaves [was] carried on." This forced cancellation of plans to establish free black settlements in the West Indies.[29]

What did the new arrivals see upon disembarking? Only a few of the islands, namely Providence, Harbour Island, Long Island, Exuma Island,

Eleuthera, Turks Islands, and Abaco Island were inhabited in 1784. The white population, roughly about 1,750, was mainly English, Scotch, and Irish. The nonwhite population numbered about 2,333, most of whom were slaves. The Out Islands (presently called the Family Islands) generally consisted of uninhabited and uncultivated farmland.[30] In Nassau, on the other hand, the new arrivals were greeted by the sight of a town whose only public building was a delapidated courthouse and jail.[31] Much to the dismay of the Loyalists, the Bahamas was not as developed as the places in North America they had left behind, but at least it was a permanent home.

Arguably, 1784 was the first major turning point in the history of the Bahamas, and 1834 was the second. The former witnessed the advent of the Loyalists with its attendant accomplishments and changes, some positive and some negative. The physical, political, cultural, and religious landscape changed after 1784 as the Loyalists introduced new types of architecture, a newspaper, and cultural events; they built churches, roads, government buildings and introduced dissenting religious groups. They tried to fashion the economy in a manner and direction similar to the plantation system in the American South, but failed. Without trying to do so, they contributed to the destabilization of race relations by resisting efforts of the Colonial Office to implement reforms beneficial to blacks and coloreds, both slave and free. Moreover, they fostered racial polarization through the laws and the social customs that were introduced to herald the triumph of king cotton.

Thus, unlike the previous century and a half, to which the plantation system was foreign and disagreements with Great Britain over race relations were uncommon, the fifty years from 1784 to 1834, bracketed on one end by the advent of American Loyalists and on the other by passage of the Manumission Act in the Bahamas legislature, were marked by a succession of disagreements between Britain and the Bahamas over race relations, with Britain prevailing in each instance and the dire predictions of colonial leaders failing to materialize. Moreover, conditions for free blacks and persons of color became more favorable in the Bahamas than in the American South, and Bahamian slaves generally endured less suffering than their counterparts in the other British West Indies colonies. Finally, although disagreements between Britain and the Bahamas over race relations were often heated, they were never violent. Consequently, those fifty years marked a nonviolent transformation from a slave to a free society.

CHAPTER I

Politics and Economics in the Cotton Kingdom, 1784–1815

Free people of color do enjoy the same rights of Property . . .
as white inhabitants, and are secured in their persons and property
by the same laws, which protect the white inhabitants.
—Peter Edwards, December 1815

The British permitted the Bahama Islands to exercise control over its political affairs; it was the only nonplantation colony to achieve this status. In the sugar colonies, in contrast, all early ones had their own planter-controlled legislatures by the end of the seventeenth century.[1] Authorized by the Privy Council in 1728, the General Assembly of the Bahama Islands first met on September 29, 1729.[2] By the time the Loyalists arrived in 1784, Bahamians had become accustomed to representative government, and the size of the assembly had grown to twenty. New Providence Island had the largest delegation (eight), representing Nassau and the Eastern and Western Districts of the island. Abaco Island and Exuma Island each had three assemblymen, Andros Island and Harbour Island each had two, and Long Island and Eleuthera each had one.[3] Turks Island steadfastly refused to send a delegation, though authorized to do so. The governor appointed the council, the other house in the bicameral legislature, and, in turn, the Home Government appointed him. Free blacks and persons of color did not sit in the legislature or vote for its members, although no laws barred them from participating. This de facto disfranchisement was nonetheless as binding as if there were laws prohibiting the practice. Furthermore, they could not testify in court, except in cases involving debt, and were barred from jury duty.[4] From a political perspective, therefore, the Bahama Islands was a closed society dominated by the white male minority, a common practice in the English-controlled portion of the Western Hemisphere.

The economic situation was different in that free blacks and persons of color could legally own real and personal property, including slaves, and engage in different types of economic activities, but could not sell liquors and suffered from restrictions on trading and planting.[5] This was the situation when the Loyalists arrived and there were no policy changes afterwards. The political and economic scenes offered contrasting pictures about blacks and persons of color. In the former, they were not an integral part of the process, but in the latter, they were highly visible.

The Loyalists and Governor John Maxwell, who replaced Governor Browne, had a mutual dislike for each other. The governor was highly critical of the manner in which some Loyalists disregarded agreements made with slaves, to whom they had promised freedom upon reaching the Bahamas. He alleged that "some of the venders came to the possession of them [slaves] in no other way than that of plunder and false promises."[6] For their part, the Loyalists accused the governor of being an enemy of American Loyalists who had settled in the Bahamas and said that he "greatly retarded and obstructed the settlement and population" of the Bahamas.[7] One group of Loyalists, the East Florida group who formed the core of opposition to him and his successor, also criticized Governor Maxwell for acting tyrannically and attempting to deny them the right of trial by jury. They also criticized some of the laws, claiming they were repugnant to British laws and demanding their reform.[8] Responding to these as well as other criticisms, the governor said, "I am sorry to say it, the cap fits a great many of them (altho there are some exceptions) but certain it is there are many it will fit without making their head ache, tho it might their hearts."[9]

These Loyalists were divided into two camps: the one from East Florida composed of merchant-planters and the one from West Florida that was snubbed by the easterners.[10] The East Florida group warmly praised Governor Patrick Tonyn of East Florida and probably hoped that he would become governor of the Bahamas.[11] This was the perception of the new governor of Florida, Manuel de Zespedes, who, at any rate, accused Tonyn of delaying his departure from Florida because he expected to be appointed governor of the Bahamas.[12] Given the partiality of the East Florida Loyalists toward Tonyn and their dislike of Maxwell, a feud between the two was almost inevitable. The Conchs (older white settlers) and the West Florida group formed an alliance with the governor against the larger East Florida Loyalists.

The bickering led to Governor Maxwell's recall in 1785. Although he retained the title of governor, he never returned to the islands after leaving, and a lieutenant governor, James Edward Powell, was sent to run the colony. Powell, who died after a long illness, served only seven months, the shortest tenure of any governor during this period.[13] He was replaced, temporarily, by the senior member of the council, John Brown, until the next governor arrived.

Thus in the short span of two years, 1784 to 1786, the Bahama Islands had two governors, a lieutenant governor, and an acting governor. This pattern would prevail for much of the period from 1784 to 1815, during which seven different Englishmen were governors and on four different occasions Bahamians were acting governors. Only two of the royal appointees served longer than four years, and one of these, Lord Dunmore, is often considered the worst governor the islands ever had. This relatively frequent turnover of governors would probably have caused serious problems had the relationship between the governor and the assembly been amiable, but given the often bitter disputes between the two branches of government, the frequent changes at the top relieved tension.

Health was a major factor in the frequent changes. Among the seven royal appointees, two died in office—Lieutenant Governors James Edward Powell (1785) and John Forbes (1797)—and three complained of illness—Governors William Dowdeswell, John Halkett, and Charles Cameron. Governor Dowdeswell was permitted to return to England and was replaced by Governor John Halkett, with Robert Hunt, president of the council, taking charge until the new governor arrived. Only Governors Maxwell and Lord Dunmore did not have their administrations ended because of illness. These, ironically, were the ones against whom the loudest complaints from the assembly emanated. Governor Halkett was transferred to Tobago; and Charles Cameron, the governor who served the longest, was allowed to return to England on two separate occasions, the first leave lasting from 1808 to 1812.

John Earl of Dunmore, more commonly known as Lord Dunmore, was approved for his appointment on April 26, 1787, and the Privy Council forwarded the recommendation for royal approval, marking the beginning of an administration that lasted from 1787 to 1796, longer than any other except Charles Cameron's.[14] Following a spate of runaways and law violations by blacks, in October 1787 Lord Dunmore issued a proclamation asking those who had fled to return. The proclamation was extended in November with a promise to address the apprehensions of those who claimed that they were free but had been denied their freedom, and if their case had merit they would receive a certificate of freedom. This stirred passions against him.[15] This accomplishment was overshadowed, however, by his mishandling of land grants; he often gave the land to favorites and snatched huge parcels for himself. The immediate offshoot of this was a hotly debated resolution condemning the governor; it passed in the assembly by a count of eleven yeas and nine nays.[16] The resolution graphically revealed that the anti-Maxwell faction had transferred its animus to Lord Dunmore.

The anti– and pro–Lord Dunmore camps seemed to be identifiable by geography. Assemblymen from Abaco (three), Exuma (three), Long Island (one), Nassau (three), and the Western District of New Providence (one) supported the resolution condemning the governor; and those from Andros (two), Eleuthera (one), Harbour Island (two), Nassau (one), and New Providence (Eastern District, two, and Western District, one) opposed it. In short, regionally and economically, the cotton-producing islands further to the north and south of New Providence opposed the governor, whereas the noncotton-producing islands nearer to New Providence supported him. Thomas Forbes, William Wylly, and Judge John Kelsall, who were among the leading cotton producers and hailed from East Florida, led the anti–Lord Dunmore faction. Much of the tension between the two groups was probably grounded in economics, borne of perceptions that the governor was insensitive to their concerns.

The enmity between Lord Dunmore and the assembly did not prevent his signing bills that benefited cotton growers,[17] and he sided with the assembly in its discriminatory treatment of refugees fleeing the carnage in Saint Domingue. He issued a proclamation barring blacks and mulattoes from that island from entering the Bahamas. Those whom privateers brought there were confined aboard prison vessels in Nassau Harbor. The whites from that island, on the other hand, were given provisions and allowed to sail to America.[18] Those who wished to stay were welcomed, while a tax was placed on blacks and mulattoes to discourage them from coming to the Bahamas.[19] Both Lord Dunmore and the assembly displayed insensitivity to the black and mulatto victims of the Haitian Revolution whose lives were in just as much danger as the whites in the atmosphere that pervaded the revolution, and their anguished cries were ignored.[20]

The partnership that formed between the governor and the assembly against blacks and mulattoes from Saint Domingue quickly dissolved once that issue was behind them, and the parties returned to their old positions. Since the governor had the support of the Colonial Office, his appointment was safe, but he lost this support over his alleged mishandling of funds, and this led to his recall. Besides showering favors upon his cronies, he indulged in nepotism and used his privileged position to speculate in land. His greatest mistake was expending huge amounts of public funds to build forts, none of which had a shot fired from it. Chief among these forts was Fort Charlotte, which took seven years to build and cost eight times the original estimate. He also built Fort Fincastle and named it after one of his family's subsidiary titles.[21]

Lord Dunmore procrastinated an inordinately long time before leaving his post. Meanwhile, the Colonial Office took the unusual step of appointing his successor, without informing him, and publishing the news in the *London Gazette* in February 1796.[22] When Lord Dunmore finally arrived in Portsmouth, England, in April 1796, he was greeted with the news of his firing. Obdurate as usual, he requested reasons for his dismissal but was told that the king never provided reasons for dismissing servants when they did not serve him properly.[23] Lord Dunmore thus may not have gotten the specific reason for his firing, but he got the message loud and clear that he had not done the job.

He was allowed to keep the title governor of the Bahamas and his replacement, John Forbes, assumed the title lieutenant governor. Forbes did not fare any better with the assembly, which he derisively called "contemptible low fellows," and he considered dissolving the body to rid it of the misfits.[24] Forbes incorrectly blamed Lord Dunmore for packing the assembly, but he was wrong on that score. During the session, the assembly passed legislation to protect those islands that the chenille and red bugs had attacked and rewrote the slave code by passing the Consolidated Slave Act. Forbes signed these bills and appointed William Wylly as chief justice of the Supreme Court.[25] Wylly, who had opposed Maxwell and Lord Dunmore, would become an able civil servant and would later become a target of the assembly's wrath. Wylly's appointment and the fact that Forbes associated assembly detractors with Lord Dunmore suggest that Forbes was not a supporter of his predecessor. Forbes was quite pleased with the Consolidated Slave Act and complimented the legislature for exhibiting "an earnest device to advance the cause of humanity." John Forbes died on June 3, 1797, less than a month after signing the act.[26]

Before enactment of the Consolidated Slave Act of 1797, slaveholders had a legal and absolute right to dispose of their slaves and punish them at will. Two magistrates and three freeholders tried slaves, and the only crime against slaves for which masters were held accountable was murder; otherwise, slaveholders could subject their slaves to untold cruelties with impunity. Slaves were allowed Sundays for themselves and a patch of land to farm, but no law guaranteed this. A positive note in this was that slaves tended to live as long as whites, about sixty to seventy years, in spite of the inhumane conditions to which they were subjected.[27]

The Consolidated Slave Act was the first major piece of legislation on slaves since 1780. It contained provisions increasing and improving subsistence allocations to slaves; for instance, it required masters to give them "good wholesome and sufficient provisions with proper clothing and necessaries." Other humanitarian provisions of the act called for sufficient quantity of land for slaves, protection of aged, sick, and lame slaves against abandonment, and a vacation lasting three days during Christmastide. These humanitarian provisions were overshadowed, however, by clauses restricting the movement of slaves, placing strict conditions on possession of hunting weapons, forbidding assemblage in numbers exceeding twelve, and using drums and horns for this purpose. Since runaway slaves were a major concern of slaveholders, a considerable segment of the act was devoted to this, and stiff punishment was mandated for anyone who violated those provisions. The act, moreover, created two types of courts to handle slave cases. A slave court lasting no longer than five successive days would meet on the first Tuesday of each quarter beginning in January to expedite felonious offenses committed by slaves. The other court, the general court, would try all cases that required the death penalty or transportation (removal from the islands) of slaves.[28]

William Dowdeswell, Forbes's successor, enjoyed better relations with the assembly than his predecessors, but his tenure as governor was shortened because of health problems. During his administration the assembly canvassed many leading cotton growers to learn why the cotton crops were failing so often. He prorogued the assembly in November 1800 and sailed for England the following March, never returning to the Bahamas again. Robert Hunt, president of the council, was placed in charge of the government until the new governor, John Halkett, arrived.[29]

Governor Halkett arrived in the Bahamas on January 28, 1802.[30] By December of the following year, the governor, who believed that the Bahamas was "a West India climate, though an American colony," began to experience serious health problems and enlisted the aid of friends in England to appeal to the Colonial Office.[31] In December he wrote to a Mrs. Todd, informing her that he was still having trouble with violent headaches and pain; but he either seemed resigned to his fate or was trying to solicit sympathy because he told her, "I suppose I must remain here tho' the certain ruin of my constitution will be the consequence." The governor, who was not alone in having difficulty dealing with conditions in the Bahamas, continued, "One half our troops have died here within these six months past and they are still dying six or eight per week."[32] About the same time the governor wrote the letter, the Colonial Office dispatched orders transferring him to Tobago. He probably had written others earlier about his situation. One of those persons, a W. Farquhar, interceded for him in a letter that warned officials that Halkett would die if left in the Bahamas.[33] This prompted a speedy response from Downing Street authorizing Halkett to return to England before assuming his duties in Tobago.[34] Ordinarily, the letter would have arrived too late, but in this instance it may not have because his departure was delayed until June 2, 1804; that gave the letter, written on March 10, 1804, time to arrive before he left. In the meantime, H. M. Dyer, judge of the Vice Admiralty Court of the Bahamas, assumed the helm of government until the new governor, Charles Cameron, arrived.[35]

Governor Cameron did not reach New Providence until September 25, 1804.[36] His tenure brought stability to an office that had not experienced it in many years. Less than ten years had past since Lord Dunmore had been unceremoniously removed from office; nevertheless, in that span of time four persons, including Cameron, had graced the governor's office. Besides a long tenure, Cameron brought something else that was sorely needed: a good working relationship with the assembly. This happened at a time when Britain decided to garrison the Bahama Islands with black troops from the British West India regiments and to abolish the African slave trade, two potentially thorny issues which Cameron handled without creating the kind of divisiveness that existed during the Maxwell and Lord Dunmore administrations. The deterioration in relations between Britain and the United States, culminating in the War of 1812, while the governor was in England, could have caused serious problems in the Bahamas.

Governor Cameron embarked for England on November 9, 1808, leaving William Vesey Munnings, chief justice of the Supreme Court, in charge of the government. H. M. Dyer challenged this appointment, however, claiming that he should have been selected, just as he had been when Governor Halkett departed.[37] Dyer's challenge failed; the Home Government ruled that Governor Cameron had acted properly. On June 14, 1812, Benjamin Moodie of Charleston, South Carolina, wrote to John Forbes informing him that the United States Congress had approved a declaration of war resolution by an overwhelming majority of seventy-nine to forty-nine in the House of Representatives and by a slim majority of two votes in the Senate.[38] Munnings did not receive news of this event, however, until July 24, 1812, over a month after the formal declaration of war.[39] Concern about the turn of events pervaded the Bahamas, but not to the extent of dissuading Munnings from proroguing the assembly in December for a few days.[40] The governor arrived a short while later and was pleased with the state of affairs: "These Islands appear to be in as prosperous a state as the war with America and the depreciated value of West India produce will allow. . . . The Inhabitants [are] more so [healthy] than they were when I last arrived among them."[41]

The Americans did not attack New Providence during the War of 1812, as they had done in the American Revolution; but had they done so resistance would have been much stronger because royal artillery, two European companies of engineers, 837 troops from the Second West India Regiment,[42] and three militia companies protected the island. Whether this would have been enough to defend the island successfully against an American force is arguable, but the prospect of an attack was remote. The Americans could not count on the support from the French navy, which the Royal Navy had bottled up in Europe, and they had their hands full trying to prevent dismemberment of their territory, the northwest one third of which the British had captured at one time. So the War of 1812 was just another issue that had to be addressed, but not with a sense of urgency. In the waning months of the war, death claimed Robert Hunt, president of the council and a member of that body for forty years. He was also an assistant judge and twice served as acting governor.[43] One month later, the council lost another member, Alexander Begbie, who was also deputy assistant commissary general.[44] Begbie, from Nassau, was among the faction that had opposed Lord Dunmore and supported the resolution condemning him. So as 1815 approached, the islands began to lose leaders who had been around since the 1780s. New faces would appear on the scene, but not necessarily new behavior from the assembly toward the governor. Moreover, Cameron and his family began to have health problems, which he blamed on the unwholesome climate, and he requested another leave of absence to return to England.[45]

Defending the Bahamas from an enemy invasion fell largely on the shoulders of nonwhite soldiers; but free blacks and persons of color were customarily barred from participating in the political process, nor were they allowed to give testimony against whites in court, except in matters of debt.

The governor asked a number of the leading whites whether free persons of color enjoyed full protection of the law and the responses showed lack of a consensus on the issue. One respondent replied, "[F]ree persons of colour do enjoy the same rights of property, both real and personal in these islands, without limitation as to the value thereof, as white inhabitants, and are secured in their person and property by the same laws which protect the white inhabitant's."[46] Another respondent opined that they were not prohibited from owning property, real and personal, "and that except their inability to give testimony against a white person, except in the matter of debt, they [were] protected in their persons and property by the same law."[47] The most insightful response came from William Vesey Munnings, who said, "[S]o long as the colour of a man is held to make a difference in the admissibility of his testimony, free persons of colour cannot be considered as enjoying equal protection in their persons."[48] Munnings saw in 1815 what some persons in the last decade of the twentieth century still do not see, one cannot enjoy equal protection of the law if he or she is discriminated against, either by written laws or by de facto institutional practices that have the sanction of those sworn to uphold the law. Jamaica made greater progress in this area than the Bahamas. After prohibiting free persons of color from giving testimony in court, even against other free persons of color, in 1796 Jamaica admitted the testimony of those persons against whites in certain criminal cases such as assault and battery, if they presented baptismal certificates; then in 1813 the law was changed, allowing the testimony of free persons of color against whites in all cases.[49] This was thus an area where Jamaica was clearly ahead of the Bahamas.

In light of his answer to the question, Munnings' failure to execute instructions in the case of the slave Will Sterling should not be construed as insensitivity to the plight of that slave. A slave court had convicted Sterling of murdering the slave Dick Campey, but the jury recommended mercy. The attorney general questioned the competency of the slave court to hear the case since under provisions of the Consolidated Slave Act (1797) the general court was charged with the responsibility of hearing slave cases involving the death penalty or transportation. The Supreme Court, headed by Munnings, concurred.[50] Upon receiving the ruling, Governor Cameron sent the whole proceeding to England for Lord Castlereagh's consideration, along with his recommendation for a pardon. Then Cameron departed for England. When he returned from England four years later, Cameron learned that no further action had been taken on the case, and all the while Sterling had remained incarcerated in terrible physical conditions that had eroded his health to such a state that he was near death. Much worse, he lived daily under the fearful expectation that he would be executed that day. Cameron acted immediately to activate the case and soon afterwards the pardon was granted.[51] This oversight happened on Munnings' watch since he was in charge during Cameron's absence, but it probably was not willful.

Jack Nottage, a free man of color, was also convicted of murder and the jury recommended mercy; he had better luck than the slave Sterling. Nottage was tried in the general court for murdering Nero Fowler, a free black man with whom he had an argument over a small water cask that was left aboard the *Sarah Ann,* on which Nottage was a crew member. Fowler boarded the vessel, which was docked at Eleuthera, claimed that he had acquired the cask in Long Island, and allegedly said to Nottage, "Damn you why did you say my cask was on board the *Lively* when here it is?"[52] Nottage became enraged over the accusation that he had lied and intended to steal the cask; he grabbed a pump-brake handle and struck Fowler on the head, killing him. Witnesses to the incident agreed that Nottage did not intend to kill Fowler. One in particular, John Boyd, a passenger on the *Sarah Ann* and a community leader, said that he and the others would have intervened if it had been believed that Nottage intended to kill Fowler.[53] Charged with deciding between a verdict of guilty of murder or of manslaughter, the jury convicted him of murder and recommended mercy; so did the judges. After the verdict in July 1814 the case moved relatively quickly through the bureaucratic process. The governor's request for pardon was sent to England in August, and the request was granted in October 1814, although it did not reach the Bahamas until February 1815.[54]

The criminal justice system worked more quickly for Jack Nottage than it did for Will Sterling; nevertheless, both men received pardons upon the recommendation of Governor Cameron, whose action was influenced by that of the juries in the cases and the judges. The decisions and actions in these cases did not happen in all cases involving blacks and persons of color, free and slave. Nevertheless, they show the safeguards that existed in the system to prevent arbitrary abuse of power by white Bahamians against slaves and free blacks and persons of color. The system had a long way to go, however, before it could be considered fair, because whites still made the laws, enforced them, sat on juries, and sentenced defendants. In addition to not being allowed to sit on juries, free blacks and persons of color could not vote. The franchise was restricted to male white inhabitants twenty years of age and older who had resided in the Bahamas for at least twelve months and either owned real estate or paid fifty pounds sterling in duties the preceding year.[55] Moreover, a double standard was used when punishing blacks, coloreds, or whites for committing the same crime. If a white discharged a firearm illegally he was fined ten pounds sterling, but if a free black or person of color committed that same crime he was fined twelve pounds, and the punishment for a slave committing the same offense was fifty lashes. Free blacks and persons of color were fined more heavily than whites, and slaves were punished more severely than free persons.[56]

Despite the feuds between governors and the assembly and the frequent turnover of governors, the executive and legislative branches of the Bahamas' political system cooperated to protect cotton growers, preserve slavery, and place free blacks and persons of color in a subordinate position. Did the efforts in behalf of cotton growers succeed and did Bahamians take advantage of the natural resources that abounded in the islands? Moreover, did blacks and coloreds fare better under the economic system than they did under the political system? The answer to the question of whether Bahamians took advantage of the rich abundance of natural resources on the islands is an unequivocal no. Loyalists caused much of this by deciding in advance, before getting knowledge about the soils in the Bahamas and what types of crops grow best there, to convert the islands into a cotton kingdom, though they had little agricultural experience. Thus, cotton production never prospered in spite of a very sympathetic assembly that promoted efforts to save cotton crops. The answer to the question concerning in which system the free blacks and persons of color fared better, the political or the economic, is they fared better in the economic system where fewer restraints existed. They could neither vote nor hold public office. Nevertheless, they could own property and by that amass sizable wealth. The total value of property which they owned is difficult to determine, but the wide range of the types of property—plantations, vessels, homes, shops, and slaves—suggests it was considerable. This was achieved in spite of having little, if any, say in the laws that were passed affecting the economic development of the Bahamas.

In the early 1780s, the British perceived the Bahama Islands as an extremely underpopulated and undeveloped land. This view was probably influential in George III's decision to issue a royal proclamation instructing the governor of the Bahama Islands to give 40 acres of unoccupied land to every head of household and an additional 20 acres to each member of that same household who migrated to the Bahamas. The annual rent per hundred acres was two shillings. The Loyalists, however, received a special dispensation that exempted them from paying rent for ten years and eliminated charges for the land. Between 1784 and 1789, about 114 grants encompassing a total of 42,842 acres on sixteen islands were awarded. The largest of these grants, located on Abaco Island, covered 1,460 acres.[57]

Thelma Peters has compiled a revealing profile of the typical Loyalist head of household. The person was a white male, "either first or second generation from Scotland or England, Presbyterian or Anglican, well-educated, and bred to accounting." The individual was living in the American South when the American Revolution began, working either as a merchant, an employee of a merchant, or a slaveholding planter. After the Revolution, he joined one of the volunteer British provincial armies, usually as an officer, and was forced to move because the Patriots had confiscated his land. This individual, moreover, generally had little experience or training in agriculture, and from the little time spent on his plantation (most were on the Out Islands) apparently had little interest in the hands-on operation of that enterprise, which was left to an overseer to run while the planter spent most of his time in Nassau.[58] Thomas Forbes, partner in Panton, Leslie, and Company of St. Augustine, Florida, was a typical Loyalist.[59] He subsequently became a prominent political leader in the Bahamas.

Several features of the profile contrasted with the situation in the Bahamas. First, the typical Loyalist was well educated, but the average Conch was not. Second, Presbyterians were considered dissenters on the islands. Third, persons knowledgeable in agriculture were needed more than accountants and merchants. So, although on the surface the Loyalists credentials were laudable, they generally did not meet the needs of the islands. Their ignorance of soil management and the latest techniques in soil conservation, including crop rotation, was very crucial. This shortcoming is at the core of the failure of the cotton kingdom and helps explain why so many Loyalists packed their belongings and returned to America after a relatively short stay in the Bahamas.

Lieutenant Wilson's report, alluded to in the introduction, did not conceal information concerning the rocky and rough surface of the Bahamas and the fact that only one type of soil there (three types were found there) was conducive for growing cotton.[60] The initial crops were successful, offering great expectations that conditions would improve, but this did not occur. The first year's crop prompted this glowing description of what had happened from the assembly: "the culture of cotton was soon carried to an extent which was rendering the cotton opulent and flourishing."[61] The Loyalists quickly became the dominant players in the economy. In 1788, a

State of the Population, Agriculture, etc., of the Bahama Islands in June 1788, Showing the Respective Numbers of the Old and New Inhabitants, Their Property, Occupations, etc.

Principal islands on which there are residents	White male heads of families	Planters possessing 10 or more slaves	Merchants	Number of slaves	Acres of cultivated land	Of the 3 learned professions	Further remarks
New Inhabitants							
New Providence	165	27	26	1,264	3,060	16	
Exuma	2	19	—	679	2,591	—	
Long Island	29	19	—	476	2,380	—	
Cat Island	28	16	—	442	1,747	—	
Abaco	49	10	—	198	1,837	—	
Andros Islands	22	7	—	132	813	—	
Crooked Islands	5	4	—	357		—	new settled
Caicos, Eleuthera	6	5	—	214	460		new settled
Harbour Island			—	—	—	—	
Turk's			—	—	—	—	
Total New:	330	107	26	3762	12,888	16	
Old Inhabitants							
New Providence	131	2	3	1,024	255	1	
Exuma	11	4	—	75	354	—	
Long Island	42	12	—	306	1,530	—	also 21 families of color
Cat Island	12	—	—	16	250	—	
Abaco	—	—	—	—	—	—	
Andros Islands	4	3	—	56	290	—	
Crooked Island	—	—	—	—	—	—	
Caicos	1	—	—	5	30	—	
Turk's	18	—	—	40	—	—	
Harbour Island	94	—	—	142	—	—	very old settlement
Eleuthera	119	—	—	310	725		The 310 set down as slaves are most FPC
Total Old	430	21	3	1,974	3,434	1	
	760	128	29	5,696	16,322	17	

government report on the state of economic endeavors divided the white male heads of household into two groups, old inhabitants and new inhabitants, and revealed that while only 43 percent (330 of 760) of the targeted group were new inhabitants, they comprised 83 percent of the planters owning ten or more slaves (107 of 128), owned 66 percent of the slaves (3,762 of 5,696), constituted 90 percent of the merchants (26 of 29), and 94 percent of the persons in learned professions (16 of 17), and they owned 79 percent of the cultivated land.[62]

Herein lay the roots of the conflict that existed between factions in the legislature. The Bahamas was expected to absorb this huge influx of immigrants in a relatively short period, but it did not happen. This situation was different from the one in Massachusetts Bay in the seventeenth century when within ten years (1630–1640) more than 30,000 Puritans had migrated to the colony. The Puritans who came during this "Great Migration" settled in an unoccupied area and created communities, churches, and a government where none had existed previously. The Native Americans kept their distance for good reason. In the Bahamas, on the other hand, the Loyalists moved into settled locations, such as Eleuthera, Harbour Island, and New Providence, as well as on unsettled islands; and within a short time their domination of all major facets of life was swift and complete. They even became the majority in the assembly. To counter this, and partly to salve wounded pride, the old inhabitants generally allied themselves with the governor.

One of those governors with whom the Conchs formed an alliance, Lord Dunmore, visited many Out Islands in 1790 and recorded his impression of economic activities there and in New Providence. The report also contained information from unidentified sources on islands that he did not visit. In his island-by-island report, the governor said that New Providence had cotton plantations, but they were not as successful as those on islands to the windward. Abaco, in the northern Bahamas, contained a harbor convenient for small vessels and excellent for whaling—whales could be seen in the waters from the shore all the year round—but neither cotton nor cattle seemed to thrive there. Turks Islands produced an abundance of salt, with rakers coming mainly from Bermuda. Exuma (Great and Little), Long Island, and Crooked Island, all south of New Providence, had excellent cotton crops, but Long Island's was thought to be the best; those islands also had provisions and stock of every kind and they thrived quite well. Harbour Island, just northeast of New Providence, with one of the best harbors in the Bahamas and where stock of all kinds thrived, was unusual in that it had a predominantly white population. Eleuthera, east of New Providence, had not ventured into cotton growing to any significant degree, but it grew the best oranges, pineapples, and other fruits. Royal Island contained stock. Andros Island, the largest of the Bahama Islands, had a huge quantity of mahogany, cedars, and a beautiful wood called horseflesh, as well as cotton. Although Lord Dunmore did not visit Cat Island, in the eastern Bahamas, he was told that corn and vegetables there were very good; and the island was said to have the best soil in the Bahamas, but its cotton crop was subpar. Watlings Island, in the eastern Bahamas, where Columbus first sighted land in the Western Hemisphere and named it San Salvador, had just been settled and, with the Caicos, was expected to produce a good cotton crop. Grand Bahama, the Biminis, and the Berry Islands in the northern Bahamas and Mayaguana in the southern Bahamas had not been settled and were unexplored.[63]

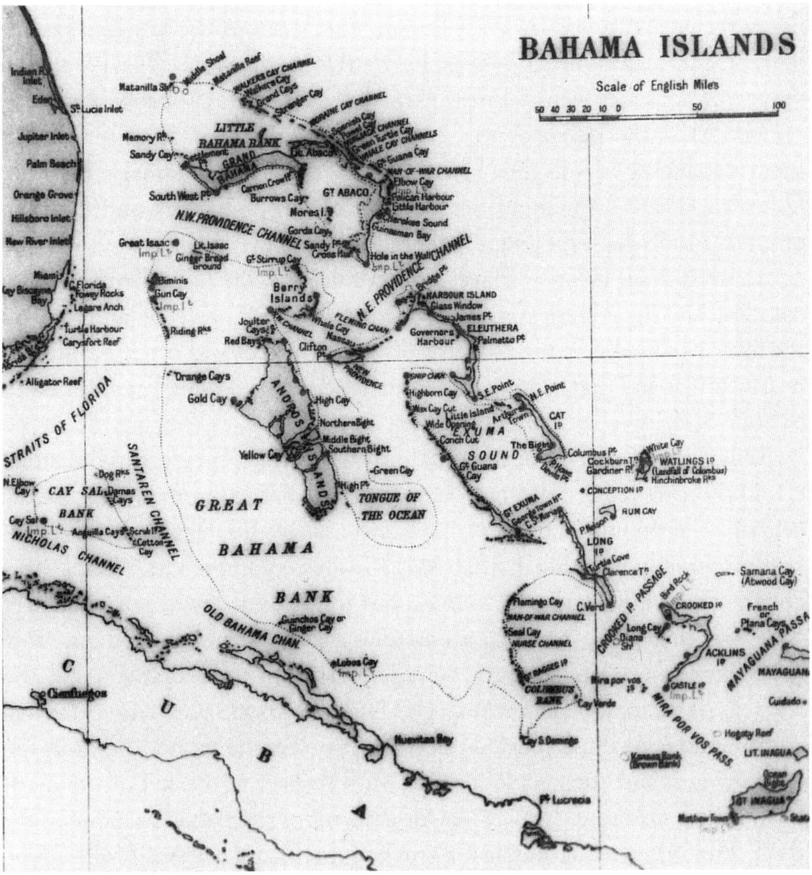

Bahama Islands. *Courtesy Department of Archives, Nassau, Bahamas.*

This detailed description of the Bahamas depicts its uniqueness, a string of islands stretching from the twenty-first to the twenty-seventh parallel, roughly the distance from Cape Fear, North Carolina, almost to New York along the North American coast, a much different geographical picture from that presented by its sister islands in the British West Indies. In 1787, the Carolina proprietors surrendered their claim to the Bahamas, thus placing the islands in the same political category with Jamaica. Both were allowed to have assemblies that passed laws governing them. Sugar dominated the economy of the British West Indies, satisfying the sweet tooth of Britain and the European continent. Since the Bahamas did not produce sugar or any other valuable exportable staples or raw materials, what good was it to Britain? The islands had strategic military value, being in the general area of French and Spanish colonies. Since the sugar economy did not define the Bahamian economy, which tended to be commercial, Bahamians did not perceive themselves as West Indian. Furthermore, the self-hire system had come into prominence by 1784. Howard Johnson wrote, "The Bahamian economic activities were primary extractive and mainly for subsistence."[64]

Slavery in the Bahamas was not completely different from that in the sugar-producing islands. For instance, a slave woman in Jamaica gave the following observation about her slave sons, "My sons work on their own grounds from which they supply themselves and me; two days in the week are allowed them for it."[65] Slaves in the Bahamas, the other British Indies colonies, and the American South were often given a parcel of land to work for their personal use; the produce from that parcel was often hawked in nearby towns and that income was either used to buy personal items or saved in hope of being able to purchase their freedom.

During the last two decades of the eighteenth century, the Bahamas' economy revolved around cotton, salt, fruits, cattle, lumber, and marine activities—economic endeavors that were basically different from those pursued regionally by other British West Indies colonies. The islands were apparently rich in natural resources, but these alone could not guarantee economic prosperity. The major obstacles that prevented inhabitants from producing an exportable staple were ignorance of the Bahamian soil and their outdated method of farming, two huge drawbacks. Governor Maxwell identified one of these shortcomings in 1783 when he wrote, "It is surprising how ignorant the people here are with respect to the soil of the many Islands that surround them."[66] As for the soils of the Bahamas, none of the three found there was suitable for growing maize, a nutritious favorite food of the slaves.[67] A telling revelation concerning the backward state of agriculture in the Bahamas is found in Lieutenant Governor James Edward Powell's responses to "Inquiry Relative to Negro Slaves in the Bahama Islands (1788)" from the Home Government. Some of the questions posed in the "Inquiry" were, How many plantations in the Said Islands use the plow? What is the manure made up of in the Said Islands? Is the labor of cattle used in the cultivation of a West Indies plantation? And cattle of what species and in what proportion? The governor's answer to the first question was that none of the plantations in the Bahama Islands used the plow; to the second he answered that manure was not used in farming; and to the third he said that cattle were scarce in the Bahamas and none were used in cultivation. When, moreover, the governor was asked whether any European implements of husbandry had been introduced in the Bahamas, he replied, "The Bahama Islands are too rocky to admit of many implements of European husbandry, the hoe excepted."[68]

Bahamians generally were not at their best when working the land. They practiced soil butchery, which robbed the soil of its nutrients, cut and burned the trees and shrubbery, depriving the soil of its cover, and did not use manure to fertilize the soil. Furthermore, they did not use the plow or introduce European farm implements to help prepare the land, neither did they evince familiarity with recent technology in agriculture. They did not, for instance, practice crop rotation, which was the latest means for preventing soil exhaustion. It was used in England. George III, an avid farmer who in later life was affectionately known as "Farmer George," reputedly used crop rotation. These shortcomings would have been surmountable if the land had been richer, thicker, and conducive to growing the staple of choice, cotton; unfortunately, it was not. Did heavy investment in slaves encumber addressing the shortcomings? It may have, because planters were probably not amenable to spending additional sums on labor-saving implements or beasts of burden after having spent large sums on slaves.

Tending the land was the Achilles' heel of Loyalists; roaming the seas was the strength of Conchs. Wrecking was very profitable because the "very great number of rocks and shoal in the area made traversing nearby waters difficult and dangerous."[69] During the course of a year many ships ran aground in Bahamian waters or nearby, and Bahamians became proficient at recovering the valuable cargo from those vessels. In this instance Bahamians took what could have been a negative and turned it into a positive, which may have compensated somewhat for what could be called the islands' unfavorable geographical location. The Bahamas was further away from the French and Spanish settlements than some of the other British West Indies colonies, and this made trading very difficult.[70] Much of the islands' trade, therefore, was with the United States, from whom supplies of livestock and provisions were received.[71] Governor John Halkett called the Bahamas an American colony, a comment that suggests that the islands depended greatly on the American trade.[72]

Some of the responsibility for trade difficulties lay with the Bahamians' failure to capitalize upon the available opportunities. Over a decade after Governor Browne (1774) had complained about the failure to develop the whaling industry, little effort had been directed toward developing that industry. Lieutenant Governor Powell reported in 1783 that the seas surrounding the islands abounded with whales, and he encouraged the British government to offer a small bounty for spermaceti to create interest in whaling.[73] At the time, other than a partnership of eight merchants, no other Bahamians were engaged in whaling. In a piece entitled "Observations of the Bahama Islands" (1792), it was believed that Exuma Island had better harbors than New Providence.[74] In 1793, Lord Dunmore suggested that Abaco Island could support a flourishing wine enterprise to replace the void occasioned by the abandonment of the island by cotton planters, who believed it was too cold to grow cotton there. Lord Dunmore said that wines had already been tried on Abaco and the result was amazingly successful.[75] A whaling industry, developing Exuma into a major seaport, and estab-

The *Galvanic,* queen of wrecking. *Courtesy Department of Archives, Nassau, Bahamas.*

Wreckers at work. *Courtesy Department of Archives, Nassau, Bahamas.*

lishing a wine enterprise in Abaco were ideas that were never given serious attention in the marketplace. Failure to act upon these probably hindered the islands' economic development. Another hindrance was the absence of financial institutions from which money could have been borrowed to build whaling ships and a winery or loaned to planters to purchase farm implements and beasts of burden. The first bank in the Bahama Islands was not established until 1835.[76]

Profitable marine ventures alone could not keep the economy afloat. The successful British colonies, whether in North America or in the West Indies, achieved this status by producing an exportable staple. The North American colonies produced tobacco, rice, and indigo; the West Indies colonies produced sugar. These crops helped Britain achieve a goal of mercantilist nations, a favorable balance of trade. Before 1784 the Bahamas did not have an exportable staple, but the Loyalists intended to change that by converting the islands into a cotton kingdom. Although most of the Loyalist planters lacked experience operating a cotton plantation, this should not have presented a major problem because their slaves, the primary source of labor on the plantation, were familiar with growing cotton, a crop that grew in Africa. It did not matter that the seed used initially was Persian cotton or that later planters switched to Anguilla cotton, which had a longer staple and grew all the year round, reaching the height of small trees, unless pruned.[77] What mattered was the poor condition of the soil and the planters' ignorance of it. The planters knew the business end of plantation operation very well and the slaves knew the planting end, but neither knew much about soil conservation.

William Wylly, a Loyalist who migrated in 1784 and subsequently became a planter and prominent political figure, published a work in 1789 in which he inaccurately credited the Loyalists with planting the first cotton crop in the Bahamas. He also raved about the cotton crop production: " [It] has infinitely exceeded their most sanguine expectations."[78] This work has led scholars to paint a rosy picture of the early cotton-producing endeavors of the Loyalists, without questioning the accuracy of Wylly's statement. But were the Loyalists the first to plant cotton in the Bahama Islands? In 1721, the first slaves brought to the Bahamas, 295 slaves imported from Guinea, were distributed among a small number of plantations where they cultivated cotton and other produce. In 1729, the legislative assembly passed several acts establishing clear title to land and encouraging economic development. One of those acts encouraged cotton planting on the islands.[79] In 1768 it was reported cotton and coffee had been planted in Nassau, and permission was requested to give the venture a few years to see if the crops would become exportable staples.[80] Moreover, Judge Kelsall, a Little Exuma cotton planter, in answering a questionnaire from the assembly concerning the causes of the consistent crop failures, lamented that Loyalists were "unable to procure from the few cotton planters whom they found in the country, any information that could be relied on."[81]

Obviously, cotton was planted in the Bahamas before the Loyalists arrived. What about Wylly's depiction of the early crop? He said it exceeded their expectations. Unless their expectations were very low, this is an exaggeration. Writing in 1785, Lieutenant Governor Powell reported, "The inhabitants overall, a few exceptions, have been unsuccessful in their crops." The governor said that the planters complained about the lack of rain in the past six months and the sterility of the soil. He also reported that those same persons only ten months earlier had given the most "flattering accounts of the Bahamas."[82] In September 1785, a severe hurricane struck the Bahamas wreaking havoc upon Harbour Island, Eleuthera, and Abaco.[83] None of these islands were known for their cotton production, but they may not have been the only islands hit, just the ones that sustained the most damage. From these accounts, 1785 was not a very good year for most cotton plantations, in spite of what Wylly would have us believe.

It was probably generally known that the planters had very limited experience, if any, in managing cotton plantations. Realizing this, John Wells, pub-

Joseph Eve, inventer of the cotton gin, and cotton gin.
Courtesy Department of Archives, Nassau, Bahamas.

lisher of the *Bahama Gazette* and the first person to publish a newspaper in the Bahamas, printed two articles that could be considered crash courses in planting cotton. In the first article planters were told how to plant cotton. The soil should be prepared in the middle of April, using a hoe to plow the land; plants should not be grown higher than five feet, and if caterpillars appeared on the crop early in the year they should be ignored and allowed to fly away since they did not pose a threat to plants at that stage of the season. If, on the other hand, caterpillars came when plants had begun to blossom, they must be destroyed, or else the crop would be ruined.[84] The second article discussed pruning plants and applying manure to the soil. Planters, moreover, were advised to top the brushes and to use manure. Readers were informed that the few planters who had used manure had reaped benefits.[85]

Cotton production had experienced fluctuations almost from the beginning of conversion to a cotton kingdom. The problems in 1785 were discussed earlier, but they did not end there. In August 1787 a hurricane struck Exuma and almost destroyed the cotton plantations.[86] There was a consensus that cotton on the islands was a failure in 1788. Both the general assembly and Lord Dunmore, two parties which agreed on very little during this period, voiced disappointment over the crop failure that year.[87] Conditions on cotton plantations reached such a low point in the late 1780s that an ad hoc committee of the assembly was appointed to look into the situation. The committee reported that 2,470 acres were planted in 1785 and they produced

124 tons for export. The acreage planted in 1786 increased to 2,900, and there was also an increase in the tons produced for export, 150 tons. The acres under cultivation increased again in 1787 and 1788, and so did cotton exports in the former, 219 tons, but not in the latter when the cotton exported dropped to 112 tons because of a chenille bug attack.[88] The picture painted of the 1787 crop seems to gloss over the losses at Exuma that year.

Even as cotton production was on a roller-coaster ride, there was a technological breakthrough in the cleaning process of cotton, a breakthrough that had the potential to thrust the Bahamas into a leadership position in the industry, even ahead of the American South, which technologically was behind the Bahamas because of Joseph Eve's machine. Eve, a Cat Island planter, announced in February 1788 that he had built a cotton machine that could clean three hundred pounds of cotton per slave each day. Either a horse or the wind could power the machine, and in addition to a greater cleaning capacity it was also less expensive to maintain than the common gin.[89] What this suggests is that the idea of a cotton gin was not new. Slaves on cotton plantations were using a machine that was probably similar to the one used in Africa and may indeed have been made by those slaves based on their African experience. Eve improved upon that machine, allowing it to be mass produced. He did not invent the cotton gin, neither did he lay claim to this feat. This by no means reduced the potential importance of his machine. Ironically, Eve's mother was a Quaker, a religious group that was in the forefront of the battle to abolish slavery, a practice his machine was perceived as intended to perpetuate. [90]

By 1792, the Caicos, Crooked Island, Long Island, Cat Island, and Exuma Island were the leading cotton producers in the Bahamas.[91] In 1795, William Wylly, who chaired an ad hoc committee of the assembly to investigate Eve's petition for aid from the government, reported that Eve was in financial trouble from exhausting his resources in a ten-year effort to perfect a cotton gin. Operated by two men, Eve's machine could clean more cotton, and do it better, than ten men using the common foot gin; and there were presently 140 machines operating in the Bahamas. Eve was willing to sell the rights to the machine to the government for 4,000 pounds sterling, which the committee thought was a modest amount; but mindful of a revenue shortfall in the government, Wylly proposed to give Eve an annuity of 840 pounds sterling for seven years. This would cover the principal and interest. Wylly, moreover, proposed to give Eve a monopoly on manufacturing the machine in the Bahamas.[92] By this time Eli Whitney, a Yale

College graduate, had built a cotton gin while visiting in Savannah, Georgia; this doubtless was known to Wylly, who, being a lawyer, may have been interested in protecting Eve against competition from Whitney. The assembly did not subscribe to this bailout of Eve, and shortly afterwards, in about 1800, Eve sailed for Charleston, South Carolina, where he lived until moving to Augusta, Georgia, in 1810. Although he returned to the Bahamas for short visits, Eve's departure dealt a severe blow to cotton producing in the islands because no one on the islands could repair the cotton machine.[93]

Eve left the Bahamas because he recognized the futility of attempting to create a cotton kingdom there. He had much company both in his perception of the future of the cotton kingdom and on the return trip to America. More crop failures in the 1790s followed the failures of the 1780s. It was probably obvious by then that the islands would never produce abundant cotton crops. This was well before the passage of the Abolition of the Slave Trade Act (1807), which further hampered efforts to create a cotton kingdom. Neither action, however, influenced the other. The collapse had nothing to do with abolition of the slave trade, and Britain did not take action against the slave trade only because of cotton's failure in the islands. Some planters continued to plant cotton well beyond 1800, but the number was smaller than in the 1790s.

The roller-coaster production continued in the 1790s when intermittent good and bad years prevented a consistent income flow from year to year. The only certainty appears to have been the likelihood of a crop failure lurking on the horizon. This was bad news for planters, who depended on the income to pay for the expensive provisions and clothing they used. For instance, 1788 was a bad year for the crop,[94] but 1794 was not.[95] The chenille bug destroyed the cotton crop in the Middle District of Long Island in 1796, but the other islands were not affected, raising expectations of a bumper crop exceeding fifteen hundred tons, an amount double that of any previous year.[96] The year 1796, therefore, had a mixture of good and bad. Bahamians probably would have settled for more of the same in 1797, but it did not happen; that year a decline in the tonnage of cotton produced resulted in a distressful situation for cotton planters.[97]

By the mid-1790s the legislature had begun to enact legislation to address the insect problem on an island-by-island basis. Accordingly, the Cat Island Bug Act covered the first beneficiary of legislation, Cat Island, (1797).[98] In due time, Long Island, Watlings Island, Exuma Island, and the Caicos were subjects of similar legislation. Thus by the late 1790s legislation covered the principal cotton-producing islands, protecting them against the chenille and red bugs, thought to be the major encumbrance to successful cotton production in the Bahama Islands.[99]

As events would subsequently show, the bug infestation over the years caused a number of crop failures, but the principal reason for the collapse of the cotton kingdom was more complex than that. Meanwhile, petitions from distraught planters who complained about their hardships and requested relief prompted Governor William Dowdeswell to appeal to the council for help.[100] The council responded positively, but it was the assembly that took the most enlightened step when it sent questionnaires to twenty-five leading cotton growers soliciting their opinion on the causes of the persistent cotton crop failures.[101] All the parties responded, but some of the responses were more insightful than others. After reading the responses, the assembly concluded that there were two principal causes of the collapse: the propensity of planters to cultivate more acres than they could protect against the chenille bug, and the failure to take proper care in clearing and laying out the land.[102]

Judge Kelsall presented one of the more insightful responses to the assembly's questionnaire. In answering questions relating mainly to the causes of the crop failures, he wrote,

> The principal cause of our failures, for so many successive years is, in my opinion, unquestionably the exhausted state of our soil, arising from constant unintermitted culture: there has doubtless been much injudicious planting, nor is it, I apprehend, to be wondered at, that men, very many of whom are unused to agriculture, all of them strangers to the soil and climate, and unable to procure from the few cotton planters whom they found in the country, any information that could be relied on, should, in cultivating cotton for the first time in their lives, fall into error.The first and most fatal was the indiscriminate cutting down of trees, thus forming one large field, in as much as, exclusive of the physical effect of such measure, a very great proportion of every tract and that, in many instances, the most valuable; has been rendered wholly unfit for the cultivation of cotton; this plant as it is well known, requiring shelter from the winds, which can only be attained by very small fields. Another serious error, which the embarrassed circumstances of the loyalists unfortunately induced them to commit—was clearing and planting more land than they could cultivate well.[103]

Judge Kelsall did not include chenille and red bug attacks on the crops among his reasons. Although his crops had suffered from such attacks, Kelsall did not believe they constituted a major problem. He said that in

November 1788 the chenille bug struck his plantation; nevertheless, the following spring he produced between 14,000 and 16,000 pounds of cotton. In 1791 and 1792 the chenille bug struck again with similar consequences. The judge continued, "In the present year, 1800, without any the least injury from the red bug, or chenille, with much greater quantity of land in cultivation than in 1788, I have great fear that its produce will not exceed 8,000 or at most 10,000 weight in cotton."[104] Kelsall believed the bugs were nuisances that could be readily overcome. Soil exhaustion, however, was not a mere nuisance, and there was no easy solution to correct it.

The other leading cotton planters generally did not share Kelsall's perception of the bug infestation; they tended to believe that the bugs contributed to the decline in cotton. William Wylly, owner of plantations in New Providence and Long Island, listed some of the same reasons Kelsall did, but he identified bug infestation as a cause. Joseph Eve, who completed the questionnaire before leaving for America, gave one cause: the bugs. Similarly, John Anderson of Long Island gave one: soil exhaustion. Most of the other planters included both soil exhaustion and bug infestation as causes, but none alluded to the inexperience of Loyalists as farmers and the absence of knowledgeable persons on the islands with whom they could consult.[105]

The assembly apparently agreed with those who believed soil exhaustion was a major cause of the decline. One of the ways to combat this, the body opined, would be for the Colonial Office to open new lands. In addition, the assembly believed that other steps should be taken. Therefore, it enacted a strict law regulating the cultivation of cotton, limiting the area cultivated from perhaps three to six acres for each "taskable hand." The assembly also created large margins of woodland in the proper direction to protect the cotton fields and limited cultivating the same field to no longer than three consecutive years, after which the land would lie fallow for up to eight years. Planters were encouraged to plant other crops after the cotton had been harvested that season and to breed cattle to provide manure needed to fertilize the fields. The assembly, moreover, encouraged the discovery of an insecticide that would kill the chenille and red bugs.[106]

While the assembly was wrestling with the issue of failing cotton crops, private individuals also sought answers to the problem. The result of this concern among individuals was the creation of the Bahama Agriculture Society in 1801. At the society's initial meeting, a committee consisting of Lieutenant Colonel Brown, Judge Kelsall, and Wylly was appointed to draft bylaws for the organization and a call was issued for papers on agriculture and natural history of the West Indies in general and the Bahama Islands in particular.

The society contained thirty-two charter members from the Bahamas and associate members from the other British West Indies colonies and the United States.[107] One of the papers submitted came from Lieutenant Colonel Brown, who criticized Nassau residents for apparently showing little sympathy for the plight of planters on the Out Islands who were struggling to survive at a time when Nassau residents were enjoying a wartime economic boom. Privateering became very profitable and the economic fallout from this attracted new residents to Nassau. Meanwhile, the Out Islands were experiencing a population decrease. Brown reminded Nassau that the present wealth, increased population, and commerce resulted from a temporary situation that would vanish as quickly as it had appeared as soon as the war ended and the "Spanish colonies return to their prewar trade practices."[108]

Brown also stated his reasons why cotton production had declined, and in doing so he hit upon a reason which Judge Kelsall had given: the inexperience of Loyalist planters. Brown argued, "[The Bahama Islands was] in every sense a new country to planters, there was not a resident in it, who could give us any information (from experience) respecting the nature of its soil, or what it would produce. In other countries the planters have profited by the experience of others, in this, we never found a person of skill or experience, to direct our agricultural pursuits."[109] One need look no further than the British North American colonies for proof of this. Jamestown, Virginia, did not prosper economically until John Rolfe latched onto tobacco, a crop that the Native Americans planted with great success. The Plymouth colony in New England enjoyed a Thanksgiving in October 1621 only because the Native Americans in that region taught the "Pilgrims," as William Bradford called the settlers, how to plant corn. In both instances the transformation was achieved because of linkage with the past. The Loyalist cotton planters could not find the important linkage with the past.

Bahamian planters did not establish a link with the past, and they were probably influenced less by this than by an opportunity to get wealthy. Need-ing cotton to supply its nascent manufacturing industry, Britain encouraged cotton cultivation in some of its West Indies colonies by offering a bounty for the successful planting of the crop. Bermuda, for example, tried to grow cotton. Just before the first crop was to be harvested a hurricane ruined it. Undaunted by this initial failure, as many as two hundred acres were cultivated in 1789, and two years later several growers received bounties from the British government for successful crops. Subsequent cotton crops nonetheless failed and, realizing conditions in Bermuda were not conducive for growing abundant cotton crops, Bermudians turned to other economic endeavors.[110] The Bahamas was not alone, therefore, in attempting to grow a crop that conditions did not favor; but slaveholdings in Bermuda were not increased to meet anticipated labor demands, whereas they were in the Bahamas, leaving slaveholders with a supply and demand imbalance.

Many prominent planters had left the Bahamas by 1800, and the prognosis was that the hemorrhaging would resume as soon as the war ended. Among those taking permanent leave of the islands were three members of the assembly. A fourth member, Alexander Wylly, former Speaker of the assembly, gave formal notification that he, too, planned to leave.[111] Conversely, James Moss and his neighbors on Crooked Island agreed to stay on another twelve months. During the interim, his slaves would be employed raking salt, since there was little work to be done in the cotton fields.[112] In a long overdue move, the Land Office was reopened in 1803, after being closed for twelve years.[113] The move that considerably eased the hemorrhaging of the planter population, however, was the embargo that the Home Government placed on the removal of slaves from the colonies; it was one of the provisions of the Abolition of the Slave Trade Act (1807). Slaveholders no longer could take their slaves from the Bahamas to the United States or to Cuba, for instance, but they could still take them to another British West Indies colony, for example, Jamaica or Barbados, where plantation slavery was still thriving. This is what they did.[114]

The involuntary constriction of the cotton kingdom somewhat changed the nature of the slave experience. Slaveholders found themselves in the unenviable position of having a slave workforce with little plantation work to do. What was perhaps even more troubling was the decline in the value of their land and slaves. Land which formerly had sold for two and three guineas (one guinea was worth twenty-one shillings) an acre now sold for not more than two and three shillings an acre, and slaves once valued at from fifty to sixty pounds sterling now were valued at just one half that amount.[115] While this was not tantamount to having worthless money, it was not like hitting the lottery either. The year 1800 is usually cited as the time when the lights went out on the cotton plantations.[116] When they went out is less important than whether they did. Abandoned plantations throughout the Bahamas were ample proof of that, and this sent shock waves through an economy that had become even more dependent on slave labor after the arrival of the Loyalists than it had been previously. With fewer chores to do, slaves had more time to work in their plots of land. With less means to provide for the maintenance of their slaves, slaveholders shifted much of this responsibility to the slaves, who were now expected to eke out a living from the provisions produced on their plots.[117] To cut their losses, some slaveholders on the Out Islands employed slaves to raise crops and livestock for the Nassau market since residents there were not in the same economic straits.

Before the downsizing of the cotton kingdom, the task system was the traditional manner of working slaves and they were divided into four classes: seamen, slaves of small farmers, plantation slaves, and domestic slaves.[118] The division into seamen and domestic slaves is quite clear, but the separation into small farmers and plantation slaves is not. According to Howard Johnson, the Loyalists probably introduced the task system. In the case of drawing, weeding, and pruning, slaves were assigned tasks rather than organized in gangs, but gangs were used in specific chores such as planting and harvesting.[119] The task system was probably employed more on small farms than on the plantations, which is not to suggest it was not used there. B. W. Higman said that some work, such as that done by watchmen, fishermen, and domestics, was not adaptable to the task system, which means that a significant segment of the slave workforce in the Bahamas was employed neither in the gang nor the task system.[120]

Conditions under which slavery operated in the Bahama Islands were regarded as less demanding and degrading than elsewhere in the British West Indies.[121] This occurred because a much smaller percentage of the slaves in the Bahamas, especially in New Providence Island where Nassau, the capital, is found, were field hands than in the other colonies in the region.[122] Higman argued that the mortality rate of slaves in the marginal colonies, which included the Bahamas, was lower than in the sugar colonies.[123] Commenting on the food intake of slaves, Richard Sheridan stated "that slaves of Jamaica and Barbados received approximately 500 calories per day from the imported food they consumed." In contrast, Bahamian slaves, as a result of the Consolidated Slave Act (1797), were entitled to approximately 3,275 calories daily; and slaveholders conformed fully to the law.[124] The Bahama Islands, moreover, employed a higher percentage of slaves in domestic service jobs than any other British Caribbean colony. In 1806, the Bahamas had about 7,736 slaves, of whom 4,202 worked in the fields and 2,434 worked in the domestic services, giving a ratio of domestics to field hands of one to two. In Nevis, for example, an island with a comparable slave population (7,225), the ratio of domestics to field hands was one to four. The average ratio of domestics to field hands in the region was one to six, which placed the Bahamas well below the average. Looking at the practice of employing slaves from the standpoint of percentages, 31.5 percent of the slaves in the Bahamas were employed in domestic work, the highest percentage in the British West Indies, where the average for all colonies was 12.75 percent.[125] Furthermore, the self-hire system was more widespread in the Bahama Islands than elsewhere in the British West Indies.[126]

The failures among cotton plantations shifted emphasis toward hiring out slaves, and the self-hire of slaves increased. Slaves were transported to Nassau from the Out Islands where work was scarce. Slaves preferred self-hire to either the task system or hiring out because under self-hire they selected their employers or type of work, provided for their own needs, and managed their own household, in return for which they paid their masters a weekly stipulated amount. A major attraction of the practice to the slaveholders was that it produced a steady income and relieved them of maintenance expenses.[127] The agreement between slave and slaveholder was usually oral and the length unlimited, if the slave kept his part of the agreement and kept out of trouble. The other form of slave hire, where the slaveholder hired his slave to another party, was often a written agreement; and the hirer was obligated to provide subsistence, clothing, and medical care for the slave if the agreement covered several months or maybe a year. With New Providence having a larger proportion of the slave population than formerly, and slave hiring replacing the task system as the most widely used method of employing slave labor, the nature of the slave experience changed significantly in the Bahamas. Perhaps no other colony in the British West Indies experienced a change in slave management as significant as that in the Bahama Islands, in the wake of the involuntary constriction of the cotton kingdom.

Although slaves made up the largest group of nonwhites on the islands, they were not the only such persons. The population of free blacks and persons of color continued to increase after the turn of the century. Some of the free blacks and persons of color did well economically, although this was the exception rather than the rule. Identifying individual free blacks and persons of color, especially the property owners, is not at an easy task because government documents on the Bahamas do not include annual tax digests of Bahamians and sometimes lists of persons were not classified by race, but papers of religious organizations usually were. It is thus difficult to determine on a consistent basis the size and number of real estate owned by free blacks and persons of color. In spite of this, sufficient evidence exists to support contemporary accounts that allude to free blacks and persons of color as among the property owners. For instance, Johann David Schoepf, a visitor to the Bahamas in the 1780s, said that he saw many free blacks and persons of color, some of whom owned houses and plantations.[128] Writing in

1804, Moses Franks, chief justice for the Bahamas, said of the group, "[N]ot a few are possessed of property in these Islands."[129] Similarly, in 1815 Wylly wrote, "Our Free People of Colour form a large proportion of these Islands—The Heads of families are in general freeholders, some of whom are opulent planters."[130]

A significant portion of free blacks and persons of color apparently lived well and had a visible presence on the islands, but unfortunately the actual number of those who fell into this category is unknown. Since extant records contain the names of some of those persons, they can thus be removed from their long state of anonymity and enjoy the light of day. Many of these individuals enjoyed free status on the islands long before the Loyalists arrived. Amelia Smith, recipient of 325 acres on Great Exuma Island, was among the persons to whom Lord Dunmore granted tracts of land in April 1788. The names are not classified by race but the *C* beside her name suggests this may have been a free woman of color.[131] Rose McLeod, owner of 180 acres on Exuma Island, had the words "a negress" written beside her name indicating that she was a free black woman.[132] Robert Hunter owned a 20-acre plantation, which may have contained three slaves, on Crooked Island. In the case of Hunter's white counterparts, determining whether they were slaveholders is easy because there was a column designated whites and another designated black and colored. George Farquharson, for example, was the lone white on a 140-acre plantation that had thirty-five persons listed under in black and colored. Farquharson was a planter on a plantation which probably had thirty-five slaves (a few of the nonwhites could have been free). In the case of Hunter, however, he is listed in the black and color column along with four other persons who could have been family but could have included one or more slaves.[133]

A 1788 survey of New Providence revealed that free blacks and persons of color owned thirteen lots in the city of Nassau, thirteen in the western part of New Providence Island, and eight in the eastern part. Hannah Marshall, a free woman of color, owned one lot in Nassau and another in the eastern part of the island. Jeremiah Tinker and James Knowles, two free men of color, and Timothy Cox and Thomas Marshall, two free black men, also owned multiple lots, with Cox owning the most (three).[134] Between 1789 and 1791, six new nonwhites became real estate owners and Thomas Wallace received more land when Lord Dunmore granted tracts of land to seven free blacks and persons of color: George Watkins (a carpenter), Thomas Wallace, Edward Cox, Eve Cooba, William Cain, John Simms, and John Williams (a stonemason).[135] Since free blacks and persons of color lived in Nassau as well as in the eastern and western parts of New Providence and they did not live in nonwhite enclaves in these areas, they were not segregated residentially.

Similar housing patterns were followed on the Out Islands. When the township of Harbour Island was laid out in 1791, there were two free blacks and two free persons of color among its landowners, William Simms (black), Rebecca Sweeting (black), Thomas Lightbourne (free person of color), and Samuel Patrick (free person of color).[136] Their lots were scattered throughout the township. Moreover, the two free black males listed in an 1805 Abaco return were probably home owners.[137]

Over time the number of free black and colored real estate owners continued to increase. The index of wills does not provide a person's race, but the will usually does, when he or she is not European. Once the race of a person has been obtained from other sources, for example, either from Christ Church parish records or petitions drafted by free blacks and persons of color, the index becomes a valuable source for determining how much property and what kind the free blacks and persons of color owned. Betty Watkins, a free woman of color who lived in the Eastern District of New Providence Island, owned a lot, a house, and a female slave. Her occupation is unknown, but she may have been either a seamstress, washerwoman, or a cook, the traditional occupations opened to women of that day. She, moreover, made her mark with an *X* on the will, indicating that she could not write.[138] John Williams, a free black, had five lots in the Eastern District of New Providence and three slaves, two males and one female, at the time of his death in 1818. Williams, who also could not write, acquired three lots from the forty acres originally granted to Ohoff Patterson and another was purchased from John Stevens.[139] John Simms, a free black in Nassau, was among the successful carpenters, and he used this to become a landowner and to join the ranks of black slaveholders. In addition to the house and lot in which he and his wife, Phillis, lived, Simms owned "a lot of land known by the name of Delancey's number 67" and four slaves—three prime males, whom he may have also trained as carpenters and had working in the business with him, and one female.[140] Andrew Frazer, a free black man, operated a successful butchering business and he, too, was slaveholder.[141] Benjamin Lightbourne, a New Providence shopkeeper and free person of color, owned at least one slave in the 1790s and acquired at least six additional ones, all of whom were baptized in Christ Church.[142]

Well-to-do free blacks and persons of color were among the persons to whom liberated Africans were apprenticed to acquire job skills and to prepare to enter society as unencumbered free persons. In May 1811, a twelve-year-old liberated African female was apprenticed to Chloe Bode, a Nassau seamstress and free woman of color. Selecting this woman to become the guardian of little Sophia—the European name given to replace her African one, Massay (she was only four feet six inches tall)—reveals the confidence and respect whites had for Chloe Bode, who must have been well situated financially. The following September, a thirty-year-old liberated African named Cuffee was apprenticed to Timothy Cox, a successful free black Nassau ship carpenter. Cuffee, a rather tall man—he was five feet eleven inches—was expected to serve an eight-year apprenticeship.[143] Cox, an Anglican, had several slaves baptized in that faith, one of whom, a ship carpenter named Dick, he allowed to hire his own time.[144] In Cox's household, therefore, was a mixture of the three groups of nonwhites in the Bahama Islands, free persons, liberated Africans (who were legally free and occupied a middle ground between slaves and free person), and slaves.

Another indication that blacks and coloreds either owned or rented land in the Bahamas is gleaned from a grand jury presentment in the late 1780s: "We present as a grievance, the law not being put in force against Negroes and others hawking goods in baskets, trays, and other wise about the stall."[145] Hawkers were producers of the wares and produce they sold; whether they owned the land is less certain. Rather than depend upon handouts, the hawkers became independent small entrepreneurs, in a sense, much to the dismay of the grand jury, which probably would have complained just as strenuously had those persons opted to accept public assistance rather than work.

As among whites, a very small minority of free blacks and persons of color did accept public assistance. Christ Church Parish was given charge of administering to the poor, and its 1810 records show that the total number of colored men and women who fell into this category was nineteen, the men (eleven) constituting the larger group. The next year, the number increased to twenty-seven, with the women (fourteen) constituting the larger group. That year, moreover, white women (sixteen) outnumbered all other adult groups on the public dole and white men (five) made up the smallest group. After 1811, the number of colored paupers, who had previously outnumbered whites, declined because the colored paupers were dissatisfied with the manner in which the program was administered. According to the Reverend John Stephen, rector of Christ Church and president of the Board of Commissioners of the Poor House, which managed the facility, coloreds were "not equally willing to submit to the proper and necessary restraints imposed upon persons admitted . . . and to the service required of those who are able to work."[146] Coloreds probably objected to being assigned menial tasks that the whites either refused to perform or were not asked to do.

Free blacks and persons of color (and their enslaved brothers and sisters) constituted a significant part of the agricultural workforce, but this by no means was the extent of their involvement in the Bahamian economy. Many free blacks and persons of color worked on seagoing vessels. This often caused problems for census takers, who on several occasions noted at the bottom of returns that the number cited probably was an undercount by as much as 10 percent because so many were at sea. Similarly, commanders of militia companies often had to conduct drills while most of the company was at sea. Since marine occupations provided a livelihood for many of them, free blacks, persons of color, and slaves became expert pilots, navigators, and commanders. "Our black seaman are perhaps equal to any in the world," wrote Wylly, and he continued, "Our Island vessels are principally manned by them; and many of our droghers, tutlers, and fishing vessels are commanded by them."[147] These black crewmen and commanders received a percentage of the profits from each cruise or voyage they took; this doubtless amounted to a substantial sum at times. The same vessels used in peacetime for fishing, wrecking, and smuggling ventures were converted into privateers during wartime, and the profits were usually even greater.[148] In addition to working on and commanding different sizes and categories of vessels, blacks and coloreds were involved in their building at the various stages of production, from carting and boating timber used in their construction to working as blacksmiths, ship carpenters, and laborers in constructing them.[149]

Another area of employment for free blacks and persons of color was in the building trades, working as carpenters, stonemasons, and laborers. Sometimes they worked as employees and other times as independent artisans, as with George Watkins and John Williams. Skilled free blacks even plied their trade while serving an indentureship, as is seen in an advertisement which appeared in a Nassau newspaper offering a reward for the return of two runaway servants, one of whom was a mason and the other a carpenter.[150]

By 1815, therefore, Bahamians were in search of new economic ventures; conversely, the political system was on the verge of enjoying a stability in the executive branch that had not occurred in the Bahama Islands since the Loyalists arrived.

CHAPTER II

Blacks and Coloreds: The Society They Created, 1784–1815

Brother Amos is at [New] Providence, he writes that the Gospel has taken good effect And is spreading greatly; he has about three hundred members.
—Baptist Annual Register, 1790–1793

The year 1784 marked a turning point in many aspects of Bahamian life, especially among blacks and coloreds, both free and slave. Their numbers increased significantly, threefold as opposed to twofold for whites; they commenced to observe social customs that gained in popularity over the years, organized schools and churches, and generally created a society that intersected with whites at points and was distinctly separated at others. It was during this time that the British, African, and American social practices, educational principles, and religious institutions were combined to form a distinctly Bahamian way of life. Much of this resulted from white ostracism, but some evolved from a normal course of events where persons with similar physical features who also worked together and lived in close proximity formed kinship networks, participated in social functions, and organized religious institutions.

By no means were white-black relations analogous to the apartheid system found later in South Africa, or to the Jim Crow practices of the American South. Moreover, color differences among blacks and coloreds were much more meaningful in the Bahamas than they were in the United States, even if free persons of color were not given special legal privileges. The major reason for this was because mulattoes in the Bahamas were the result of legal commingling between the races. On the continent, on the other hand, where antimiscegenation laws were common, mulattoes were not the result of an accepted practice. Winthrop D. Jordan attempted to explain why Englishmen with the "same cultural baggage" developed divergent attitudes towards miscegenation and concluded that those living in areas with white majorities became antimiscegenationists and those living in the West Indies with its black majorities did not. Englishmen in North America tended to plant deeper roots in their new homeland than their counterparts in the British West Indies who still perceived themselves as English and returned to England at the slightest pretension. Those on the continent, moreover, argued Jordan, tended to replicate the moral climate in the mother country. This is a plausible explanation. It does not, however, address the question of extinction. One would expect the minority to be more sensitive to the need to avoid social interaction with the black majority in order to preserve its racial purity and avoid extinction. Jordan incorrectly assumed that even in the West Indies the liaison between whites and blacks did not lead to the altar and declared unequivocally that white women were not parties to these liaisons: "I have found no cases of white women sleeping with colored men in the West Indies," said Jordan.[1] But white women did.

Enforcement of the abolition of the slave trade led to the creation of a new group of blacks, the liberated Africans, who formed yet another separate group of free individuals. Within the English-speaking Western Hemisphere, "liberated African" was a uniquely British West Indies term, since no such group existed in the United States. The Bahamas probably was the British colony in the region where most of the African slaves were brought after the ships transporting them were intercepted before reaching their destination in the Spanish and French West Indies.[2] Those Africans were liberated and placed in an apprenticeship program for a stipulated period. Similarly, American slave ships that were either blown off course or inadvertently sailed into Bahamian waters, some landing on shoals, while traveling from one American port to another, were brought to New Providence where the slaves were freed. They, however, were not called liberated Africans.

The Bahama Islands, therefore, had a diverse group of people of African origin. Liberated Africans ranked above slaves, but they occupied a lower position on the social hierarchy than the free blacks and persons of color. The three free groups tended to subscribe to endogamy, with liberated

Africans more likely to marry slaves than the other two groups. On the other hand, free persons of color were more likely to marry whites than free blacks; and whites, when involved in interracial relationships, tended to select free persons of color as their mates, rather than either free blacks or liberated Africans. So the social practice that emerged was significantly different from that which the Loyalists had left in America, perhaps due in part to the imbalance that existed between white males and females, with the latter being in a decided numerical minority.

Blacks and coloreds, especially those who were free, increased throughout the period of 1784–1815, but the white population did not, partly due to the failure of cotton plantations. According to an unofficial 1790 population count, in 1784 there were about 1,750 whites and 2,300 "Blacks of every description" in the Bahamas. The figure for both groups increased in 1790, the whites by twofold and the blacks by threefold, the estimated count being 3,500 whites and 6,500 blacks, including people of color, for a total population of about 10,000 inhabitants.[3] A census taken by the Assembly of the Bahamas also reported that the whites had increased twofold and the blacks threefold since 1784, but the actual figures were different. The assembly's figures showed whites at 1,700 in 1784, a number that increased by 1,200 the next two years and by 400 the next three. Similarly, the black population, which numbered 2,300 in 1784, increased by 3,600 the next two years, and by 2,100 the next three.[4] The figure for whites is consistent with a twofold increase, but not the one for blacks since an increase from 2,300 to 8,000 is greater than threefold. A third eighteenth-century population count also cited the twofold and threefold increases among whites and blacks, respectively, during the five-year period from 1784 to 1789, but its actual figures differed from the two others given above. In 1789, William Wylly, the source for the third count, gave the following breakdown: whites 3,100, slaves 5,696, and free people of color 500, "making in the whole about nine thousand two hundred and ninety-six souls."[5]

The different figures of the various sources point up the need to avoid placing great stock in the counts of that day, other than as an indicator of population movement in a certain direction, either by the general population or by a certain group within it. A fourth population count underscores this. After visiting Long Island in 1790, a Reverend W. Gordon reported that the population was about 2,000 persons, over 1,500 of whom were slaves.[6] The figures are inflated because at no time during the period did the population of Long Island reach 2,000.

In addition to differences concerning the actual size of the population, contemporary sources also differed on the number of islands that were inhabited in 1784. The Missionary Report (1790) listed Abaco among the inhabited islands, but the assembly's did not. The latter also stated that Harbour Island (5 whites and 5 coloreds), Eleuthera (10 whites and 5 coloreds), and Long Island (8 whites and 21 coloreds) were the islands where the old inhabitants outnumbered the new; Harbour Island, Eleuthera (two neighboring islands), and Turks Island were the only ones with white majorities; and whites outnumbered blacks in Harbour Island 512 to 147, the largest imbalance by far, favoring whites. Conversely, on Exuma blacks outnumbered whites 638 to 66, the largest imbalance blacks enjoyed in the Bahamas. Moreover, Andros Island, the largest island in area, had the smallest population, 61—2 whites and 59 coloreds.[7] Thus, the five years from 1784 to 1789 witnessed an increase in both the population and in the number of inhabited islands.

New Providence Island led the Bahamas in population growth between 1801 and 1810. In 1801, Nassau had 1,599 whites, 752 free people of color (probably including blacks), and 3,861 slaves.[8] Among free persons on the island, whites and blacks/coloreds, the numbers for men, women, and children contrasted. While adult males composed the largest group of whites (620) and children came next (542), it was just the opposite among free blacks/coloreds, with the women (269) being the largest and the men (221) the smallest. Furthermore, the slave figures were different than those for both groups of free persons, with children (1,390), men (1,358), and women (1,093) ranking in descending order.[9] The relatively small number of slave women is indicative of their lack of importance in the workforce, their major value being procreative; and the abundance of children indicated that there could be a glut of hands in the future since it was becoming apparent that the plantation economy was not going to survive in the Bahamas, at least not that aspect of it that was geared to growing cotton. Although the need for slave labor would decrease, the level of natural increase continued. If this practice persisted, it portended ill for slaveholders, who would have more slaves than their labor needs required and their weak financial situation could sustain. The fact that this occurred in New Providence rather than on the Out Islands reduced but did not eliminate the seriousness of the situation.

Between 1805 and 1810, the slave population decreased while that of the free persons of color increased. In 1805, Governor Charles Cameron, who had arrived a year earlier, ordered a census taken of the "free people of color and negro slaves" on New Providence Island. Since all free people of color were required to register before receiving badges, which they were required to wear, the census taker used the Police Book, in which this information was kept, to gather information on the number of free persons of color. The breakdown of the group showed men (356), women (334), and children (302) for a total of 972. The numbers for the men and women were almost equal, but surprisingly, children constituted the smallest group. The slave population of 3,556 was less than the figure in 1801 and this caused William Chisholm, the census taker, to question the accuracy of the count and complain about the lack of cooperation from slaveholders. Believing that the slave population had been undercounted by one-sixth, Chisholm added 506 to his original count of 3,050, hence the number 3,556.[10] All the slaves were not available when the count was taken because some slaves were at sea and in other instances slaveholders did not know where they were, perhaps because these slaves had been allowed to hire their own time and no longer lived with the slaveholder. Surprisingly, the number of aged males (those above sixty years of age), 120, far exceeded that of aged females, 57. These figures were increased to 141 men and 66 women to compensate for the alleged one-sixth that Chisholm did not see.[11] It may have been plausible to adjust for the unexpected shortfall in the number of prime male slaves, believing those slaves had been undercounted, but to apply this equally to the aged slave population was unwise. If that group was out of place, it was more probably because the persons had died. Furthermore, the figures in the Bahamas are the opposite of what they were in slave societies in the Lower South, where throughout the region slave women outlived men. Savannah was just one example of this.[12]

In 1810, the white population of New Providence was 1,720, the free black/colored, 1,074, and the slave, 3,190.[13] On the basis on these figures, one may conclude that all segments of the population increased, except for the number of slaves. The census taker continued to complain and his frustration shows clearly in the document. He believed the undercount of the slave population was even greater than before, this time 10 percent, and that of the free blacks/coloreds was "very great . . . because many have no fixed place of residence their being employed in wrecking and other vessels belonging to the port." This return gave separate figures for free blacks (565) and free persons of color (509).[14]

Thus, in the Bahamas free blacks outnumbered free persons of color, a situation that differed from that in both the American South and the larger British West Indies colonies. Free mulattoes greatly outnumbered free blacks in New Orleans, Charleston, South Carolina, and Mobile, and to a lesser extent in Savannah, Georgia.[15] Similarly, free persons of color in

Jamaica and Barbados outnumbered free blacks. Edward Brathwaite said there were about 4,000 free persons of color in Jamaica in 1793, "including free blacks." In consecutive chapters entitled "Blacks" and "The (Free) People of Colour," Brathwaite discussed "nonwhites." The chapter entitled "Blacks" dealt only with slaves; the other one alluded to free blacks only in passing, which suggests that free persons of color outnumbered free blacks, who were not worth discussing, or that blacks generally were slaves.[16] Moreover, according to an 1825 estimate, Jamaica had 30,000 free persons of color and 10,000 free blacks.[17] That same year in Barbados free persons of color outnumbered free blacks 2,066 to 1,760.[18]

The preponderance of blacks among free blacks/coloreds resulted from a large imbalance between mulattoes and blacks in the slave population and the readiness with which Bahamian officials approved manumission requests. In 1810, for instance, blacks constituted 95 percent of the slave population—3,044 out of 3,190—in New Providence.[19] If most of the slaves were black and manumissions were granted relatively liberally, then most of those receiving manumissions were black, and this tended to blacken the free population of nonwhites. In the American Lower South, on the other hand, even though slaves were also predominately black, whites generally outnumbered African Americans in the general population, manumissions were more difficult to obtain, and when they were granted the recipients in significant numbers were mulatto relatives of the slaveholders. Many southern states enacted legislation mandating that manumitted slaves must leave the state.[20] The law was often circumvented, but its presence on the books inhibited expansion of the free African-American population through manumission, which was the intent of the legislation.

The population picture in New Providence was different from the one in the Out Islands. The total free black/colored population in the Bahama Islands in 1805 was 1,344, with 82 percent of these living on two islands, New Providence Island (999) and Eleuthera (110). More specifically, 74 percent of the free black/colored population lived on the former and 8 percent on the latter. The greatest concentration of free blacks/coloreds was in New Providence. It was the economic and political center of the Bahamas, a magnet for persons seeking employment, as opposed to the Out Islands, many of which were undeveloped even though inhabited. If one did not farm on the Out Islands, it was hard to make a living. As this situation did not offer much attraction for free blacks/coloreds, five of the Out Islands, about one-third of all the inhabited islands, had individual black/colored populations of less than 10.[21]

The slave population figures, however, were different. In 1805, only 27 percent of the slaves in the Bahama Islands lived in New Providence (3,045 out of 11,093). Turks Islands (1,348), Exuma (1,087), Eleuthera (1,071), and Caicos (1,069) each had more than 1,000 slaves; Crooked Island (871) and Saint Salvador (694) each had more than 500.[22] The large slave population on these islands cannot be explained solely in terms of the cotton plantation system, because only two of the islands with over 1,000 slaves grew cotton, and the out island with the largest slave population in 1805, Turks Islands, was a major salt producer. Regardless of the main economic endeavor pursued on the Out Islands, the mind-set was oriented toward slave labor. As a result, the slave population multiplied.

More whites lived on the Out Islands than in New Providence, but the free black/colored population of New Providence was more than double that of the total on the Out Islands.[23] New Providence, with its large free black/colored population, provided the leadership and set the standard for the Bahama Islands, but over time each out island developed its own idiosyncrasies which became clearly identifiable and associated with that island by other Bahamains. To this day, Bahamians know an Andros man from one, for instance, who was reared in Gregory Town, Eleuthera. It was during the nineteenth century that these characteristics came to epitomize Bahamian society and culture.

The black and colored leadership in the Bahama Islands was provided by those persons who were free. This status was achieved mainly by birth; nevertheless, a number of other avenues were available to achieve freedom. During the American Revolution, the British military command issued a proclamation freeing any "negro slave" who deserted his Patriot master and entered British lines. At the conclusion of the war, many of those who responded to the proclamation and reached British lines were evacuated along with the British forces that moved to East Florida; and from there they were uprooted when Britain ceded that territory to Spain, causing yet another move, this time to the Bahamas. They expected to live the remainder of their lives as free persons, only to discover that American Loyalists made ownership of a certificate of freedom a prerequisite for enjoying freedom in the new land.[24]

In order to gain their freedom, those persons who did not have certificates had to petition the receiver general to validate their claim. One such case involved a black woman named Rose, alias Binah, who applied to George Barry, receiver general, on February 19, 1787, claiming that Thomas Ross was holding her in bondage illegally. Responding to Rose's petition,

Barry summoned Ross to his office to address the allegation.[25] In another case the following October, "a negro fellow named Matthias" petitioned for his freedom. The following excerpt from a letter of John O'Halleran, justice of the peace, to William Green lays out the law regarding the matter: "As the Laws of these Islands direct that in all cases Where the freedom [of] any Negro shall be in contestation the same shall be determined by the Receiver General for the time being and two Magistrates; and it appearing to me that this fellow's pretensions to freedom are well grounded, I am to desire that you will attend at the courthouse of Friday next at twelve O'clock to show cause good and sufficient, why the above mentioned Negro should not obtain a certificate of freedom agreeable to his Majesty's Proclamation and the Said Act."[26]

The clause requiring Green to provide proof of why he was entitled to enslave Matthias got to the heart of the matter: the slaveholder was not presumed to be right. If the slave presented corroborated evidence supporting his case, the slaveholder was then required to provide compelling evidence to the contrary. Rose, Matthias, and four other slaves won their freedom that term of the court. In fact, between 1783 and 1787, eleven slaves were manumitted by proclamation; during the next nine years forty-one slaves gained freedom in this manner, but after 1796 only seven gained freedom by proclamation.[27] The peak period for gaining freedom by proclamation came, therefore, during the governorship of Lord Dunmore, who commanded a black unit during the American Revolution and promised freedom to slaves who joined the Loyalist cause.

Proclamation was just one of many ways that slaves gained freedom in the Bahamas. Natural love, gift, claim of right, sentence of the Admiralty Court, forfeiture, military service, faithful service, fidelity, and natural service are key terms that appeared in documents granting freedom to slaves.[28] For instance, in his will a slaveholder may have written that the natural love he had for the slave compelled him to free the slave. Some slaves, doubtless, purchased their freedom after accumulating money earned from working jobs or selling (hawking) produce in the market. These manumissions do not appear in the Register of Freed Slaves. The multiplicity of ways for slaves to gain manumission and the manner in which officials handled manumission requests reaffirm the earlier statement of the part manumissions played in the steady growth of the free blacks and persons of color from 1784 to 1815.

The courts exercised the same diligence in cases involving cruelty to slaves. From 1800 to 1811, fourteen cases were heard in the general court dealing with violation of the "Law made for the protection of Slaves." The most serious violations were committed by Abraham Grange, a white, and

James Stewart, a free man of color. Grange was convicted of wantonly and cruelly beating and mistreating his male slave; for this he was fined eighty pounds sterling, incarcerated in jail for three months, and required to provide security for good behavior for twelve months. Stewart was also convicted of cruel treatment of a slave, a girl whom he beat and mistreated, loading her with chains and irons. In spite of committing the more serious violations, Stewart received a lighter sentence than Grange. His punishment was six weeks in the workhouse and a security for good behavior for twelve months. In other cases, fines of fifteen, twenty, fifty, eighty, and ninety pounds sterling were imposed.[29]

Color was a major barrier to commingling between Bahamians.[30] Whites generally associated with persons of the same color and so did free blacks and persons of color. No law granted persons of color special privileges; they were discriminated against just like their free black counterparts.[31] Nonetheless, a mind-set prevailed which encouraged persons of color to segregate themselves socially from free blacks. The Bahamas was not unique in this regard because a similar attitude about color pervaded the English-speaking Western Hemisphere, especially in slave societies. The practice was etched so deeply into the way of life that gradations of whiteness existed in the law in many British West Indies colonies. Accordingly, the child of white and black partners was called mulatto; the child of white and mulatto partners was a quadroon; the issue of white and quadroon partners was a *mustee,* and that of white and *mustee* partners was a *musteefinos.*[32] In the Bahamas, persons three degrees removed in lineal descent from their black ancestors were deemed white.[33] All those nearer to being completely black were mulattoes or persons of color in the eyes of the law.

Marriage registers of the parishes, containing in many instances the color of the mates, are invaluable for determining the extent to which the Bahamas subscribed to the social convention of the rest of the British West Indies. Christ Church, for instance, held 281 marriages for blacks and coloreds, both free and slave, from 1791 to 1828. In 8 marriages involving slaves, 1 involved a male slave and a free woman of color, 4 involved a male slave and a free black woman, 2 involved a female slave and a free man of color, and 1 involved a female slave and a free black man. From the perspective of the total marriages performed, the number involving slaves was very small. In those marriages, moreover, the husband was usually a slave and the wife a free black woman. In those marriages in which both parties were free, 11 included a free man of color and a free black woman, and 2 consisted of a free black man and a free woman of color. Given the total number of 273 marriages involving free persons, 13 was very small, less than 5 percent. In those marriages, the husband usually was a person of color and the wife was black. More significantly, however, in the free black/colored marriages, the overwhelming majority (260) were between parties of the same color and only 13 were not.[34] This is a telling commentary of how strictly Bahamians adhered to social convention.

One cannot look at these numbers without wondering if it was by chance that people of the same color tended to marry or if other factors were at play. For instance, was economic status a factor? Was education a factor? Did the faithful tend to marry within the faith? Doubtless these were all factors, but the greatest factor was still probably color. Does this mean that blacks were proud of their blackness and disdained tainting it with European blood, so to speak, or did persons of color view blackness negatively and place social distance between themselves and their black brothers and sisters? In short, who ostracized whom? Both camps, blacks and coloreds, probably were guilty, but persons of color more so than blacks, if early twentieth-century vestiges of it in the United States are indicative of practices of that day.[35]

Color also figured very prominently in interracial marriages. Christ Church identified parties by complexion until 1789 when the practice was abandoned. When the practice was in vogue, it was easy to identify interracial marriages; after this, it was not. Whether interracial marriages ceased after that date cannot be determined from the record, although one doubts that they did. Using 1773 and 1788 as cutoff dates, we find that twenty-one interracial marriages were conducted, all involving whites and persons of color. In a majority of the marriages, fifteen, the husband was white and the wife was a person of color, and in the remaining six the husband was a person of color and the wife was white.[36] Therefore, white men participated in interracial marriages almost three times as often as white women. Although Winthrop D. Jordan reported that he "found no cases of white women sleeping with colored men in the West Indies," these church records show otherwise. Jordan probably overlooked Bahamian sources. The disparity between white men and women in these interracial marriages could have stemmed from a shortage of white women in the colony and the silence of the law of the subject. It was not illegal to marry outside one's race. The twenty-one marriages, moreover, refute Jordan's characterization of these interracial relationships as mere liaisons. Those twenty-one couples did more than merely live together; they made a lifetime commitment to each other.

Additional instances of interracial commingling are found in the record of baptisms from 1795 to 1828. The infants' parents were interracial in six baptisms and in each instance the father was white and the mother was a free woman of color. Only one couple indicated they were married. Moreover, one of the white parents was a governor, Lewis Grant, the father of a baby girl born to Susan Sherman, a free woman of color. The baby, born on February 28, 1825, and baptized on June 5, became the godchild of Charlotte Dillet, a free woman of color and wife of Stephen, a prominent free man of color and successful tailor.[37] This type of liaison between prominent white males and free women of color may have happened more often than can be documented. Another case that can be documented, however, involved Henry Yonge of Andros. Yonge was expelled from the assembly in 1803 after he fled the Bahamas in a vessel registered to his colored mistress, but which he probably owned, leaving behind huge sums of unpaid debts.[38]

These marriages and liaisons send very strong signals that whites harbored stronger prejudices toward blacks than toward persons of color, and persons of color were more willing to marry a white than a black. Neither white men nor white women married blacks. Only two marriages performed in Christ Church involved a free woman of color and a black man. In another marriage involving a free woman of color the mate was a slave whose color was not stated. He, too, could have been a mulatto. On the other hand, no less than sixteen of the interracial marriages (including the one in the baptisms) involved a free woman of color. It was not a situation where these women were outnumbered and presented a numerical match for white males who outnumbered white females. At least one census placed free black/colored males as being slightly more numerous than their female counterparts. In light of this, free women of color were not forced by numerical circumstances to look outside. Rather, signs point to a color bias among free women of color that was stronger than the one among free men of color. Furthermore, recently arrived persons of color also subscribed to the social convention, as seen in the marriage of William Turton, a mulatto from Barbados and a Methodist missionary, to a white woman who was his first white convert.[39] Thus, racism and color bias colored relations in the Bahamian society. On this, the record is quite clear.

Since the record reflects such little social interaction between free persons of color and slaves, it should not come as a surprise that they formed companies that hunted runaway slaves hidden in the woods. In December 1803, two companies of "free persons of colour," under the command of a white officer, John Jennings Smith, searched the woods for runaways.[40] The patrol cost the government £13.8s which included funds for provision and refreshments. The assembly minutes expressly referred to the units as "Two companies of Free People of colour."[41] Whether this should be taken literally, meaning that free blacks were excluded from the excursion, is difficult to determine. What is less difficult to discern, however, is that the units were not composed of whites, leaving one to conclude that slaves wishing to escape bondage in the Bahamas were often apprehended by their own kind who happened to be free. This must have been disturbing to slaves.

Most slaves in the Bahamas, like elsewhere in the British West Indies, came from West Africa, and the situation in the Bahamas was conducive to the preservation of African customs and practices.[42] As noted earlier, most of the Out Islands were inhabited predominately by slaves, who, in light of their numerical superiority and the geographical isolation of the islands, were ideally situated to maintain their culture. Even on New Providence this was possible after the creation of separate communities for the liberated Africans. Once the initial cultural shock that resulted from their uprooting and transportation to a different part of the world had run its course, slaves created a society over time that clearly bore the stamp of Africa, although the society was not purely African.[43] This is evident in their new names, the African names having been replaced by "Christian" names provided by their captors.

Perhaps the most distressing part of the name change was the whites' propensity to give several slaves the same first name, a practice that was alien to the African experience, where each name was special and unique to the villager who possessed it. In West Africa, where most of the slaves in the Bahamas were from, children were named most frequently for the day of their birth; in addition, they were named for specific events or places, lineages, occupations, attributes, proverbs, and gods. Had whites been aware of the practice and merely substituted an English translation of the African name for the slave's new name, the shock may have been less traumatic, but whites either were ignorant of African culture or insensitive to the feeling of their captives, or both. So a slave who may have had an African name that represented bravery may have been saddled with a so-called "Christian" name of an English or Scottish city; the slave who may have subscribed to worshiping idols could have received as a new name a Biblical character; a slave to whom the concept of months of the year was foreign may have found himself named after a month of the year; a slave who may have been the village historian may have been renamed for a Greek of Roman personality.

The women, moreover, were not spared, except that none in the Register of Freed Slaves was named for either a month or a place. The names which appeared most frequently were Hannah (twenty-four), Cleopatra (nineteen), Phoebe (twelve), Patience (ten), and Chloe (ten). The men had a longer list of names and the ones which appeared most often were Isaac (twelve), Prince (eleven), Cuffee (seven), Pompey (six), and Ceasar (six).[44] Phoebe was the Caribbean female name for Friday among the Akan people, and Cuffee was the male name for that day. In Laurie A. Wilkie's anthropological study of slaves on Wade's Green Plantation on Caicos Island, occupied mainly by Creoles who were allowed to name their children without outside pressure, the names fell into four types: unaltered African names, Anglicized Africans names, Creolized names, and European names. The vast majority of the slaves (over 70 percent) had European names and about another 25 percent had either Creolized names or Anglicized African names. Wilkie believed that the loss of African naming patterns resulted from the replacement of African languages with English.[45]

Most Africans lost their names but retained many of their customs. In fact, slaves in the Bahamas were more successful in retaining their culture than their American counterparts, and this was generally the case throughout the British West Indies. Although the English generally had a low regard for African culture, actions which resulted in stripping Africans of some of their culture probably were not so much deliberate attempts to do this but were the result of efforts to shape Africans into efficient, obedient laborers. In his award-winning work *White over Black,* Winthrop D. Jordan observes, "In England perhaps more than in southern Europe, the concept of blackness was loaded with intense meaning. Long before they found that some men were black, Englishmen found in the idea of blackness a way of expressing some of their most ingrained values. . . . Black was an emotionally partisan color, the handmaid and symbol of baseness and evil, a sign of danger and repulsion." This negative view of blackness was transferred to Africans and to African culture, Jordan subsequently argues.[46] In the clash of cultures that ensued in the Bahamas, those parts of African culture that encumbered achieving the goals the English had established became casualties of the African Diaspora. The slaves, for their part, did not cooperate entirely with the whites' grand design to remake them; nevertheless, they did cooperate enough to make the system function.

Celebration of Christmas was one of those practices which did take hold among the slaves. The Consolidated Slave Act (1797) mandated a three-day holiday for slaves during Christmastide; this probably came after the fact

Renaming Africans (Females)

African Names [11]		Biblical Names [6]		Egyptian, Greek, Addjectival Names [8]		Other Roman Names [5]		Famous Persons [2]		Names of Places [0]		Calendar Names, or Days and Months [0]	
Phoebe	12	Hannah	24	Patience	10	Sophia	19	Lucretia	4				
Chloe	10	Esther	6	Charity	4	Venus	6	Priscilla	4				
Sukey	5	Rachael	4	Tulip	1	Cleopatra	1						
Hagar	4	Hester	2	Lady	1	Delia	1						
Binah	2	Rebecca	1	Comfort	1	Juno	1						
Dinah	2	Mariah	1	Temperance	1								
Agar	2	Prudence	1										
Rinah	1												
Rhina	1												
Minah	1												
Qua Sheba	1												

*Source: Resgister of Freed Slaves, Eighteenth and Nineteenth Century

Renaming Africans (Males)

African Names [6]		Biblical Names [4]		Names of Places [15]		Adjectives, Titles, Famous People [13]		Greek, Egyptian, and Roman Names [14]		Months [3]	
Cuffee	7	Issac	12	Edinburgh	5	Prince	11	Pompeii	6	March	3
Juba	2	Jacob	6	London	3	Hercules	3	Caesar	6	November	2
Quash	2	Amos	1	Bristol	3	Sambo	3	Cato	3	July	1
Congo	1	Abraham	1	Dublin	3	Smart	2	Scipio	2		
Cudjoe	1			Liverpool	1	Sampson	2	Othello	2		
Zuba	1			Halifax	1	Kill	1	Apollo	2		
				Britain	1	Gabriel	1	Augustus	2		
				Warwick	1	Uriah	1	Pharaoh	2		
				Boston	1	Napoleon	1	Nero	1		
				Trafalgar	1	Fly	1	Bachus	1		
				Essex	1	Mustapha	1	Constantine	1		
				Belfast	1	Savage	1	Titus	1		
				Castle Town	1	Yellow	1	Brutus	1		
				Scotland	1			Romeo	1		
				Lancaster	1						

*Source: Register of Freed Slaves, Eighteenth and Nineteenth Century

because slaves may have been enjoying this privilege before the act was passed. Instead of enjoying it as a privilege, as they formerly did, after 1797 slaves enjoyed the three-day holiday as a right. The timing was right for this celebration because the favorite food crops, maize, yams, plantains, bananas, and sweet potatoes, were harvested and cattle were slaughtered in the late fall. Several pounds of meats were given to each adult slave and large shipments of foodstuff arrived from abroad, ensuring that more food was available at Christmas than at any other time of the year.[47] Slaves prepared tasty meals, engaged in frolicking and merriment, including performing "rushin," a celebration similar to the ring shout in America.

The Junkanoo may have also been performed at this time, although it was not until much later (the 1830s) that we find documented proof of what could be called a Junkanoo celebration. A celebration which the Methodist reverend W. Dawson, a missionary, observed among blacks on Turks Islands in 1811 could also have been a Junkanoo. The blacks were said to have beaten tabourines and danced for a whole day. The Junkanoo has definite West African roots; there celebrations from which it evolved were found in places under different names. The Ibo called their celebration the "Yam Festival," the Yoruba observed recreational activities of the Egungun Secret Society, and the Ga peoples practiced the Homowo harvest festival. In the Mno Secret Society dancers were masked and impersonated ancestral spirits. The Egungun Secret Society, composed of all males, had members who adorned themselves in splendid masks and costumes. Bahamian Junkanoo, a close relative of the John Canoe and Jonkonnu celebrations in the West Indies, is a synthesis of old African secret societies' celebrations rather than a direct derivative from one particular celebration.[48] This perhaps accounts for the wide range of practices and different, though phonetically similar, names throughout the Caribbeans. Only in the Bahamas, however, is it called Junkanoo, which is phonetically close to the word *dzonkonu* from the Ewe people of Eastern Ghana and Togo.[49]

Story telling, foods such as mi mi, foo foo, and accard, ring play, the fire and jumping dance, warri, and asu(e) also have African roots. Warri was played by women. The warri board was usually carved from mahogany wood with fourteen wells. Each end of the board had a well called a bank with six on each opposite side of the board. The game was played by two persons with the board held tightly between the knees.[50] Asu(e), a means of pooling money, has a direct link to the Yorubas, unlike Junkanoo, which is eclectic. Among the Yoruba, the practice was known as esusu, and Samuel Johnson defines it as a "universal custom from clubbing together of a number of persons for monetary aid. A fixed sum is given by each at a fixed time [usually every week] and placed under a president, the total amount is paid to each member in rotation. This enables a poor man to do something worthwhile where a lump sum of money is required. There are no laws regulating the sum."[51] This practice came in handy in the Bahamas where there was no bank from which money could be borrowed. Moreover, low-income workers who probably did not have sufficient credit to get a loan would not have been helped had there been a bank. Asu(e) obviated this. By pooling their resources, ten persons were assured of receiving a payment ten times what they contributed each week, when their hand came. The money could have been used to buy seeds, a farm animal, tools, or cloth to make garments. Asu(e) was also practiced elsewhere in the British West Indies under different names: susu in Trinidad, and partners in Jamaica. Asu was not practiced, however, in the United States where, for instance, in Philadelphia an insurance company was started but failed.[52] Furthermore, Bahamian secular music with its strong emphasis on drumming and dancing, generally also came from Africa, but not the religious music, which was imported from the United States.[53]

The practice of African medicine in the Bahamas probably did not vary much from that found throughout the Caribbean. Slaves on Caribbean plantations were affected by African medicine in a variety of ways. The impact doubtless was more significant prior to the ban on the African slave trade when African-born slaves predominated on the plantations than it was afterwards. A number of features of African medicine were continued on the plantations: (1) folk medicine was divided between good and bad medicine men, with some blurring of the line; (2) herbal and other remedies were used extensively and transmitted from generation to generation; (3) charms, spells, fetishes, incantations, and poison were used; and (4) women played an important role. Planters inadvertently contributed to the preservation of African medical practices by refusing, for a long time, to introduce their slaves to European education and religious training.[54] This supports the position that the primary purpose of planters was not to de-Africanize the slaves.

Obeah was the name given to bad medicine in the West Indies, the term originating from the West African word "obeye," meaning a spiritual being or minor god.[55] It fell under that category of sorcery whose primary intent was to harm others, upon request, by using "shadow catching" charms and poisons. Obeah was an individual practice, performed by a professional who expected to receive a fee for his, or her, service. Obeah persons, with few exceptions, were aged Africans of both sexes who mastered knowledge of medicinal and poisonous plants, using this knowledge to exert influence over their subscribers who, while simultaneously revering and abhorring them, nonetheless sought their advice.[56] People especially sought Obeah men when sudden unexpected events occurred in their lives, or after the mysterious death of a loved one, or to gain revenge for insults or mistreatment. Obeah men were also blamed for some of the very pain they were hired by others to assuage.[57]

Concomitant with the presence of a mind-set that supported primitive and distasteful practices such as obeah was support for education among free blacks/coloreds. At no time did the government outlaw the operation of schools for blacks/coloreds, nor did it pass laws requiring separate schools for the races. Education among blacks and coloreds received a boost with the arrival of the American Loyalists, among whom was an able black educator and Methodist minister named Joseph Paul Sr., who had been educated in South Carolina. Paul, his wife, Susannah, and their three children sailed for the Bahamas on a vessel commanded by Captain Patrick Kennedy, with whom they indentured themselves. His indenture to the captain suggests that Paul did not have sufficient funds to pay for the passage of his family. A convert of the stalwart Great Awakening evangelist George Whitefield, Paul arrived in Abaco in 1783 and remained there a few years before moving to New Providence.[58] The time spent in Abaco may have been devoted to working off his indenture, leaving him free to move away. Shortly after Paul arrived in New Providence, he built a Methodist chapel and opened what is believed to be the first private school on the island for blacks and coloreds.[59] He evidently was a competent teacher because Dr. Bray's Associates, an affiliate of the Society for the Propagation of the Gospel in Foreign Parts (S.P.G.), invited him to head a school which it opened in March 1793. The school had twenty-four or twenty-five free children of blacks from America, who paid tuition of twelve pence to attend classes and receive instruction in reading, writing, and arithmetic, the basic core courses of primary education of that day.[60]

Paul taught in the school for nearly a decade before he died in April 1802. The torch was then passed to the older of his two sons, Joseph Paul Jr.[61] We do not know how old the elder Paul was at his demise, but he had lived in the Bahamas for nearly twenty years. The older son who replaced him must have been in his forties, at the least. Joseph Paul Jr. did an outstanding job of teaching his seventy scholars—only thirty of whom were funded by Bray's Associates—in what must have been crowded conditions. After visiting the school in 1806, Richard Roberts reported to the S.P.G. that "the scholars shewed [showed] a readiness in writing and cyphering beyond my expectation." When John Stephen, rector of the Christ Church, visited the school about four years later he "found it was a rule to exercise them [scholars] once every day on the Church Catechism and to explain it to them from *Lewis'* Exposition." Furthermore, he said that the scholars read a portion of the New Testament with great readiness and correctness and "[t]heir writing Books and Cyphering Books, likewise, in point of neatness, regularity, and correctness very far exceed[ed his] expectation." Stephen, however, was "at a loss to conceive how he [Joseph Paul Jr.] would find leisure in so numerous a school."[62]

Since Paul was compensated for teaching the thirty scholars that Bray's Associates funded—he received an annual salary of eighteen pounds sterling —in addition to income obtained from his forty private students, his financial situation was solid.[63] This was not the case with the struggling school founded by William Turton, a Methodist missionary who opened it in 1803 for the instruction of youth and from which he expected to receive income to support his missionary work.[64] About the same time Turton opened his school in New Providence, William Darrell started a free Sunday school on Turks Islands.[65]

Joseph Paul Jr. died in June 1811, and his younger brother, William Paul, a ship carpenter and head of the chapel his father had built, replaced him.[66] Stephen initially was apprehensive about recommending William Paul for the position because he was inexperienced, but Paul proved to be a chip off the old block, relieving Stephen's apprehension and causing him to conclude that "the school will be a gainer by the change of master."[67] William Paul's tenure as master of the Bray's Associates School was much shorter than those of his father and brother who preceded him in the position. He died on August 23, 1813, after a brief illness, slightly over two years after his appointment.[68] This death created a problem for the S.P.G. because apparently there was not a suitable pool of candidates from which a new master could be selected. The last Paul, William, exhausted the list of qualified persons for the position. Thanks to Joseph Paul Jr. however, the situation was not hopeless. He had identified Joseph Gould Watkins, a young man who attended his school, as a future master and had further contributed to Watkins' development by hiring him as an assistant in the school. There was just one problem, the S.P.G. preferred masters to be at least twenty-five years old, but Watkins was only in his late teens in 1813. Nevertheless, Stephen suggested to Watkins that he open a school for tuition-paying scholars until he could secure approval for the appointment from the S.P.G. This subsequently came and Watkins was offered the position commencing on January 1, 1815; he accepted the appointment, foregoing an opportunity to work in the more financially rewarding vocation of ship carpenter for which he had been trained.[69] Thus the torch was passed to another generation to continue the work that Joseph Paul Sr. had begun in 1793.

The early effort of Joseph Paul Sr. in the field of education perhaps caught the eye of the public officials who saw the need to have schools operating in the Bahamas. Accordingly, the assembly became involved in education in the mid-1790s after an absence of nearly a half century. In 1795, it passed a school act for the first time since 1746, the provisions of which placed all schools under a central authority. Four years later, another school act was passed, this one providing for the establishment of ten schools which were to be administered by the rector, church wardens, and vestry in each parish where a school was located. In 1804, the assembly passed yet another education act, this one providing for the establishment of a high school.[70] Thus, in the span of less than ten years the legislature enacted three education acts, pushing the Bahamas forward in the field of education.

The public school system that was created posited administration of the public schools in the hands of the Anglican Church, and with good reason: the rectors, collectively, were the best trained professionals in the Bahama Islands. On some Out Islands, rectors may have been the only literate persons, and if not they were the best trained and the only ones capable of running a school. In New Providence, the residence of most of the learned men in the Bahamas, the rectors of Christ Church and St. Matthews, on the eastside, ranked among the best educated. This ensured that public schools in the Bahamas would have the best qualified professionals at the helm, but were schools opened to all children regardless of color? The assembly posed this question while attempting to ascertain the status of slavery, using the standard instrument of the day, an inquiry, but the questions were intended to gather information on free blacks and coloreds. In addressing question 12, which dealt with the school issue, the respondents declared that children of free blacks and persons of color were not denied access to the public school in Christ Church parish. Respondents generally passed, however, on the section of the question that dealt with whether the same number of those children attended as whites. The response of one T. Matthews, "This examinant . . . cannot take upon himself to say what proportion the number of coloured children generally bear to the number of white childen educated at the public expense in those schools," mirrored the views of most respondents.[71] The one respondent who did address the question, the Reverend John Stephen, rector of Christ Church, said, "During a great part of last year, and the whole of the present, the number of Blacks and Coloureds have been nearly equal to that of the white."[72]

The Reverend Stephen's reply leads to a number of observations. First, the answer is consistent with that of the other respondents concerning the public school's admission policy: children of all colors were admitted. He also said that the number of black and colored scholars was nearly the same as that for whites. This is remarkable in light of the 1815 population figures, which showed that whites in New Providence greatly outnumbered free blacks and coloreds combined. One should not race to the conclusion that the proportional representation of black and colored children enrolled in all schools, public and private, was larger than for whites because the answers to the inquiry reflected the situation in the public school only. Private schools in the Bahamas, Bray's Associates School excepted, were probably all white, and when these numbers are added to that of the public school the picture changes. The third observation is that blacks and persons of color attended the school, not just persons of color. Since black children attended the same school as persons of color, and since many of the teachers in New Providence were black—namely the Pauls and Joseph G. Watkins—free persons did not monopolize education and they did not have a privileged position in the church. Since free persons of color did not dominate the religious and educational institutions, the two most important institutions on the islands, there is no basis for arguing that they constituted a mulatto aristocracy.

Respondents did not say whether slave children attended the public school. They may not have because slaveholders were not disposed to surrender them for the length of time demanded by school attendance policy and because the curriculum did not enhance the value of slaves; if anything, educated slaves lost market value. The public school referred to its pupils as scholars, strongly indicating its educational objective. An institution that perceived its pupils as scholars was also one that taught a classical curriculum rather than trades, certainly not the type of institution that slave children were expected to attend in appreciable numbers. The exceptions to this were children of slaves who hired their own time and may have earned sufficient income to pay their masters the weekly amount demanded and still have money left to pay tuition. Even in cases involving hired slaves, slave children who attended school were probably the exception. It appears that the first priority would be to save enough money to purchase the family's freedom.

The assembly's willingness to expend public funds to educate black and colored children placed the Bahamas well ahead of the United States and most of the other British West Indies colonies in the field of primary and secondary education. No American state had established an effective public school system in 1815, not even for white children, and the private schools were opened to one race, not to both, a situation that existed in both the North and South.[73] The schools in Jamaica were superior to those in the Bahamas. In Barbados, however, there were no public schools for free blacks and coloreds until 1818 and the schools usually were not integrated. Similarly, St. Kitts and Grenada did not create schools for blacks and coloreds until the mid-1820s.[74] The West Indies enjoyed the advantage of having an established church staffed by English university-trained clergy to run its public schools. Although the First Amendment freedom of religion clause applied to the Congress of the United States, not to the states' legislatures,[75] the poorly trained American preachers, especially in the South where the untrained Baptist and Methodist preachers had gained a foothold, could not emulate the Anglican Church–run public schools, even if the American South had attempted to follow the Bahamian model. Furthermore, the Bahama Islands' policy of offering education to free blacks and coloreds exposed the shallowness of the conventional wisdom of the South—that educating blacks and coloreds would portend ill for the perservation of slavery and the perpetuation of white dominance.

Creating schools and opening their doors to black and colored children did not pose a threat to slavery and white domination; instead, it facilitated the perpetuation and expansion of free black and colored leaders and assured that their good English education would make them loyal subjects of the Crown. That was the crux of the matter. Since the schools trained this small group of black and colored children to be English at a time when the untrained masses retained a significant portion of their African hertiage, a cultural gap was inevitable between the educated free blacks and persons of color and the slaves. Moreover, many, if not most, of the educated free blacks and colored leaders were Anglicans while the masses, especially the slaves, shunned that faith and cast their lot with the Baptist missions and Wesleyan Methodist societies, creating further distance between the free black and colored leaders and the rest of the black and colored population. In short, education completed the assimilation of free blacks and persons of color.

Blacks and coloreds in the Bahama Islands were mainly unchurched prior to the arrival of the American Loyalists, partly because the Anglican Church was undermanned, and hence did not provide clergy of any consequence to minister to the inhabitants, and partly because the church was indifferent, showing little concern about religious instruction for the slaves and the spiritual needs of whites. All suffered from this, both Europeans and people of African descent. The arrival of the Loyalists elevated awareness of the religious situation in the Bahamas; and soon not only the Anglican Church but other Protestant churches moved to establish churches, especially the Anabaptists (Baptists) and Wesleyan Methodist societies.[76] The Anabaptists have their origin in the Protestant Reformation when a radical wing of the movement rejected the practice of infant baptism and argued that persons should not be baptized until they were old enough to know its significance. Consequently, those adults who had been baptized as infants had to do it over again, hence the prefix "ana." By the eighteenth century that prefix had long since lost its significance, but the group was still called Anabaptists by Anglicans who had a low regard for the Baptists, who by this time subscribed to total immersion at baptism, distancing themselves from the basin Christians (i.e., Anglicans, Catholics, and Lutherans). The Wesleyan Methodist societies were of more recent vintage, having arisen from the eighteenth-century efforts of a small band of Anglican priests led by the Wesley brothers, John and Charles, and George Whitefield. While in college, they had formed the small Holy Club at Lincoln College, Oxford, and were called "Methodists" in derision because of the methodized discipline of the club. They subsequently became priests in the Anglican Church but never lost the fervor of their faith as manifested in college as members of the Holy Club visited the sick and the poor, prayed, and tried to inject emotion into the frozen Anglican Church. John Wesley remained an Anglican priest (the churchyard at Saint Paul's Cathedral contains his statue) but his ministry gave birth to a new faith, the Wesleyan Methodists.

The Baptists, or Anabaptists, attracted the largest following among blacks/coloreds for a number of reasons: (1) the simplicity of their worship service; (2) the fire and brimstone style of preaching; (3) the lack of strict educational requirements for the ministry, with emphasis upon being called to preach rather than upon educational preparation; (4) the congregational structure of church organization, facilitating the organization and operation of an independent church body; and (5) the distance it allowed them to put between themselves and the often highbrowed Anglican Church officials. Even though the Baptist Church in the Bahamas was congregational, the church in New Providence had a close, though informal, connection with those in Kingston, Jamaica; Savannah, Georgia; Nova Scotia, Canada; and Freetown, Sierra Leone.

This close informal connection originated in Savannah during the American Revolution. George Liele, a slave preacher who once lived in Silver Bluff, South Carolina, and prior to the Revolution moved to Savannah with his master, was allowed to travel to plantations along the Savannah River to preach to the slaves. He remained in Savannah during the war and allegedly was manumitted by his master, who subsequently died in the war. The decedent's family rescinded the manumission. Fearful of being returned to bondage, Liele indentured himself to a British army officer who befriended him. When the British army evacuated Savannah, Liele accompanied the officer to Jamaica; but just before he left, Liele converted Andrew Bryan, a slave on Brampton Plantation outside Savannah, along with others.[77] Liele was assisted in his Savannah ministry for two months by David George, who had heard him preach in South Carolina and was converted. At the beginning of the siege of Savannah, George moved there, setting up residence in Yamacraw.[78] Also in Savannah at the time was a black man known to us only as Brother Amos, and he also came under Liele's influence. Liele left Savannah in 1780 for Jamaica and shortly after arriving founded the first Baptist Church on that island.[79] George left Savannah for Nova Scotia in 1782 and founded a Baptist church at Shelburne before leaving for Sierra Leone where he founded another Baptist church in 1792.[80] In the meantime, Bryan filled the void created by Liele's departure and on January 20, 1788, founded the first Baptist Church in the Savannah area. This church eventually acquired the name First African Baptist Church. Furthermore, Brother Amos may have moved to East Florida with the Loyalists and from there came to New Providence and established a Baptist church.[81] Hence that church was linked to an international body of independent black Baptist churches.

In 1784, Samuel Kelly, a seaman who visited Nassau, said that "a man of colour frequently preached to the eastward of the town under a large spreading tree."[82] This could have been Brother Amos, who stayed in contact with Liele, as did George and Bryan, after settling in New Providence and starting a church. Brother Amos organized that group of worshipers into a congregation with a reported forty members.[83] The number of worshipers increased rapidly, and in 1791 Brother Amos wrote to his friend George Liele that he had about three hundred members.[84] At the time, this was the only Baptist Church on record in the Bahamas.[85] There is no known evidence of Brother Amos's age or of how long he continued to preach after 1791.

The only other Baptist preacher in New Providence was Sambo Scriven, a black runaway slave from St. Augustine with knock knees and a "remarkably long under lip and chin." He came to New Providence in late 1784 and probably began preaching shortly afterwards.[86] Scriven acquired his freedom in 1790.[87] Since Scriven was not directly associated with George Liele he doubtless came under the influence of Brother Amos, either in East Florida or upon arriving in the Bahamas. Unfortunately, there are no extant papers that could shed light on the matter. We learn from a petition of Prince Williams that he joined the Baptist Society shortly after he arrived in New Providence, either in 1801 or earlier, and that Sambo Scriven was the preacher.[88] According to a local newspaper advertisement, however, Prince Williams ran away from his master in July 1785.[89] Whether Sambo Scriven succeeded Brother Amos is unclear. In spite of the uncertainty concerning the answer to this question, a few facts are quite clear about the early Baptists: (1) they started informally in 1784, (2) they were nonwhite, (3) they began under the leadership of Brother Amos, and (4) they did not worship in a permanent building until 1801 when Prince Williams spearheaded the move to buy a lot and build an edifice.

Another factor points toward the existence of one Baptist church in the 1790s: Baptists churches in Savannah and New Providence were not schismatic in their formative years. The Baptist Church in New Providence stayed intact from 1801 to 1826, a quarter of a century, which was a lifetime for many blacks and coloreds of that day. That year, 1826, a dispute between Williams and persons who questioned his alleged unethical behavior led to a schism that resulted in Williams leaving the church and organizing another one that worshiped the next six years without formal sanction, this not coming until in 1832.[90] Similarly, after the founding of Second African Baptist Church of Savannah in 1802 to relieve crowding at First African Baptist Church, no other black Baptist church was started in Savannah until a schism in First African Baptist Church in 1832 led to the formation of Third African Baptist, afterwards renamed First Bryan Baptist Church.[91] These are only two examples; they, nevertheless, lend strong support to the position that Sambo Scriven may have been the successor of Brother Amos.

Since there are no extant sources, public or private, describing worship service at the church, or minutes of its monthly conference, one must depend upon what is known about the churches with which Brother Amos had ties and surmise that they mirrored the situation in New Providence. The preaching was probably expository, focusing on the themes of sin, redemption, salvation, and the importance of Christian conduct in daily living, and the scriptural passages were probably drawn primarily from the New Testament. The music was imported from America, with the deacons lining verses and the worshipers joining in singing these since the majority of the members could not read and even if they could, did not have hymnals, which were scarce. The services were filled with emotion, with songs of joy resonating through the edifice. The business of the church was conducted at its monthly meeting where financial matters and those related to behavior were dealt with. Wayward members could expect to be punished for sinful conduct, such as intoxication, adultery, fornication, fighting, illegitimacy, and profanity. The duration of the punishment depended upon the severity of the misconduct. In instances of expulsion, these could last for years. Moreover, majority rule was applied with all members in good standing having voice and vote in matters brought before the conference.

Because there was no other Baptist church in New Providence and because the nearest Baptist Church was in the United States, Sambo Scriven and his members probably did not belong to a Baptist association. In fact, the churches which Liele and George headed were in a similar situation, but not the black Baptists in Savannah, who belonged to the same association as the white Baptists in south Georgia. Similarly, the "invisible institution," as Albert J. Raboteau referred to the secret slave worship services held on, or near, plantations, sometimes in the woods, but out of sight and hearing of slaveholders and overseers who prohibited them from worshiping, was not as common in the Bahamas as it was in the American South because Bahamian slaveholders generally did not emulate their American counterparts in this regard.[92] The high percentage of absentee masters who preferred life in Nassau to the isolation of plantation life worked against a successful system of religious oppression, even if masters thought that denying slaves an opportunity to worship was a good idea. Furthermore, Bahamian officials apparently were not concerned about the situation, unlike Savannah, where Andrew Bryan and his followers, who did not go underground, were whipped publicly for worshiping God in their own way.

The first Baptist edifice that can be documented was built in 1801. In August 1801, Prince Williams, John Williams (no relation), and their associates agreed to buy two lots in Delanough in the southern suburbs of Nassau, and on September 24 they paid Benjamin Lord $245 for the property. The money for the purchase was collected from "individuals composing the society of Baptists" who had pledged to build a meeting house. About the same time, Prince Williams, who could read and write, was elected assistant to Sambo Scriven.[93] The church's leaderhip contained free blacks and persons of color, but were slaves counted among its members? The number suggests that large numbers of slaves attended the black Baptist

Church. Brother Amos claimed he had almost 300 worshipers in the early 1790s, probably including free blacks/coloreds and slaves; New Providence only had 753 free blacks and persons of color in 1801. If all the members of the church were free, this would place the churched at over 40 percent of the population; when allowances are made for those who attended the Anglican Church, the percentage climbs to over 50 percent. It is unrealistic to believe that 50 percent of the free black/colored population of New Providence was churched. A plausible conclusion is that both slaves and free persons attended the Baptist Church. These persons represented the disaffected who were turned off by the Anglican Church, which did not develop regulations for slave marriages, baptize slaves, provide religious instructions for them, or send missionaries to them.[94] Furthermore, those blacks and coloreds upon whom good fortune smiled, and who were lucky enough to enter the Anglican Church to worship, were crowded into segregated cramped quarters.[95]

The Baptist Church spread from its New Providence base to the Out Islands. From an unflattering account of a baptismal scene on Long Island, reference to "their preachers" suggests that there may have been more than one church on the island. This account, with its strong Anglican bias and antipathy for Baptists, alleged that the blacks "had been misled by strange doctrines." The account describes black preachers as being "artful and designing making merchandise of Religion." The description of the baptism sheds light on how and where total immersion was conducted and the Anglican perception of it: "at certain time in the year the black preachers used to drive numbers of Negroes into the sea, and dip them by way of baptism for which they extorted a dollar, or stolen goods."[96] The tone and tenor of this account contrast noticeably with that of an account of a Savannah baptism in 1793: "After morning services they [blacks] went to the River to dip. Several numbers of white people had Assembled to see them. After that ceremony was performed they returned in procession to their place of worship singing psalms, their deacon reading [lining] every line, all the men with their hats in hand."[97] In the absence of baptismal pools at the church, Baptists usually conducted baptisms in a nearby body of water, if one was available. As the Savannah account states, the procession was generally orderly and pensive on the way to the water and festive on the way back to the church.

Baptists had a higher percentage of blacks and coloreds than any other religious denomination. In fact, the Baptist Church in the Bahamas was either all or nearly all black/colored; even so, it appears that only a small fraction of the black/colored population was churched at the beginning of the nineteenth century, with the Baptists attracting most of these and the Wesleyan Methodists societies running a distant second. The Baptist preachers, moreover, by the very absence of information on them, seem to have been ordinary men; indeed, Sambo Scriven was in such an economic bind at the time of his death that he did not leave sufficient funds for his burial. And Prince Williams, who was better off economically than Scriven, had lapses of moral character that probably reflect what a weak person he was. The Baptist Church, therefore, was not a very strong institution. The best thing that could be said for it was that it was black/colored owned and operated.

Whereas it is difficult to determine when the Baptists started in the Bahamas, tracing the origin of the Methodists is less challenging. Joseph Paul Sr., a leading educator, brought Methodism to the Bahama Islands. When he moved from Abaco to New Providence in the mid-1780s, Paul proselytized among blacks and coloreds and, buoyed by the responses to his evangelism, built a small wooden chapel on the corner of Augusta and Heath Field Streets.[98] His early appeals to American Methodists for help went unheeded for a while, and when help did arrive the persons sent were so depraved that Methodism suffered a setback both from standpoint of access to the governor and assistance from supporters, some of whom left the movement.

William Hammett, the first Methodist missionary to Jamaica, returned to America after a short stint. Later, disenchanted with the Methodists, he left the society and formed an independent religious organization which subsequently sent, on separate occasions, three missionaries.[99] The first of these missionaries, known to us only by his surname, Johnson, clashed with Joseph Paul and later ousted him from the leadership of the movement, at which point Johnson assumed control of the chapel which Paul had built. Johnson then applied for and received a license to preach from Lord Dunmore, but he ran afoul of the law when he performed marriages, which his licensing did not authorize. This professional breach was compounded by trouble in his personal life. He assaulted his wife and that landed him in jail.[100] Johnson's successor, a black man similarly known to us only by his surname, Rushton, did not fare any better and was replaced by yet another man, the surname of whom, Melody, is all we know. He suffered an undisclosed moral lapse and voluntarily returned to America.[101] These bad choices brought shame to the Methodists without causing lasting damage. To their credit, they introduced in the Methodist church a liturgy that was similar to the Anglican's.

The removal from the scene of these scoundrels paved the way for the reemergence of Paul. The small group which had remained with him after the bout with Johnson moved from the schoolroom where they had been worshiping and reclaimed the chapel. After Joseph Paul Sr.'s death, his son William succeeded him. The Sunday morning worship service usually began with a prayer by William Paul after which the worshipers recited a few psalms; Paul followed this with readings from some English books, then explained the passages in language that was understandable to his worshipers. At the completion of the service, Paul led his congregation to Christ Church to attend morning service and partake of the eucharist. Paul held evening prayer meetings on Sundays and twice during the week. Stephen appealed to the S.P.G. for financial assistance for Paul, who worked as a ship carpenter to support himself and his family because the only income the chapel provided was the receipts from the annual pews sale. Stephen gave Paul books that he had requested and was happy that Paul rejected overtures from "a wild Methodist Missionary" to join that denomination.[102] Paul retained close association with Christ Church and demonstrated the same kind of foresight that his older brother, Joseph Jr., had done by training Joseph Gould Watkins as his replacement. The Watkins family attended the chapel, as did many of the other "well disposed Negroes and People of color," and George Watkins Sr., Joseph Watkins' father, was one of the most respectable members of the chapel. Although an elderly member of the chapel conducted services during Paul's illness, Stephen did not believe he was qualified to lead the society permanently. When William Paul died in August 1813, an influential member of the chapel approached Stephen about appointing Joseph G. Watkins to succeed him, which Stephen did. Watkins probably had less problems with conducting the service than he had finding a place to worship since the chapel's roof had been destroyed and the walls severely damaged by the July 26, 1813, hurricane, the most powerful one to hit New Providence in memory.[103]

The Pauls began as Methodists but switched to the Anglican Church, carrying a group of their followers with them. The larger group of Methodists had gravitated towards Anthony Wallace, a free black man, out of protest against the deplorable trio from America; this group worshiped in Wallace's home.[104] Although he was not a missionary, Anthony Wallace held the small group of about sixty persons together until help arrived from England. The Methodist incursion into the Bahamas went through three stages. The first stage began when Joseph Paul Sr., an unaffiliated Methodist who had been converted by the Great Awakening stalwart George Whitefield, built a chapel in New Providence and called on Americans for help. When help did arrive after a short delay, Paul was pushed aside in the ensuing struggle between himself and the first American sent. After successive efforts to jump-start the movement had failed, the Americans lost interest and did not send another missionary. In the meantime, the Anglican Church used its immense influence and muscle to win the Pauls to the faith, leaving Anthony Wallace and his small group without a sponsor. After a few years in this state, which could be called stage two, help arrived from England at the turn of the century. This marked stage three.

The first two stages of the Methodist venture into the Bahamas were similar in some respects to that of the Baptists, yet there were also differences. Black/colored American Loyalists who came to the Bahamas after the Revolution started both groups, and neither group received overwhelming support from blacks/coloreds. While the Baptists did not suffer from infighting as the Methodists did, the Methodists leaders, the Pauls and Anthony Wallace, were a cut above the likes of Sambo Scriven and Prince Williams. The Baptists, moreover, who initially had ties with other black Baptists outside the Bahamas, eventually lost communication, perhaps after the death of Brother Amos, and from then on were isolated from Baptists beyond the borders of the Bahama Islands. The Methodists, on the other hand, remained in touch with other Methodists outside the Bahamas. This enabled the Methodists to draw upon talent outside the Bahamas, bringing experienced and committed missionaries to the islands, the results of which made a significant difference in the ministry of the two churches. All signs pointed to the Methodists exceeding the Baptists.

Before proceeding with the third stage of the Methodists' mission in the Bahamas, it would be useful to look at the instructions that Methodist missionaries to the West Indies received. These stated that the objective of the mission was "to convert and instruct young negroes in the British West Indies Islands in the principle of the Christian Religion." Missionaries were given specific instructions not to target whites and free persons of color (probably meaning free blacks as well): "You are not to undertake the instruction or education of any of the white inhabitants, or free persons of colour, or to interfere in the smallest degree with the ministerial duties of parochial Clergymen." Missionaries were also instructed to get permission from slaveholders before attempting to instruct or educate slaves. Teaching young slaves, moreover, was perceived as a means to an end, "not as a primary and principal object in their education." The targeted group of young slaves were those between five and six years of age who probably were not assigned permanent tasks. If this was not feasible, the missionaries were instructed to establish Sunday schools similar to those in England.[105] In short, the early English Methodist missionaries were warned against taking any action that might draw the ire of the two heavyweights in the West Indies, the slaveholders and Anglican clergy. These instructions were not followed to the letter.

In 1799, the British Methodist Conference Meeting in Manchester, England, selected William Turton, mulatto son of a white Barbadian planter, to be its missionary in the Bahamas.[106] Turton left Antigua on May 31, 1800, and reached Turks Islands on June 4, 1800. What had been a swift and smooth journey to that point changed. Shortly after arriving in Turks Islands Turton learned that it did not have transportation linkage with New Providence Island, his destination. He waited two months before boarding a vessel to New York, where he hoped to get passage to New Providence. This he did, arriving there weak, tired, and sick from fever and ague on October 22. Now that he was in New Providence his work was cut out for him because the actions of the American trio were still fresh on the minds of officials. Turton's initial effort to get an appointment with Governor Dowdeswell failed, but the governor subsequently relented, agreed to meet with him, and at that meeting, issued Turton a license to preach. Having overcome a major hurdle, Turton was now in a position to right the wrongs of his American predecessors by restoring to health the Methodist Society, which "was in a weak state."[107]

Before Turton could restore the health of the society, however, he had to get situated. Anthony Wallace, whom he had met shortly after arriving on the island, made the task less daunting by moving him to a suitable and less expensive place to live than the inn where he was living, locating a convenient room where he could preach, and relinquishing control of the small band of Methodists who had been meeting in his house. With these initiatives completed, the new year, 1801, held good promise for his mission, and he did experience success. The downside of this, however, was that he came under closer scrutiny from public officials and the Anglican clergy, the latter accusing Turton of offering the "sacrament." When the police visited him with an order to stop, Turton did so immediately. Dissenting preachers, the label placed on Baptists, Methodists, and some of the other non-Anglicans, were not allowed to administer the eucharist (holy communion) and perform marriages. In spite of the limitations and protests, Turton gained the confidence of powerful figures, namely, Judge John Kelsall and Assemblyman Thomas Forbes, who invited him to instruct slaves on their Out Islands plantations after trying unsuccessfully to get the Anglican clergy to offer their slaves instructions. Once these gentlemen placed their stamp of approval on Turton, the opposition became silent.[108]

The Methodists gained so much respect that whites and free blacks/coloreds started to join the society, especially those on the Out Islands where the Anglican Church did not have clergy. In directing their ministry toward whites and free blacks/coloreds, Turton and his fellow Methodist missionaries violated the letter of their instructions, although the intent of the instructions may not have been to turn away free persons. The instructions were probably intended to prevent the established church from persecuting the missionaries. This could best be achieved by allaying fears that the missionaries intended to eat from the table of the established church; rather, the missionaries would only gather crumbs that Anglicans left. Methodist societies on Rock Sound, Tarpum Bay, and Palmetto Point all had white majorities, and the one at Savannah Sound had twenty-six whites and forty-five blacks and coloreds. The society on New Providence, which had only a few whites, including Turton's wife, its first convert, was a different matter. Somewhat disappointed by his failure to make significant inroads among whites, Turton wrote, "[T]he whites keep at a distance, there are but few brought to join us."[109] New Providence was a tougher nut to crack because, unlike the situation on the Out Islands, the Anglican Church did not surrender it by default; the church instead maintained a strong presence with two parishes, Christ Church and Saint Matthew's. Consequently, it was unreasonable to expect the same results in New Providence as had been achieved on the Out Islands.

Turton did an outstanding job and was highly regarded by whites, blacks, and persons of color. Elizabeth Hamilton, a white convert, said of him, "I love him for his work's sake. May the Father of Mercies assist me to follow him as he follows Christ."[110] Just as Anglican tardiness and in some instances apathy toward establishing a presence on the Out Islands provided opportunity for the Methodist Societies (really for dissenting sects generally) to become the dominant church body on some of those islands, so did the Anglican clergy's indifference to the religious instructions of slaves on plantations far removed from Nassau create similar opportunities for Methodist missionaries on New Providence. For example, William Wylly, attorney general of the Bahamas, invited Turton to preach to his slaves on Clifton Plantation, about seventeen miles from Nassau, with a promise that he would be invited to continue the practice, for which he would receive "a certain allowance per annum."[111] In 1812, Turton was one of the five recognized dissenting preachers in the Bahama Islands—three Methodists and two Presbyterians. In the Bahama Islands, the Presbyterians were the only dissenting preachers paid from the public coffers, indicating the level of respectability that church had vis-a-vis the Methodist Societies.[112] Furthermore, the Baptist preachers, all of whom were black/colored, were not even listed among the dissenting preachers, a sure sign that the Baptists were the low group on the totem pole.

Stage three marked the coming of age of the Methodist Societies in the Bahama Islands. After a slow start that almost ended in disaster, Methodists were able to correct the course with the arrival of William Turton and other missionaries from England. In addition to converting many slaves, they gradually made inroads into the traditional Anglican base of support and soon surpassed the Baptists, becoming second in size only to the established church. Moreover, although the first Methodist Society in the Bahamas was a black/colored operation, the Methodists extended their ministry to whites, who gained control of the movement, leaving the Baptists as the only black/colored church.

In summary, free blacks and persons of color created a subsociety within the larger slavocracy, despite the earlier perception of free blacks in America who scoffed at suggestions that they settle in the West Indies with its slaveholding societies. Free blacks and coloreds started schools and churches, including an independent Baptist church and a Methodist society, and increased their numbers at a time when the slave population was decreasing. African slaves, for their part, contributed by retaining much of their culture and concomitantly imbibing British customs and traditions. When, moreover, the sprinkling of American customs was added to the mix, the rich vibrant way of life for which the Bahamas subsequently became known emerged. The society that was created among blacks and coloreds had its warts, however, paramount among which was the social distance that free persons of color placed between themselves and their free black counterparts and slaves. In spite of the vicissitudes, polarization, and unlevel playing field associated with their Bahamian experience, blacks and coloreds, both free and slave, did not become alienated to the extent that they did not perceive of themselves as Bahamians, unlike their counterparts in America who through the years have had difficulty calling themselves Americans without a reference to color preceding it. Finally, the social, educational, and religious changes combined with the aforementioned economic changes from 1784 to 1815 made this era an age of transition.

CHAPTER III

Race Relations in an Age of Transition, 1784–1815

It is not easy to conceive a more general panic than the appearance of these [black] Detachments . . .
—Robert Hunt, President of the Council, May 9, 1801

The period from 1784 to 1815 witnessed many significant changes in the Bahama Islands. A major increase in the population, an expansion in the number of inhabited islands, a sudden shift in its racial makeup from having a slight black and colored majority to a decided one, and a transformation of the economy all occurred at this time. These changes in turn produced others, such as the establishment of black churches and schools, the coalescing of African, English, and American practices into something different and new in Bahamian society, and the collapse of the cotton kingdom with its attendant effects upon the size of the slave population and the manner of managing it. All these changes happened inside the Bahamas and were caused primarily by events that directly related to the situation on the islands. The events that shaped race relations, however, were largely the result of decisions made elsewhere, particularly in Britain.

Garrisoning the Bahamas with troops from the West India regiments (all black units) and the abolition of the slave trade were the major events that shaped race relations in this age of transition. The use of black troops caused greater tension than the ban on the slave trade, because the collapse of the cotton kingdom had already dampened enthusiasm to import additional African slaves into the Bahamas. The presence of troops from the West India regiments was a new experience for whites, who could not walk the streets by day without being reminded of their presence or sleep peacefully at night in the wake of their daytime experience. Those opposed to the use of armed black troops adorned in their Zouave uniforms claimed that the presence of the soldiers had an undesirable effect upon the behavior of slaves. In his highly regarded work on West Indian planters, Lowell Ragatz said, "A deliberate arming of the bondsmen to defend their masters marks the opening of a new epoch in interracial relations in the Caribbean."[1] Thus, this age of transition marks a turning point in race relations in the Bahamas.

Soon after the American Loyalists arrived in the Bahamas, they concluded that the mechanism of social control was unsatisfactory, especially the permissive air that pervaded the islands relating to the behavior of free blacks and persons of color. This permissiveness annoyed a Loyalist-dominated grand jury to such an extent that it devoted much of its presentment to the reigning in of blacks and coloreds. The grand jury recommended the construction of a "proper work-house for the punishment and confinement of disorderly and criminal negroes" and complained about the absence of proper laws and regulations governing the behavior of "free negroes" and the practice of allowing many of them to gather behind "Government-House and elsewhere." The grand jury perceived this gathering as a nuisance. Finally, the grand jury criticized local officials for not enforcing laws against "Negroes and others, hawking goods in baskets, trays and otherwise about the street."[2] Writing in 1789, William Wylly shared the grand jury's perception of the situation in New Providence, "The town of Nassau is actually overawed by a considerable body of runaway and other negroes, collected and kept together in the neighborhood of Government House and about Fort Charlotte in open and flagrant violation of the laws of the colony."[3] Wylly did not separate free blacks from persons of color; whereas the grand jury identified the persons as "free negroes." Since American Loyalists, who were accustomed to lumping free blacks and persons of color into a single category, dominated the grand jury that called them "free negroes," both Wylly and the grand jury could have intended to include free persons of color among the "free negroes" to whom they referred. The grand jury, moreover, did not say that the persons who gathered in those places violated the law; rather, it said they created a "nuisance."

The grand jury presentment sent a strong signal that race relations in the Bahamas would be different after the 1780s than they had been previously. The Loyalists evidently associated the workhouse with blacks and coloreds. Free blacks and persons of color were subjected to special criticism from a grand jury that probably was not accustomed to seeing blacks and coloreds live as free people. The grand jury believed these persons should not be allowed either to socialize in public or to make a living by selling their wares. Many men on that jury were either in the assembly or subsequently were elected to that body. Similarly, Wylly was later appointed attorney general of the Bahama Islands. In short, the grand jury presentment and Wylly's account were anti-black/colored and represented the future conventional wisdom on racial matters.

Free blacks and persons of color were also early targets of opponents of those governors whom they perceived as too sympathetic to blacks/coloreds. Soon after Lord Dunmore issued his proclamation, armed whites stormed into homes of a number of free blacks and persons of color, wounding several women; and they were on the verge of damaging property and inflicting additional injury to the inhabitants of those dwellings when Lord Dunmore, who was awakened from his sleep, appeared and ordered them to stop the mayhem. The mob justified their behavior on the grounds that they were looking for runaway slaves. Lord Dunmore received the gratitude of the victims of this outrage for his stand, but the perpetrators joined his opponents.[4]

More evidence that free blacks and persons of color were in for a rough time is found in the text of a proposed road bill that the assembly considered in 1789. John O'Halleran, justice of the peace and assemblyman, proposed that free blacks, mulattoes, *mustees,* and Indians should register, pay ninety pounds sterling in tax, and be given the necessary tools, implements, and other conveniences, then drafted to work on the public roads, highways, and paths until they had been completed. In return for this labor, those persons would receive an allowance of two shillings each day they worked. Once the projects had been completed, the workers would be allowed to keep the tools and they would also receive a certificate from the governor. Moreover, the Bahamian government would suspend the ninety pounds sterling tax while the road act was in force. Persons who refused to work would forfeit their freedom after the third refusal. The bill was forwarded to the council, which made the following changes: (1) it exempted all blacks, mulattoes, *mustees,* and Indians who had been born in the Bahamas, and (2) allowed those who refused to work to pay a maximum of ninety pounds sterling rather than lose their freedom. The bill passed with these revisions.[5] This was a blatant attempt to reduce free blacks and persons of color to the status of villeins. Instead of hiring slaves from their masters and self-hired slaves, the legislature of the Bahamas would rather force free black/colored businessmen to close their shops or dispense with their trade, as the case might be, to work on public projects; and if they refused, they could lose their freedom, unless they had ninety pounds sterling. Creoles were exempted. The mere fact that such an idea saw the light of day was troubling.

Considering the atmosphere that pervaded the Bahamas immediately after the Loyalists arrived, it was not surprising that occasionally civil disturbances erupted. Lord Dunmore was confronted with one shortly after he took office in 1787. It was reported to him that many slaves in the outlying areas of Abaco used muskets and fixed bayonets as they went on a robbing and plundering spree. Whites organized a party to confront the slaves and succeeded in wounding and killing a few and taking most of the others as prisoners, three of whom were executed.[6] Upon hearing of the unrest, Lord Dunmore went to Abaco where he held a hearing at which slaves were invited to attend and air their grievances. Only thirty slaves appeared, and twenty-nine of these were adjudged to be slaves.[7] The uprising thus originated over the issue of whether the blacks brought to Abaco had been promised their freedom. Many of the slaves did not appear because they doubtless knew what the decision would be; it was probably this very fact that led to the uprising.

The most talked about conspiracy of the day occurred in New Providence in 1797: the French Negroes Plot. The plot's leaders, Baptiste Perpall, Baptiste Tucker, Tom Bethune, Police Edgecombe, and Tom Lockhart, were slaves from Saint Domingue whom privateers had captured and brought to New Providence. Thus, all participants were slaves. They planned to unite French and English blacks, siege the ordnance stores, kill the sentries, and, after arming themselves, attack Forts Charlotte and Fincastle, start diversionary fires on the east end of Nassau to attract the attention of whites, then capture Nassau while the whites were busy fighting fires.[8] Blacks in Saint Domingue had used this tactic—starting fires—successfully to capture Cape Francois. The first act in the plot began with Baptiste Perpall hosting a dinner at the house he rented in the western suburb of New Providence from a free black man named Stephen Rogers; the ostensible purpose of the dinner was to seek reconciliation with his wife after a domestic dispute. The dinner was followed by another one the next Sunday. In the aftermath of that dinner, Tom Lockhart, Tom Bethune, Baptiste Perpall, Baptist Tucker, and other unidentified persons met and decided to fight the whites and capture New Providence.[9] The group met again the next Saturday night at a gathering that was expected to draw about seventy persons, but only about twenty attended, including two African slaves who went only as informers for their masters. Though the attendance at that meeting was disappointingly low, the leaders decided to meet again the following Monday.[10]

During the interval between the last meeting and the next scheduled one, the slave informers told their masters about the plot. When the conspirators met that Monday, the slaves who had revealed information about the plot led several white slaveholders to the site of the meeting and they broke into the house where they found the surprised conspirators gathered around a table with a lighted candle on it. One conspirator tried unsuccessfully to hide an object under the bed. Once the conspirators, seven men and one woman, were secured, the slaveholders searched the dwelling and found a fuse, a musket, or sword, and a powder horn hidden under the bed. They then marched the group off to jail to await trial.[11]

At the trial, which was held on September 7, 1797, only five of the persons arrested were prosecuted and they were all convicted, but only three were subsequently executed. The "French negroes," Baptiste Perpall, Baptiste Tucker, and Police Edgecombe, the three who were executed, remained defiant to the end, refusing to confess or beg for mercy. The two other convicted conspirators, Tom Bethune and Tom Lockhart, were respited while whites tried unsuccessfully to extract additional information from them. They both blamed the "French negroes" but did not provide any other useful information. Since information here did not implicate other blacks, Bethune and Lockhart had their sentences commuted to transportation with the understanding that if seen on the islands again they would be executed. The bodies of two executed conspirators were ordered hanged in chains at a public place on Hog Island (the former name of Paradise Island, located across the bridge on the east side of Nassau).[12] The assembly paid the two slave informers a total of forty pounds sterling.[13] The trial transcript gives neither the names of the three other blacks whom they apprehended at Perpall's house nor what became of them. Since they were not major players in the plot, the authorities may have released them in the custody of their masters to be punished.

Did the whites overreact to this plot? The leader of the plot, Baptiste Perpall, was a responsible slave whose master allowed him to hire his own time and set up a separate home with his family away from his master's watchful eyes. Perpall rented a dwelling from Stephen Rogers, a responsible free black man who later joined the ranks of the slaveholders.[14] Little is known about the other "French negroes" who were executed. One has to wonder how seriously to take a plot whose brain trust had so few weapons and literally no support from the slave community. Their plan to attack the ordnance warehouse to get weapons made sense only if the rebels had enough people and firepower to overwhelm the Thirty-second Regiment's guards.

From the size of the group of whites—Rigby Lindsay, John Wildgoos, and two unidentified white men—who broke into the meeting place of the conspirators, they did not expect to encounter much resistance, and they did not. Those slaveholders did not seek the help of either the police or the royal fusiliers to suppress the intended revolt, thus how real was the threat? Sure, the "French negroes" may have wished to wrestle control of New Providence from the white minority; but this would have been difficult for this group of ambitious rebels to achieve, in light of what they had going for them: virtually nothing. Whites were probably aware of the limitations of the intended revolt and that it was an isolated incident; therefore they did not hassle Stephen Rogers, Perpall's colored landlord, martial law was not declared, and the black population was not placed under closer scrutiny. Moreover, they did not prosecute three of the conspirators, and two of the five that were prosecuted did not receive even a whipping for their transgressions before they were transported. Saying that the whites' reaction to the plot was low-key thus would be an understatement.

The reaction of whites reflected less a concern about a widespread slave uprising than it did revulsion of French Negroes and apprehension that the uprising in Saint Domingue might spread to the Bahamas. Years before this plot, Lord Dunmore and the legislature on the Bahamas showed where they stood on the issue when they imprisoned mulattoes and blacks from Saint Domingue on ships in the harbor while they provided whites from that island succor and either sent them on their way to America or encouraged them to become landowners in the Bahamas. If the fear of a general uprising was small, did the punishment given to the three "French negroes" fit the crime? If Bahamians wished to send a message to Toussaint L'Ouverture and his compatriots, did they use the most effective mechanism?

Ironically, before the slave insurrection in Saint Domingue the slave system there was perceived more favorably than the ones in the British West Indies. The French slaves probably lived on a modest-sized estate supervised by a resident who avoided encumbering his property with heavy debt. Conversely, British plantations were larger, built on an elaborate structure of commercial credit, and encumbered by salaried management under absentee ownership. Since French masters fed their slaves better, they worked harder than the British ones. While a liberal constitution created a laissez-faire policy by the British government toward British colonists in the management of their slaves, the French monarchy promulgated a legal code that prohibited the worst abuses on the French islands. This perception of the French and British plantation systems became widely accepted, even if it probably was not accurate.[15] Both systems were remarkable for their production of wealth and notorious for their treatment of slaves.[16] The crucial point, however, is that the Haitian Revolution left a bitter taste in the mouths of whites in the Bahamas toward French Negroes. Thus, the three conspirators whom they executed for being associated with the French Negroes Plot died because of whom they were more so than because of what they did.

Whereas there was little difference in the treatment of slaves in the French and British colonies, there was a marked difference in the Bahamas and the American South in the use of free blacks and persons of color in the militia and the reliance upon slaves to help defend their boundaries. The American South generally did not allow African Americans to serve in the state militias because whites feared arming African Americans, arguing that this could result in a race war. In the Bahamas, on the other hand, free blacks and persons of color were required by law to serve in the militia and slaves defended the Bahamas when it was attacked. The Militia Act (1796) mandated that free blacks and persons of color should form separate militia companies from whites, but the officers of those units must be white.[17] Officers of the colored militia companies were forbidden from issuing weapons owned by the public to free blacks and persons of color unless they had called them to active duty. The lone exception to this policy were members belonging to the Creek Company, whom they permitted to keep their weapons, if the officer could confide in them.[18] In 1801, the three colored companies had a total strength of 623, of whom 453 attended training.[19] This was a sizable force that compared favorably in number with the total strength of the white units.

Free blacks and persons of color gained a well-deserved good reputation in combat situations. In 1804, Moses Franks, chief justice for the Bahamas and colonel in chief of the military, stated in a memorial that during the American Revolution he had commanded "three companies of infantry composed chiefly of free people of color, and one company of canoniers, [*sic*] all able bodied men—this last company formed almost entirely of confidential slaves, amounting in the whole to upwards of three hundred men within the Island of New Providence." Franks also stated that he formed an entire battalion of slaves with their masters' blessing.[20] Furthermore, armed slaves from plantations defeated two crews of French privateers that landed on Exuma Island. He added that on one or two occasions colored troops under his command had succeeded in subduing "hordes of runaway" slaves of New Providence who had plundered inhabitants and generally made life miserable on the island. These colored troops had succeeded, continued Franks, where "several similar attempts made by the whites as well as Regulars Militia" had failed.[21] H. M. Dyer, in a report to Lord Hobart in 1804, supported Franks's account of the role slaves played in defending Crooked Island. Dyer said that the island had been in a state of constant alarm, and after praising the militia he stated "that the slaves in all these attacks ha[d] conducted themselves with great bravery." [22]

Franks referred to the slave cannoneer company as able-bodied men, not as hands; and throughout his memorial the message came through very clearly that blacks and coloreds, free and slave answered the call to defend the Bahamas whenever it came, no matter how often that was. Blacks and coloreds throughout the Bahamas—in New Providence Island and the Out Islands—were loyal to the Crown. This loyalty was not something American Loyalists introduced. For instance, free blacks and persons of color served in the militia a decade or more before the American Revolution and when the Bahamas was attacked during that war blacks and coloreds, both free and slave, answered the call to arms. Since the Bahamas was situated near colonies of France and Spain, two perennial enemies of Great Britain dating back to the ascension of the Bourbons to the throne of Spain during the reign of Louis XIV, whites wisely recognized that their number was too small to form a fighting force of sufficient strength to repulse invading armies of these nations. They soon learned, moreover, that black and colored militia companies were more effective in subduing and apprehending runaway slaves than whites. The actions of public officials, whether in legislative acts or in memorials, provide ample proof that the Bahamas depended upon its blacks and coloreds, both free and slave, to help provide its military needs; history has shown that they delivered.

This contradicts conventional wisdom in the American South where it was believed that arming African Americans would invite an insurrection. Even after the uprising in Saint Domingue, white Bahamians continued to arm blacks and coloreds and to maintain militia companies consisting of free blacks and persons of color; and when French privateers invaded an out island, whites called upon slaves to help defeat the invaders and drive them from Bahamian soil. White Bahamians thus drew a distinction between French Negroes and their Bahamian counterparts. Whites obviously did not believe a universal bond united blacks everywhere. It was this perception of blackness that kept whites from making the costly mistake of driving blacks/coloreds in the Bahamas into a league with the French Negroes. This was evident in 1797 when the French Negro insurrectionists were executed but their black Bahamian conspirators were spared. The sentence of transportation allowed owners of the convicted slaves to sell them in a foreign market, maybe even at a profit. In this instance, the judges probably made the sentence with slaveholders in mind.

By the time the French Negroes Plot had run its course, the British government was well on the way to implementing a new policy concerning the defense of the West Indies colonies, a policy that would cause great consternation throughout the region, especially in the Bahama Islands. The British would raise black regiments, called West India regiments, for duty in the West Indies, replacing the European regiments. The decision could not have come at a worse time for the Bahamas, where whites still lived in constant fear over the situation in Saint Domingue where the French had been defeated and the mulattoes and blacks, the latter led first by Toussaint L'Ouverture, were locked in bloody battles for control of the island. To make matters worse, some of the French Negroes who escaped from that rebellion and came to New Providence had been implicated in a plot to start an uprising in New Providence. Why did Great Britain decide to station black troops in its West Indies colonies and remove the European ones, for the most part? Given the unenlightened attitudes toward Africans (many of the soldiers in the regiments were born in Africa) and the huge preponderance of black slaves in the population of those colonies, placing armed blacks as the primary military presence in the region was either a stroke of genius or an act of desperation. Considering the large number of Africans who would be introduced in the region as free persons as a result of the ban on the slave trade and the high mortality rate among European troops in the West Indies, manning the West Indies with black troops was a logical move to take; but what makes sense logically does not always work, especially when the potential minefields were so plentiful.

The European regiments in the British West Indies suffered an astronomically large number of deaths. Lowell Joseph Ragatz said that "of 19,676 men sent to the British West Indies in 1796, no less than 17,173 died within five years."[23] Slightly more than 87 percent of those soldiers died. Understandably, a tour in the Caribbean became tantamount to death because so few soldiers survived and returned from duty there. Many reasons accounted for this, but they generally fell into five categories: (1) biological, (2) geographical, (3) sanitary, (4) dietary, and (5) administrative. The immune system of the typical British soldier was conditioned to endure the cold damp weather found in the British Isles, and it was not equipped to fight tropical diseases. The hot weather was unbearable and this was exacerbated by the unwholesome location of barracks in low swampy areas that were breeding grounds for infectious insects. Yellow fever took its toll. The unhealthy outside conditions matched the unhealthy conditions inside—barracks were neither spacious, airy, nor clean. The soldiers did not help matters any by avoiding taking a bath as if it were a plague. The foods served were the standardized old-world rations of salt meat served five times weekly and complemented with the traditional libation, a poisonous new brand of rum. The soldiers' uniforms, moreover, were made of heavy wool more suited for Britain and much colder climes than for the West Indies.[24] The litany of mistakes were made from ignorance, not from indifference. Unfortunately, the result was the same for the officers and men who were its victims.

Ragatz's mortality figures covered all the West Indies colonies, the Bahamas included. Peter Edwards, a prominent Bahamian, wrote in 1798, "[T]he remains of the 32nd [a European regiment] are very weak."[25] Conditions had not changed two years later when between June 1 and November 5, 1800, eighty-six soldiers and two officers died.[26] Writing from Whitehall in 1801, the Duke of Portland talked about the "great mortality" visited upon the Bahamas, as reported by Governor Dowdeswell, and he ordered three hundred men from one of the West India regiments stationed in Honduras to the Bahamas.[27] These were the first black troops assigned to the Bahamas. In 1804, Moses Franks commented on the weak military state of the Bahamas occasioned by the high mortality among British troops.[28] Also that year H. M. Dyer, interim governor until the new governor arrived, informed the Colonial Office that the troops were hit hard by deaths that summer, leaving only ten men that were fit for duty at Fort Charlotte.[29] These contemporary accounts of the military situation in the Bahamas all have a recurring theme: European troops were losing the battle to survive in the tropics. What the accounts did not say was that each soldier's death put the colony at risk of an invasion.

So, Britain had a major problem to resolve: should it change course and stop the hemorrhaging of the regular army or continue? In his authorative work on the British West India regiments, Roger Norman Buckley discusses at length the problem Britain faced at a time when Europe was aflame and the sovereignty of Britain was threatened. Since dead troops could not be reassigned, it was not a case of shifting troops from the British West Indies to Europe on temporary assignment and replacing them with black substitutes. The West Indies must be placed in a special category and left for black troops to defend well beyond the French revolutionary wars. Even if Britain had wanted to continue the policy of garrisoning the West Indies with European troops that would have been difficult to accomplish because word of the large number of deaths among white troops there had spread within the realm, hampering recruiting. Buckley gave other factors that were at play and worked against maintaining the status quo; included among these were the unpopularity of lifetime service, successful competition from the metropolitan militia for recruits, preference of some for the civilian workforce over the armed force, and the dwindling supply of recruits from debtor prison. These all combined to have an adverse effect upon the size of the British regular army that in 1793 had fewer than forty thousand men.[30] This came at a time when Britain faced expanding responsibilities because of its expanding empire.

The proposal for creating the black regiments received serious consideration in December 1794. The black regiments would be organized along the line of the European regiments, with the same size companies (one hundred men), regiments (ten companies), and command staff (officers and noncommissioned officers). The troops would be recruited from the ablest slaves in the West Indies, and if the number there was insufficient, free blacks would be recruited. If sufficient troops could not be obtained from these two sources, then Africans right off slave ships would be recruited. From 1795 to 1808, the British government bought an estimated 13,400 slaves for its West India regiments at a cost of about 925,000 pounds sterling.[31]

Employing slaves as soldiers in the West India regiments raised questions concerning their legal status. Lack of a clear-cut policy on this issue caused confusion because the colonies generally believed those soldiers were subject to their slave codes, whereas the black soldiers believed they were free, thus superior to the slaves and equal to the white soldiers. Black soldiers consequently were both proud and jealous of their unique position. The manner in which their officers treated them reinforced this perception. Black soldiers, who wore colorful Zouave uniforms, received the same pay, privileges, and allowances and were treated in the same hospitals as white soldiers. Furthermore, their white officers told these soldiers that their status was superior to that of the slaves because they served the Crown in a military capacity. The confusion was clarified in 1807 when the Mutiny Act was passed, containing a clause that declared all blacks in the King's service free to all intents and purposes. This act enfranchised about ten thousand troops of the British West India regiments.[32]

Stationing black troops in the colonies was generally resisted with a few exceptions. The policy received the least resistance from colonies that had experienced a slave rebellion in which whites had been massacred. There, inhabitants were more concerned about the protection provided for their families and property than they were about the color of their protectors. St. Vincent, for example, was one colony that did not resist garrisoning black troops on its soil. Conversely, islands spared the ravages of war, with its attendant loss of life and damage to property, were often willing to help with recruiting blacks for the army as long as they were stationed elsewhere. Jamaica, for instance, went to great lengths to prevent being garrisoned with black troops, and it partially succeeded because only a small number of blacks enlisted from there. The Bahamas had the distinction of being the last British West Indies colony to have black troops stationed on its soil. In 1801, six years after they formed the first units of the West India regiments, the Colonial Office sent a unit to the Bahamas.[33]

Based upon the performance of blacks and coloreds in the defense of the Bahamas, one could expect the Bahamas to be in the forefront of the colonies that welcomed the West India regiments. In the memorial alluded to earlier, Moses Franks said that many blacks knew how to use "arms, muskets, as well as great guns." Franks added, "[T]o some extent, they worked the same batteries with white troops and remained in the field under the

Soldiers of the Second West India Regiment.
Courtesy Department of Archives, Nassau, Bahamas.

scorching heat while white troops wilted."[34] Written three years after the first units of the West India regiments had landed in the Bahamas, this memorial provided strong evidence of why black troops were the soldiers of choice to defend the Bahamas and, by extension, the British West Indies.

Bahamians may have become accustomed to seeing armed black and colored militia companies, but they were not ready to accept West India regiments as their defenders. Upon receiving the news that units of the West India regiments formerly stationed in Honduras were being transferred to New Providence, residents reacted in the usual fashion when faced with a displeasing situation: they wrote a petition. It did not matter that the action was long overdue since black troops had already been stationed in other colonies. In a petition addressed to Robert Hunt, president of the council and interim governor, the petitioners expressed consternation and dismay while arguing that the consequences of the decision were "too obvious for [them] to enumerate." The petitioners asked Hunt to follow the lead of Jamaica, which had refused to accept the troops. Otherwise, the petitioners continued, "[W]e see no other alternative to adopt for our safety but to abandon the Colony with our families and property."[35]

Hunt tried to dissuade the Colonial Office from stationing black troops in the Bahamas and resorted to a little French Negro bashing. Describing the situation into which the West India regiments would be sent as very volatile, Hunt told his superiors that the European garrison in the Bahamas, part of the Forty-seventh Regiment, was weak, consisting of less than 200 effective troops and three officers. Using an approach that others would repeat, he contrasted this small force of white defenders with the 2,000 blacks in New Providence, saying, "[M]any of whom are French of evil disposition." It was rumored that of the 272 black troops who would be stationed in New Providence about one-half were French. Hunt lamented that because of the large population of French already present on the island and the weakness of the European regiment and white militia, sending black troops with a heavy proportion of French Negroes was appalling. Hunt said whites were fearful that "what had happened in Saint Domingo" would be repeated in New Providence. Hunt then continued, "Merchants and traders live in apprehension of having their stores and property destroyed by fire. The planters fear a spirit of Licentiousness will disseminate among their slaves. In short, Sir, there is scarcely an inhabitant of this colony who is not alarmed at the arrival of those Black Troops."[36]

Two days later, he sent another letter in which he repeated, in principle, the argument advanced and elaborated upon earlier. The initiative behind the second letter is unknown. It could have been the result of members of the council prevailing upon Hunt to use the opportunity he had while occupying the governor's chair to good advantage by pressing hard on the issue, or the initiative could have come from Hunt himself. The intent of the letter, however, was clear and unchanged from the first letter. In the second letter, Hunt again expressed his concern about the French Negroes: "[T]he large number of recently arrived French Negroes and others from different countries may ingratiate themselves with the Black troops, which would be truly alarming." As he described the excited crowd that gathered at the port where the black troops arrived, Hunt attempted to make his argument more compelling by injecting the name of the dreaded Toussaint L'Ouverture, writing that "the public mind could not have been greater had Toussaint himself come with all his force."[37] What Hunt forgot in his analogy was that Toussaint's army was not led by white officers, but the West India regiments were, a point that probably was not lost on the astute professionals who read his letter in the Colonial Office. Hunt, nevertheless, begged the Colonial Office to keep the Forty-seventh Regiment in the Bahamas and, if practicable, send more European troops.[38]

Hunt was among the vocal majority in the Bahamas who disagreed with the decision to defend the islands with black troops, some of whom had just been taken off slave ships. Bahamians viewed the decision from a different perspective than Britain, which watched its West Indies colonies become a virtual cemetery for thousands of British troops. Bahamians and others in the West Indies opined about the consequences of replacing European regiments with those of the West India regiments, but they had no hard data to support these predictions. Britain, on the other hand, knew firsthand the consequences of continuing to staff its colonies in the West Indies with European troops. The West Indies probably claimed the lives of more British troops than European battlefields, a situation that could not be allowed to continue, given the perilous situation in Europe where the political situation in France had come unglued and the new French leaders had embarked upon a military venture that could end in French hegemony over Europe. In times like these, Britain needed to be strong militarily if the challenges were to be met successfully. This point may have been lost on whites in New Providence who surveyed the scene from their distant corner of the British Empire.

Almost before the ink had dried on Hunt's letter, 143 white males attached their names to a petition complaining about the policy. They, too, harped on the disparity between the white and black population and questioned the character of the black troops, emphasizing that their propensity to revolt would be fueled by "so much value and treasure" occasionally deposited in Nassau. The openness of Nassau, where a large diverse group of foreigners came to trade "by means of the Spanish licensed trade," further made the colony vulnerable to plunder.[39] Hunt, who had sent one petition to the Colonial Office, sent this one also and stated in the cover letter that the hysteria had not subsided; thus, he needed four brass six-pounder artillery pieces.[40] Similarly, Major James Cuming of the Forty-seventh Regiment voiced derogatory remarks about black troops, only his letter was intended for Governor Dowdeswell, whom he told that black troops were "composed of a description of people who have contracted bad habits that eradicating will be difficult."[41] Major Cuming advocated shipping two companies of the West India regiments to Bermuda.

Major Cuming did not command a black military unit and his view of black soldiers did not jibe with that of white officers who commanded these men. The major had established roots in the Bahamas and wished to remain there, but if the Home Government switched to an all-black defense force he would be transferred. He, moreover, shared the stereotypical characterization that Hunt and others had of French Negroes and was opposed to garrisoning the Bahamas with the West India regiments, but expressed his objection with less passion than the civilians. Determining whether other British officers who did not command black units shared the major's position is difficult. His experience in the Bahamas influenced the major to some extent, but a combination of factors probably accounted for his position. There were perhaps other British officers who felt the same way, some of whom may have been stationed in the West Indies and some of whom may have been swayed by other considerations. The policy of forming the West India regiments and stationing them in the West Indies thus may not have received universal support within the British army.

In August 1801, Downing Street ordered Sir Thomas Trigge to reduce the number of black troops in the Bahamas, showing that the outpouring of complaints had made an impact; furthermore, the Colonial Office authorized sending the artillery pieces which had been requested. Besides these signs that London was listening to the complaints, British officials told Hunt that they would try to acquiesce to requests when "respectfully and properly expressed."[42] In spite of the conciliatory tone of British officials, Hunt did not change his perception of black troops and the need to have their numbers reduced: "The general temper displayed by the latter [blacks], appears to me to be indispensably necessary for the safety of the Colony that their numbers should be very considerably reduced and the force of the others [European] should be augmented."[43] Leaders in the Bahamas therefore continued to pursue a hard line on the issue.

Before 1802, no official or white person in the Bahamas, in any known records, said anything positive about having West India regiments in New Providence. The first positive characterization of the blacks troops in New Providence came from the pen of Governor John Halkett, who wrote in September 1802, "I beg leave to assure your Lordship that I believe there exists none of the W. India Regiments, who is more to be depended upon, or from which there ought to be less cause of alarm as the men composing it, have always behaved quietly, and properly, and are, I am confident, in every respect well disposed to their officers and the Inhabitants." Although the governor qualified his statement by placing the compliment within the context of West India regiments, the statement, nonetheless, is one that European regiments would have welcomed. Speaking of European regiments, with the departure of the Forty-seventh Regiment and the arrival of a much larger contingent from the Seventh Regiment, a European outfit, the imbalance between European and black troops was reduced; but it was not eliminated.[44]

Reducing the imbalance between black and European troops was an indication, and this was followed by encouraging news that British officials were listening to the anguished pleas of the whites in New Providence. Early in January 1803, Governor Halkett was informed of a reduction in the size of the West India regiment unit. Although British officials did not state precisely the unit's new size or when this would be achieved, the governor was told arrangements were being made and it should happen "by an early opportunity." Meanwhile, preparations were being made to send three hundred European troops to the Bahamas; they would complete the peacetime army for the islands, and by the time they arrived arrangements for reducing the size of the black troops would be completed.[45]

With April almost gone and no word forthcoming on the long-expected reduction in black troops, Governor Halkett penned a letter to Downing Street concerning this matter. The governor told the Colonial Office that although five companies of royal fusiliers had arrived as promised, six months had passed since the promise to reduce the number of black troops and no movement in that direction had occurred; this had caused uneasiness and indeed even the emigration of many planters, who took six hundred slaves with them. Calling the troop imbalance "the imprudent proportion of European and black troops," the governor admitted it was a factor, but not the sole cause of the exodus. The governor also depicted the size of the troops garrisoned in the Bahamas in unflattering terms, complaining that "the unnecessary number of troops in garrison" had placed a strain on the financial resources of the government.[46]

Several key expressions in the letter exposed the true feelings of the governor and showed that he was nearing the breaking point on the issue. He called the troop imbalance the "imprudent proportion." Similarly, the governor referred to the number of troops in garrison as "unnecessary." Distancing himself from a policy of the Colonial Office was highly unusual for a governor of the Bahamas, but nothing in this letter shows that Governor Halkett supported garrisoning the colony with black troops. In fact, the letter was a veiled repudiation of the policy. Even though he was weary of waiting, when he wrote the letter on April 20, 1803, the governor still believed that the promised reduction in black troops would occur.[47]

Then on April 24, 1803, an anguished Governor Halkett complained to Downing Street that instead of reducing the number of black troops and increasing that of whites, a frigate was in the port with 270 black troops. The troops had been transferred from Antigua to Bermuda, but the president of Bermuda's council sent them to the Bahamas. One could sense the anger that swelled inside the governor as he informed Downing Street that if those troops were allowed to land in New Providence something very detrimental to the colony would follow. The governor felt compelled, therefore, to prevent their disembarking.[48] Three days later, Governor Halkett dispatched another letter to the Colonial Office in which he inferred that a conspiracy was afoot in the British West Indies to use the Bahamas as a dumping ground for black troops instead of sending them to the designated duty station. The governor may have been alluding to Jamaica when he said, "Your Lordship have certainly reason to feel, not a little disappointed, by the delays, or obstructions of some of the other West Indies Department, or Commands." He could not understand why more troops were needed in the Bahamas in peacetime than were stationed there in wartime, or why the Bahamas, a small colony, should garrison a whole regiment when he believed there were only "four other Black Regiments, over the whole of the British colonies in the West Indies." The governor then urged Whitehall to honor its decision to keep only 100 black troops in the Bahamas. If measures were not taken to reduce their number in the colony, Governor Halkett said, "[W]hile the black troops are disembarking on one side of the Island, the peaceable white Inhabitants will be embarking on the other."[49]

So within the span of four months the situation went from promising to disappointing. Indeed, 1803 would not be the year when whites would exorcize the demons from their psyche. The governor was quick to point out that whites were not going to vent their anger by engaging in a racial confrontation or, for that matter, by defiantly refusing to let the black troops disembark. Whites, instead, would peacefully leave the Bahamas and return to America. The governor engaged in a little chicanery when he blamed the expected exodus of whites on their unhappiness with the presence of black troops when the real reason for the departure was the tough economic times the cotton plantations were experiencing.

Late in 1803, tension began to abate as the black troops that had been sent inadvertently to the Bahamas were sent to Barbados, the Sixth West India Regiment was reassigned to another post, and the Fifth West India Regiment returned to the Bahamas. The decision to reduce the size of black troops and increase that of white ones became a casualty, however, of the latest mortality figures that revealed that since July 1803 two hospital mates and over fifty soldiers of the royal fusiliers had died and about sixty were in the hospital.[50] These figures doubtless caused the Colonial Office to question the decision to increase the number of white troops in the Bahamas, although they made no immediate decision to cancel the earlier one. The only action taken concerning the policy was to place units in the Bahamas under the command of the military headquarters in Jamaica.[51]

In the spring of 1807, Downing Street reversed itself on the decision to reduce the size of the black troops in the Bahamas and went, instead, in the opposite direction. It decided to garrison the Bahamas with black troops only. The British decided they had sound reasons for creating the West India regiments and nothing had happened to change their minds. In fact, if anything, recent events had confirmed their decision. The governor was ordered to inform the legislature that one thousand black troops would be assigned to the Bahamas and the units presently on duty there—the Second West India Regiment and the Ninety-ninth (European) Regiment—would be transferred to Jamaica and the Bermudas, respectively.[52] The council, which received the news first, reacted predictably: "The Board . . . feel . . . that the proposed measure to garrison this colony solely with Black troops is fraught with the most imminent Danger to the peace, happiness and property of His Majesty's loyal subjects of the Bahamas." The council then went on to cite recent population figures that placed the black/colored population above three thousand while white males numbered a little more than five hundred. Continuing in this vein, the council averred that the disparity between the two races was too great and needed to be reduced. The body declared, moreover, that it was more conversant with the situation in the colony than "His Majesty's Advisers in the Mother Country," and so knew what was best for the colony.[53]

The council manipulated the figures to support its argument. For instance, figures for the black/colored population included women, children, and men, whereas those for the whites included only the males. If just the figures for black men were cited, the imbalance would not have been nearly as large because the combined total of women and children was much greater than that of black/colored men alone. Furthermore, complaining about a situation that it had created was hypocritical of the council. The American Loyalists had created the great racial imbalance in the population; many of them sat on the council that now complained about the situation and talked about reducing the size of the black population. Before the coming of the Loyalists blacks constituted just a slight majority. This argument was not very persuasive and probably would not have the effect of the earlier complaints.

Governor Charles Cameron, who had replaced John Halkett several years earlier, sent the council's minutes to the Colonial Office and in the cover letter expressed the following thoughts, "The consequences to be apprehended from the garrison consisting of Black troops only are in my opinion extremely alarming."[54] For the second time, a governor supported the Bahamian leadership position. This time, however, the Colonial Office was not receptive to the position.

The Colonial Office responded immediately to the council and Governor Cameron. It first repeated its position that the decision was driven by the high mortality among European officers and soldiers and that black troops were selected as an alternative because they were better suited for the environment. The Colonial Office acknowledged that the policy did not gladden the hearts of Bahamians; nevertheless, it persisted and the results were favorable. The British then went on to give these results. Deaths among European troops "have been greatly diminished and the peace subordination and security of His Majesty's West India Colonies has been as well preserved as before the institution of this species of force." The Colonial Office added that when black troops were treated properly they were as dependable as European ones.[55] The Bahamas was encouraged to reconcile itself to the policy because it was not going to change.

Whitehall had finally taken a hard-line stance on the issue. Bahamians could complain and prophesy until their chickens began to whistle, but nothing would change. Black troops had been in the Bahamas since 1801, and now six years later none of the predicted awful consequences had materialized. Stores had not been looted, treasures had not been stolen, and French Negroes had not ingratiated themselves with the slaves, staged a rebellion, and invited Toussaint L'Ouverture, the architect of the Saint Domingue rebellion, to invade the Bahamas and convert it into another black kingdom. In fact, by the time the decision to rely solely on black troops had been made the French had duped and taken Toussaint to France where he starved to death in 1803 at Fort Joux, a French prison.[56]

The hard-line stance of the Colonial Office seemed to have made a convert of Governor Cameron. On January 8, 1808, just eight months after he had opined that the situation would become "extremely alarming" if the all-black garrison policy was implemented, Governor Cameron wrote, "It gives me great pleasure to inform you that this colony is in a state of tranquility and free from contagious disorders—The Blacks troops continue to conduct themselves with the utmost propriety."[57] Similarly, almost six months after that letter was written, the governor advised the Home Government that he was returning to Jamaica the troops he had requested because his uneasiness over the situation had ended. Governor Cameron praised Lord Castlereagh for strengthening the garrison, in light of the impending conflict with the United States.[58]

Thus, by 1808 resistance to garrisoning black troops had evaporated. Did whites overact to the policy? No, theirs was a natural reaction given the huge preponderance of blacks in the Bahamas and its proximity to the turbulence in Saint Domingue. The Bahamas is physically nearer to that island than it is to Jamaica. Moreover, the flood of victims of the rebellion to the Bahamas with their tales of the atrocities placed Bahamians closer psychologically to the scene than some of the other British West India colonies. Bahamians vicariously smelled the stench that emanated from the dead bodies and saw the wanton slaughter of persons, and this shaped their perception of French Negroes, whom they associated with the horror stories. Coming so closely on the heels on events in Saint Domingue, the sight of armed black troops terrified Bahamians, a casebook example of transference. Bahamians tactfully ventilated their fears, and in the end, the policy worked well for both London and New Providence. Deaths were reduced significantly among Europeans troops, which is what London wanted, and it exorcized the ghost of the Saint Domingue rebellion from the psyche of Bahamians, which is what New Providence needed.

The British wisely rotated units of the West India regiments in and out the Bahamas, with a tour of duty lasting several years at the most, rather than assigning a unit there on permanent duty. This practice tended to discourage the close association of black troops with the civilian population, although it did not eliminate it and soldiers did marry black women. In such a liaison, the husband was usually a noncommissioned officer. The units did not stay around long enough to collect sand in their shoes, as the old saying goes. Between 1801 and 1809, troops from the Second, Fifth, Sixth and Seventh West India Regiments were stationed in New Providence, but seldom did two regiments serve together.[59] This prevented fights—which could have escalated into something more serious—between units and made it easier to identify individuals, or companies, that may have had an altercation with civilians. All uniformed black soldiers tended to look alike to whites, making identifying wrongdoers difficult when the troops numbered nearly a thousand, but when there was only one small unit in garrison, finding the culprits became less challenging.

Even though none of the chilling predictions materialized, conflicts between civilians and soldiers did occur. In June 1806, for example, at approximately 11:00 P.M. a civilian struck a sentinel as he guarded public offices in New Providence. Colonel Alexander Maclean, commandant, appealed to Governor Cameron to apprehend and punish "the perpetrator of so violent an outrage."[60] The records do not identify the assailant; nevertheless, the nature of the act and the time it was committed suggest that the person was a white male. A female, whether black or white, was not likely to be in the streets at that hour of the night. It is unlikely, moreover, that a free black male, or even a male slave, would have risked striking a uniformed soldier of the king, or that the mere presence of a black sentry would have provoked him. Moreover, a male slave probably would not have been out that time of night, unless he was a runaway who would not have risked drawing attention to himself by committing such an act. To the credit of the troops in the sentry's company, they did not march on Nassau to gain revenge, an act which a less disciplined unit would have done.

A second incident involving a soldier and a civilian occurred in August 1808 when a soldier in the Seventh West India Regiment (this was not the same unit involved in the 1806 incident) struck a slave of Alexander Begbie, assemblyman and opponent of the policy. The reaction to this incident suggests that tension existed between black troops and civilians in Nassau, in spite of the governor's rosy depiction of the situation earlier that year. The affidavit stated that the other soldiers of the regiment, who rescued their comrade from Begbie, "drew their bayonets and threatened to stab the Inhabitants, and one of them struck the High Constable with his bayonet."[61]

Begbie's slave probably imbibed his master's dislike of black soldiers and stepped over the line in voicing his feelings. Begbie used this opportunity to vent his anger and put black troops in their place, and others who shared his view joined him, including some blacks. At this point, the other soldiers intervened. This apparently was a civilian versus soldier conflict, and it was also a black versus white conflict because the whites despised the black soldiers. Blacks in Nassau did not form an alliance with the troops because they probably did not know them as persons. The black troops did not live among them, attend their churches and schools, work beside them, or consider themselves Bahamians. Since there was little opportunity to bond, black soldiers and black civilians did not. White and black civilians would later view the black soldiers less negatively, especially when the professionalism of those soldiers eventually surfaced.

Besides being disliked by many white civilians, black soldiers were discriminated against by British officers in the European regiments. A case in point, when the Ninety-ninth (European) Regiment arrived in July 1806, the season during which European troops were most susceptible to tropical diseases, Major H. C. Darling of that regiment told Governor Cameron that he did not want black troops "mixed with the soldiers of the 99th" in the so-called "Yellow hospital."[62] Major Darling did not make the request because he was afraid the white troops who became infected with yellow fever would give it to the black troops; or because the soldiers, black and white, were trained from different drill manuals, used different weapons, and wore different uniforms; or because his superiors believed black soldiers were a disgrace to the uniform they wore. The major's reason for requesting a separate health facility for white troops was the same as the one that drove whites in the Bahamas to protest against the garrison policy: prejudice.

Notwithstanding the early opposition to the policy and the prejudice of some officers in European units, the establishment of the West India regiments achieved its stated goal and provided the British West Indies with well-trained, dependable troops who maintained the high level of professionalism established earlier by European troops without putting the slave system at risk. As Roger Norman Buckley says, "[N]ot only did the West India Regiment not jeopardize the slave system, they in fact buttressed it with tough dependable African soldiers."[63] The policy also led indirectly to better relations between whites on the one hand and blacks and coloreds on the other, as whites came to realize that the black troops, just like the colored militia, could be depended upon to keep slaves in check.

The Abolition of the Slave Trade Act that Parliament passed in 1807 met similar resistance. British leaders may have reflected upon the financial cost of the legislation to slaveholders, but they did not permit that matter to affect the decision to end the slave trade. First and foremost, humanitarianism motivated the Abolition of the Slave Trade Act. The American Quakers provided the initial leadership for the movement to abolish the African slave trade. In 1783, a contingent of Quakers visited London and lobbied for action to end the slave trade. The outgrowth of this visit was the formation of a group called the Special Committee on the African Slave Trade.[64] Cambridge University became one of the first English public bodies to support abolition of the African slave trade when it petitioned Parliament to ban the trade.[65] Emergence of these supporters did not mean the end of the slave trade was assured because strong opposition existed in Parliament against such legislation and it was unpopular in the West Indies, the Bahamas included. Historian Dale H. Porter gives the following points that seem to be at play within the abolition of the slave trade campaign during its early phase, 1784–1789: (1) most of the British part of the slave trade was conducted by a few large Liverpool firms whose connections with the West Indies economies were neither direct nor extensive; (2) the primary markets for the British-carried slaves were the non-British colonies; (3) British merchants were facing increased competition from foreigners, chiefly the French, in the slave trade to non-British colonies; (4) living and working conditions in the West Indies required a constant importation of new slaves to keep up the labor force, compensate for soil depletion, and clear new land for cultivation; (5) increasing costs, financial impudence, and the recurring need to purchase slaves had reduced plantation profits and had thrown West Indian proprietors deeply into debt to their factors in England; (6) many persons in Great Britain were directly or indirectly dependent for their livelihood on West Indian enterprises and believed continued success depended on the supply of African slaves. Porter, furthermore, believes the abolition of the slave trade was "an essentially fortuitous achievement that would not have occurred were it not for the brief conjunction of a set of economic conditions necessitating restrictions on the productive capacity of the British Caribbean colonies, an unprecedented control of the slave trade industry by British subjects, and a strong abolition-minded ministry."[66]

Porter may have underestimated the worldwide strength of the movement to ban the African slave trade. The idea was in the marketplace and many other nations subscribed to it. In fact, Denmark abolished slave trade in 1792, over a decade before Parliament took similar action, and the United States abolished it in 1808, a year after Parliament acted.[67] The Americans had committed to banning the slave trade twenty years earlier when they ratified the Constitution—Article 1, section 9, authorized the United States Congress to abolish the slave trade twenty years after ratification of the Constitution. The movement did not stop with these three nations. Following on the heels of these bans, the Netherlands abolished the slave trade in 1814, France in 1831, Spain in 1835, Portugal in 1846, and Brazil in 1850.[68]

Furthermore, the legislation did not sail through Parliament overnight; instead, it took over a decade of agitating and agonizing before Parliament marshaled the will and votes to pass the act. Parliament first tried to abolish the slave trade by making it unnecessary. In 1797 legislation was introduced in the House of Commons to ask the Crown if it would instruct governors in the British West Indies colonies to recommend to their legislatures to pass acts improving the condition of slaves, to result in their becoming more productive, thus obviating the need to import slaves. Abolition would then "take place of itself from the want of demand." This ship failed to sail.[69] It was only after failure to abolish the trade through "melioration" that Parliament adopted a tougher stance on the issue. The Abolition of the Slave Trade Act was therefore hardly a "fortuitous achievement."

George Chalmers, colonial agent, was among those unhappy about the act's passage. In alerting the legislature of the Bahamas that the act had passed Parliament, Chalmers characterized the legislation as an infringement on the constitutional privileges of the Bahamas with far-reaching consequences. He advised the legislators that the act would "enfeeble [their] right to domestic intercourse." The legislation troubled Chalmers so much that he hired a lawyer to defend the colony "against the evils of this bill."[70]

Chalmers' missive preceded official notification that Parliament had passed the legislation. Bahamians argued that the act was unnecessary because they had stopped importing slaves since about 1804, as a result of the failure of many cotton plantations. If this was true, it appears as if Bahamians had little reason to complain; nevertheless, they did. David Brion Davis argues that abolitionist leaders linked the slave trade to West Indian slavery and believed the ban on the slave trade would force slaveholders to improve the condition of their slaves.[71] Bahamians probably also saw an ulterior motive behind the slave trade ban, which besides infringing on the constitutional privilege to regulate slaves would indirectly force slaveholders to ameliorate the conditions of their slaves since replacing them would be difficult. Some slaveholders, moreover, believed that the ban on the slave trade was the prelude to manumitting slaves.

The Colonial Office sent a circular letter to the West Indies in October

1807 with the text of the act enclosed. The penalty for violating the act was a fine of one hundred pounds sterling for every slave carried and confiscation of both the ship and cargo.[72] Whereas Parliament was very serious about ending the slave trade, those involved in the trade did not share this view and continued to engage in the activity, notwithstanding the heavy fine imposed for violating the act. This prompted Parliament to stiffen the penalty in 1811, making violation of the law a felony punishable by a fourteen-year transportation; and, when that did not discourage smugglers, Parliament further stiffened the penalty in 1824, declaring the slave trade a piracy and that those caught engaging in it would be executed.[73] The constant stiffening of the penalty for violating the law suggests that violations were occurring, though not necessarily by Bahamians, who were not major players in the slave trade. They were not carriers and the number of slaves that Jamaica and other large islands in the British West Indies purchased dwarfed purchases by Bahamians. It is probably fortunate that Bahamians were not the violators because Governor Charles Cameron was committed to strict enforcement of the Abolition of the Slave Trade Act.

In March 1808, the governor received communication from Lord Castlereagh with instructions to protect and maintain Africans seized from slave ships and to use money drawn from the public coffer to feed and clothe them until the Privy Council decided how to deal with the liberated Africans.[74] Apparently, even though the abolition issue had been around for at least two decades and had been debated with great passion in Parliament, all the details for its achievement had not been thought through. From the looks of things, most of the attention and energy had been directed to rescuing Africans from their captors and cutting off the flow of slaves from Africa; very little attention had been given to developing a policy and program for liberated Africans. It took nearly four circular letters to convey the essence of the policy concerning these freed Africans. One of the first steps was the creation of a new civil servant position in the Bahamas, that of chief justice of customs; he was charged with supervising the activities of Africans, who would be "condemned either as prize of war or forfeitures of His Majesty's use."[75] The piecemeal manner in which implementation was achieved did not detract from the seriousness of the British government's mission to eradicate the slave trade, and the Colonial Office found an apostle in Governor Charles Cameron, who enthusiastically orchestrated implementation of the policy.

The same could not be said about the choir to whom the governor preached—the legislature of the Bahamas, most, if not all, of whom were slaveholders who did not like the sermon nor the text from which it was taken: the Abolition of the Slave Trade Act. In an 1811 memorial, many wealthy planters expressed apprehension concerning the dangers that could arise from the number of Africans brought to the Bahamas as a result of enforcement of the act. The memorialists feared, moreover, that the presence of liberated Africans would lead to unrest among slaves who might misunderstand why these Africans had been liberated. William Vesey Munnings, acting governor during Governor Cameron's long leave of absence, reminded the memorialists that the act was passed only after lengthy debates covering many years, that care was taken to address issues raised by its "self-interested misguided opponents," and that serious thought was given to the "mode of disposing of these natives of Africa." As for the alleged dangers inherent in expanding the African population, Munnings replied, "[T]he colony has heretofore remained tranquil and undisturbed under a much larger than the present slave population." Munnings concluded his response with the commonsense advice that "any Amelioration of a man's condition will probably render him a better than a more dangerous member of the community."[76] In short, it was less threatening to the peace and tranquility of the Bahamas to have liberated Africans than African slaves. Munning's characterization of the slave trade as "this disgraceful traffick" and the Abolition of the Slave Trade Act as "this most happy event" placed him squarely in the camp of the act's supporters. He, nevertheless, promised to present the memorial to the legislature when next it met.[77]

Meanwhile, Whitehall sent another message relating to the act, this one concerning African slaves seized after the law was passed. Munnings was told that the blacks ought to be treated as free persons and should be released, except the ones born in Africa who appeared to have been apprenticed under the act. Moreover, the provisions of the Act to Prohibit the Purchase of Certain Foreign Slaves (1795) that conflicted with the Abolition of the Slave Trade Act were null and void.[78] The blacks in question were seized off foreign ships.

After suffering through a prolonged period of silence, the assembly and council drafted a petition to the king and Privy Council. The petition was critical of the recent capture of three slave ships near the Bahamas containing a total of 451 Africans. Officials inducted 91 into a British West India regiment and the rest were apprenticed. The petitioners lamented that there was not sufficient employment for the 360 who were not placed in the military. The petitioners further complained that since the Africans were not "liege subjects" of the Crown they had no natural right to a resource in any part of the Dominion. Any act of Parliament that bestowed rights among liberated

Africans in the West Indies "without the consent and against the wishes and interest of the colonies" was a violation of their constitutional privileges.[79]

Would the Colonial Office ignore this challenge to the constitutionality of the Abolition of the Slave Trade Act? Complaints about the dire consequences that would result from the act, mere conjecture at best, were expected, even if not solicited, but couching the disagreement in constitutional terms was a different matter. Surprisingly, Downing Street ignored the constitutional issue raised and instead sounded a conciliatory note. The Colonial Office told Munnings that the prince regent hoped that as greater efforts were made to recruit more liberated Africans into the West India regiments this would remove the apprehension of the Bahamians.[80] The tone and tenor of this letter placated the legislature and it did not write another petition on the subject.

Two very important observations concerning this petition shed light on the length the legislature was willing to go on this issue. First, the petition stated that placing liberated Africans in the West Indies "without the consent and against the wishes and interest of the colonies" was a violation of their constitutional privileges. The petitioners were careful, however, not to declare the Abolition of the Slave Trade Act, the basis of their disagreement with the mother country, null and void. The legislature realized its authority did not extend to nullifying an act of Parliament, even when the act violated the constitution. The petitioners, moreover, were careful to use the term privileges rather than rights when alluding to the body of liberties they enjoyed. So, the action of Parliament was a violation of their "constitutional privileges," not their natural rights. As long as the petitioners did not nullify an act of Parliament or claim a constitutional right to enjoy something, Downing Street was perhaps content to let them ventilate their frustrations. The legislature, for its part, was careful to stay well within the boundary of acceptable behavior, in spite of its anger. Ironically, the main complaint was not the end of the slave trade itself, with the attendant loss of the opportunity to purchase a species of property that traditionally was available to them. Bringing liberated Africans to the Bahamas was the problem. It was thus a black versus white issue, not a slave versus master one. Once the anger subsided and whites realized there could be a hidden advantage in the policy, the act was perceived less negatively. The hidden advantage was the apprenticeship program established for the liberated Africans, a program that Bahamians exploited to their personal gain—instead of training those Africans in some useful skill, persons to whom the Africans were apprenticed more often than not worked them as agricultural laborers.

The years 1784 to 1815 constituted a transitional period, with the multiplicity of economic, social, religious, and cultural changes that occurred, not to mention changes spawned by the garrisoning of the Bahamas with black troops and the abolition of the African slave trade. Much of the anger produced by the latter two was directed toward Britain and its policy makers. Moreover, both the garrison policy and the Abolition of the Slave Trade Act benefited blacks and coloreds. Whites lost their trump card, the royal fusiliers, who were no longer around to provide protection. They thus had to be more circumspect in dealing with the numerically superior black/colored population. Similarly, slaveholders had to take better care of their slaves because the pool of available replacements in Africa was now off limits. Although the legislature of the Bahama Islands did not pass any new laws granting additional privileges to blacks and coloreds, this age of transition marked a turning point in race relations in the Bahamas where whites, for the first time, depended upon black soldiers for protection and were forced to admit to themselves, if to no one else, a new reality—they were no longer totally in control of the situation. As disturbing as this might have been, even more troubling was the realization that white Bahamians and British leaders were not on the same wavelength regarding race relations, and the wishes of the British had prevailed. In the midst of this revelation, however, something positive surfaced. Whites discovered that blacks and coloreds in the Bahama Islands were not interested in taking New Providence from them. Since the Bahamas would not become another Haiti, whites, coloreds, and blacks could all make the Bahama Islands their home.

CHAPTER IV

Confrontation and Advancement: Politics and Economics, 1816–1834

Many of the Coloured Subjects are men of property. . . . Their property, like that of the whites, consist principally of slaves.

—Leonidas, *Bahama Argus,* April 4, 1832

The executive branch of the Bahamian government, which had been unstable for much of the early period under study because of constant changes in governors, stabilized during the long tenure of Governor Charles Cameron (1804–1820) and the relatively lengthy terms of Lewis Grant (1820–1829), who succeeded him, Sir James Carmichael Smyth (1829–1833), and Blaney Townley (B. T.) Balfour (1833–1835).[1] Two of these governors, Cameron and Smyth, dissolved the assembly and called for new elections. The assembly turned the table on Governor Smyth by submitting two petitions asking for his removal because of his insistent demands for implementation of amelioration reforms and removal of civil disabilities that encumbered free blacks and persons of color from enjoying political privileges. The economic situation for blacks and coloreds, on the other hand, continued to improve as the economy stabilized and successful persons built upon that success. In short, political rancor from the obstreperous assembly and expanded economic opportunities for blacks and coloreds characterized the almost two decades preceding the Manumission Act.

A major political confrontation was the William Wylly Affair (1817), which began as a dispute between Wylly, who was attorney general of the Bahamas, and the assembly, but spread to include Governor Cameron and the Supreme Court; through the course of events Cameron and the court found themselves aligned against the assembly. This body became angry with the attorney general over what it called his breach of privileges of the House. Wylly converted to Methodism and subsequently gained a new perspective on slavery, believing now that it could only be justified if it was reformed and slaves were brought into the Christian faith. In 1815, he published a set of regulations for his slaves on New Providence Island; these regulations contained more generous allotments than those provided by law. That same year he ordered the collector of customs to seize four blacks who allegedly had run away from East Florida. Instead of turning the case over to the Vice Admiralty Court in Nassau as Bahamian slaveholders wished, Wylly decided that the case should be heard by the High Court of Admiralty in London.[2] The straw that broke the camel's back was an allegation that Wylly told the London-based African Institution, an abolitionist organization, that the assembly had misrepresented his views on slave registration.[3] A January 22, 1817, resolution of the assembly charged that "William Wylly Esquire . . . ha[d] been guilty of a breach of the privileges of this House, by injuriously and scandalously misrepresenting the proceeding of the House, during the last Session, on the subject of a Bill then before Parliament concerning a General Registration of slaves in the West Indies."[4] This led a Bahamian to remark that Wylly was "an honorary governor for life of the African Institution."[5] The assembly authorized the speaker to have the messenger of the House arrest Wylly. Ironically, Wylly's father, Alexander Wylly, had been speaker of the colonial Assembly of Georgia and now the younger Wylly was the target of the colonial Assembly of the Bahamas.[6]

The speaker, Lewis Kerr, ordered William Chisholm, messenger of the assembly, to serve a warrant for the arrest of Wylly, who was to be brought before the assembly to address the allegation that he had breached its privileges.[7] The rift became interesting from this point. There are two accounts of what happened next, Chisholm's and Wylly's. According to Chisholm, after he learned that Wylly had left his Nassau residence for Clifton, his plantation at the western end of New Providence Island about fourteen miles from town, Chisholm proceeded there to serve the warrant; just before arriving he heard a few gunshots in the woods near the road, and once he arrived at the plantation's gate from sixteen to twenty slaves, eight or ten of whom were armed, met him and refused to let him enter. Undaunted, Chisholm remained on the plantation's grounds overnight and attempted to serve the warrant the next morning, but by that time Wylly had returned to Nassau. In addition to not being able to serve the warrant, Chisholm lost his horse, which he claimed Wylly's slaves stole. The messenger tried unsuccessfully to serve the warrant on Wylly in Nassau, but he was not at his residence. Chisholm then reported to the speaker. Angered by Wylly's "[r]epeated and daring contempt" of the assembly, the speaker ordered his arrest and incarceration in jail (gaol).[8]

Wylly gave a slightly different account of what happened. He said a slave who had been sent on an errand returned to inform him that a single rider was approaching the plantation. Since it was late, presumably after 8:00 P.M. and seeing no reason why he should voluntarily suffer himself "to be arrested, at that hour of the night, and dragged fourteen miles like a malefaction," the attorney general ordered a party of his slaves to stand guard at the gate and refuse to allow the stranger to enter. Wylly explained the gunfire by first stating that the government had supplied him with ordnance to protect the west end of New Providence and that he had taught his slaves to use firearms. That night, he ordered four muskets from storage and gave these to his most intelligent slaves. After learning that two or three of the weapons were loaded, he "ordered them to be fired off, which was done." Wylly further said that he waited a period for Chisholm and when he did not arrive left the gate, leaving strict orders that no one was allowed to enter. The next morning Wylly returned to Nassau, intending to meet with the assembly; but upon learning that it had ordered his arrest, the attorney general returned to Clifton, determined to ask for an extension of his leave. While at Clifton, Wylly received a note from Governor Cameron requesting his presence at the Government House at 10:00 A.M. on January 25, 1817, to provide legal advice to the governor "on a subject of public importance."[9] The matter in question was a request, from the assembly, that the governor prosecute the collector of customs for demanding and receiving unlawful fees. In a resolution drafted on January 23, 1817, the assembly protested that officers at the Port of Nassau were compelling persons who transported slaves from one island in the Bahamas to another to enter into bonds and pay large fees, the authority for this supposedly coming from the Abolition of the Slave Trade Act. The resolution asked the governor to "give directions to the proper law officers of the Crown to prosecute the collector of customs of the Port of Nassau."[10]

When Wylly arrived at the Government House on the date and time requested, William Bayliss, the provost marshal, accompanied by Chisholm, approached him, tapped his shoulder, and took him prisoner. Wylly reminded Bayliss that he was on the property of the king and was there on official business; this prompted the angry response from the provost marshal that he would arrest him if he were in the king's house. Wylly was led away to jail complaining that no official notice had been given to him.[11]

Wylly and Chisholm did not differ significantly on the essential details of events that evening. Wylly admitted that his slaves had weapons and were ordered to refuse Chisholm's entry through the gate. He, moreover, acknowledged that he had ordered the weapons fired. Chisholm also mentioned the gunshots. He differed with Wylly, however, over the number of slaves posted at the gate and their behavior toward him, claiming they resisted his efforts to enter the gate. The term resist may be misleading in the context in which it was used. The sight of armed slaves at the gate and their refusal to open it to him is somewhat stretching the definition of resistance. Wylly probably armed his slaves and ordered the guns fired to intimidate Chisholm and prevent his serving the warrant. His explanation that he had the weapons discharged because he did not want the slaves to have live ammunition rings hollow. He believed Chisholm would not attempt to force his way through the armed slaves, and he did not, giving Wylly time to evade him by returning to town. In short, Wylly played a cat and mouse game with Chisholm; this did not amuse the assembly, who overreacted by ordering his arrest.

At this point Governor Cameron became involved because the arrest occurred while Wylly was responding to his request to appear and provide legal advice that the assembly had requested on a matter. The arrest prevented the attorney general from giving the governor information which the assembly had suggested he receive. It appears that the assembly was acting out of pure rage and with little common sense. The governor was justified in being disappointed with the assembly and questioning its ability to discharge its duties properly.[12]

Meanwhile, Wylly applied for and received a writ of habeas corpus from the Supreme Court. Thus, the Supreme Court became involved. Wylly argued against the legality of the warrant that the speaker had issued, claiming the case was entirely unprecedented in the Bahamas. He further argued that at the time of the arrest he was in actual attendance on the king's representative "to advise him on matters of high and immediate importance to the Colony."[13] The court was impressed with this argument. It then ruled that the warrant for breach of privileges was not supported by legislative sanction and that in the few cases where the usage had prevailed in the Bahamas none had been "confirmed by the judgments of the Courts of law of this Colony." The court further ruled that the assembly could only invoke breach of privileges against members of that body and could not be permitted greater latitude. It pointed to the danger of allowing the assembly greater latitude on this issue in noting that the assembly had challenged the right of the court to issue a writ of habeas corpus to Wylly. The court declared that the general court in the Bahamas had the same power and authority to grant a writ of habeas corpus as the judges of the courts of the King's Bench and Common Pleas in England. The assembly, on the other hand, did not possess all the power that the House of Commons in England enjoyed since that body possessed "power of judicature" to a certain extent and the assembly did not.[14]

The assembly countered by requesting the immediate dismissal of Wylly, declaring that it was the sole judge of its privileges and denying the authority of the Supreme Court. The assembly, moreover, charged that the release of Wylly was illegal and ordered a new warrant for his arrest and incarceration in pursuance of the assembly's January 22, 1817, resolution.[15] At this point, Governor Cameron dissolved the assembly by proclamation and dismissed the provost marshal. The governor planned to call for new elections, hoping a new group would be elected, but he delayed taking further action until instructions came from the Colonial Office.

The assembly's knee-jerk reaction to pressure from the Colonial Office to force compliance with the Abolition Act (1807) by passing a strict slave registration act expanded into a struggle between the assembly and the other branches of government. The court's ruling restricted the assembly's ability to punish members of the executive branch by invoking breach of privileges against them. The governor dissolved the assembly, but all he got for his trouble was reelection of the old members, which was not his intention in ordering new elections. Upon returning, the assembly flexed its muscle by exercising power of the purse against the attorney general, refusing to appropriate money for his salary. The assembly made Wylly a scapegoat for its problems with the Colonial Office over slave registration legislation. It never succeeded in passing a slave registration act that met the approval of Whitehall. Governors Cameron and Grant were unable to prod the assembly into passing a triennial registration act that gained unqualified approval. One of the reasons for this was that Bahamians believed the act was unnecessary and unworkable. As Speaker of the Assembly Kerr said, "But it has already been admitted by His Highness Minister through your Excellency that there has not been any systematic violation of the Abolition Law in the West Indies."[16] Kerr characterized the law as "purely unnecessary and offensive" and complained about passing a "law exclusively to prevent the perpetuation of an offense that has, no existence." He also believed that enforcing it would be expensive.[17] Another reason for the failure to pass an acceptable act was that the governors and Bahamians did not share the same values concerning slaveholding. An 1826 report revealed that all the public officeholders, except Governor Grant and the rectors of Christ Church and St. Matthew's, owned slaves. The attorney general, William Martin, owned forty; the solicitor general, Thomas Wylly, owned sixteen; the chief justice, William Vesey Munnings, and the secretary of the colony, Samuel Nesbitt, each owned nine; and the other law officers—the associate justice, assistant justice, and provost marshal—owned four, one, and two, respectively.[18]

The assembly was slightly more successful in meeting Parliament's mandate to ameliorate the condition of slaves. William Wilberforce, a member of Parliament and one of the leading humanitarians of his day, presented his framework for the amelioration reforms in an 1823 debate in Parliament, but subsequent demands of the Colonial Office and legislation in the Bahamas went beyond Wilberforce's proposal. In that debate he proposed "the abolition of the system of female punishment; the restriction of certain days to the negroes for laboring on their own account; the discontinuance of the practice of working on Sundays; the abolition of the driving system, or of urging the field slaves to their labor by the whip; and above all, the introduction of universal establishment of a system of religious instruction, and of the moral reformation of the slaves of which marriage was of course to be one of the principal particulars."[19]

Between 1824 and 1833, the legislature enacted amelioration reforms in a trilogy of acts that included most of the major mandated reforms, except a prohibition on flogging women, a prohibition which slaveholders insisted on retaining to control their slaves.[20] The assembly said that, since the Bahamas did not have workhouses, treadmills, or places of solitary confinement, "to exempt female negroes from corporal punishment, therefore, would be at once to proclaim freedom to nearly one half of the slave population of the Bahamas." Demands for this reform were viewed as "an interference of undefined extent from Europe between the Master and his slave."[21] The assembly did consolidate the slave acts, passing legislation limiting conditions under which slave families might be separated, providing for the introduction of slave evidence in certain cases, establishing a savings bank for slaves, reaffirming their right to vacation time during Christmas, and legalizing slave marriages.[22] Legislation granting civil liberties to free blacks and persons of color was also passed. Now evidence of these persons could be introduced in certain criminal cases, and persons of color "three degrees removed from black ancestry" were deemed to be white.[23]

The House's failure to pass all the reforms angered Governor Sir James Carmichael Smyth, but he was especially exercised over the failure to outlaw flogging of women. He abhorred this practice, calling it a "revolting, degrading, and unmanly custom."[24] The governor's agitation over this matter evolved into an irreconcilable breach with lawmakers when he assailed a member of that body for twice flogging a female slave while she was in jail. John Wildgoos, assemblyman from the Western District of New Providence, ordered Phoebe, his female slave, and another female slave, this one owned by his mother, flogged with thirty-nine lashes each. About two months later, Wildgoos ordered a second flogging of thirty-nine lashes for Phoebe. Upon learning of this, Governor Smyth apprised the assembly of Wildgoos' action, expecting the body to punish him.[25] But the assembly responded indignantly to the message, declaring that it had recently passed a law protecting slaves and "preventing any abuses by their owners toward them." The assembly instructed the governor that his message should have been directed to the courts of law, which were opened to deal with such cases. In a slap at the governor, it referred to his charges as allegations and characterized his message as "unwarranted and wholly unprecedented."[26] After receiving a cold shoulder from the assembly, the governor turned to the courts for justice. Meanwhile, in an attempt to court public opinion, Wildgoos wrote a newspaper article in which he said that the second flogging did not happen immediately after the first, as the governor suggested, and that the second one came as a result of a new offense committed in the presence of the supervisor and his son. Wildgoos added that Phoebe was still "obstinate as ever."[27] Wildgoos was one of the slaveholders who uncovered the "French Negro Plot" in the 1790s, the rhetoric from which degenerated into French Negro bashing. He certainly could not be called the William Wilberforce of the Bahamas with a straight face, and the reaction of the House of Assembly to the flogging earned it a similar reputation.

As the fate of Wildgoos lay in limbo, the assembly adopted a resolution calling for the removal of Governor Sir James Carmichael Smyth. The removal resolution alleged that he abused his trust and encroached upon the assembly's rights and privileges by attempting to exercise an arbitrary influence over the proceedings of the slave courts and police of the Bahamas. The resolution further alleged that the governor attempted to encourage "a spirit of refractioness" among the slaves and that his message concerning John Wildgoos was an unwarranted and unprecedented attempt to "cast a stigma upon the Character of the House thru one of its members."[28] This allegation, buried in the middle of the resolution, was probably the precipitating cause of the resolution. The assembly obviously sided with John Wildgoos and believed the governor wanted to use him as a tool to castigate it for failing to ban the flogging of female slaves.

Sir James Carmichael Smyth, governor of the Bahama Islands, 1829–1833.
Courtesy Department of Archives, Nassau, Bahamas.

Governor Smyth replied immediately. He observed that many outstanding assemblymen had left shortly after the session was convened, leading him to believe that the harmony which should exist between the branches was likely to suffer. He criticized the assembly for failing to address the shortcomings in the Jury Act, the primary reason for his convoking the assembly. The governor also said that the moment he discovered the assembly had created a committee to enquire into the proceedings of the slave courts and other alleged unconstitutional matters he decided to let matters run their course rather than prorogue the assembly for failing to perform its duty. The governor then repudiated the allegations and chastised the assembly. Having given the body a verbal thrashing, he dissolved it in June 1831.[29]

A year earlier, Governor Smyth dismissed John Lees from the council and fired the police magistrates and two other magistrates for their action in cases involving forty slaves of Lord Rolle on Exuma Island. The slaves had seized one of his boats and headed to Nassau to complain against abusive treatment. Lees, an agent of Lord Rolle, probably aware of the liberal views of the governor and anxious to avoid subjecting the incident to his scrutiny, labeled the slaves runaways, a misdemeanor, obviating the need for a hearing in the general court, whose decisions were subject to review by the governor, who had requested that the cases be heard there. The police magistrates who heard the cases sentenced five men to a public flogging, each receiving fifty lashes; the other slaves were given less severe penalties. The governor retaliated for this slight by dismissing all the magistrates involved in the cases.[30] This further increased the bitterness of his detractors in the House.

By early 1832, Governor Smyth received insightful advice from Lord Viscount Goderich concerning the John Wildgoos matter, advice which he gave to Attorney General William Martin.[31] The governor had approached Whitehall after consulting with the chief justice, attorney general, and solicitor general of the Bahamas, the colony's law officers, who all told him that Wildgoos could not be tried under any existing law in the Bahamas.[32] After reading Lord Viscount Goderich's letter, the attorney general prepared two bills against Wildgoos and presented these to the grand jury. One of the bills charged Wildgoos with causing his slave to be punished twice for the same offense, and the other charged him with misdemeanor in common law for entering the king's "public work house and unlawfully causing and procuring his slaves to be punished with thirty-nine lashes by the whipper at the said workhouse."[33] These bills were consistent with Goderich's position that Wildgoos did not have authority over the public whipper. The grand jury refused to indict him.[34]

The governor had better success with another detractor, George Higgs, editor of the *Bahama Argus,* the antigovernment newspaper. Higgs assisted the assembly in its campaign against Governor Smyth by printing inflammatory articles containing misleading and sometimes inaccurate information. He was charged with committing libel against the government for writing an inaccurate and inflammatory article about the governor. The trial was held in general court with the chief justice presiding. The special jury which heard the case included two nonwhites, Joseph G. Watkins, a free black man, and Robert Price, a free man of color and master mariner.[35] This was perhaps the first interracial jury in the Bahamas to hear a case involving a white defendant. The verdict was guilty.

Shortly after the assembly reconvened, it passed another resolution calling for the removal of Governor Smyth and threatening not to pass any more amelioration legislation until he was removed. Free blacks and persons of color in New Providence rose to his defense, just as they had done after the first petition. John Boyd of New Providence, a free man of color, drafted the petition, which contained over three hundred names; but not all were signatures because one of the persons was George Watkins Sr., a free black carpenter who made his mark on his will years later, indicating that he could not write. Since it was not a legally binding document, the authenticity of the signature was less important than the intent of the person. George Watkins Sr. doubtless was a supporter of the governor and probably had his son, Joseph G., sign his name on the petition. The petition painted an unflattering picture of the governor's critics and stated clearly in harsh terms why they wanted him removed: ". . . deluded as are many of the ignorant, and inconsiderate white inhabitants, by the wiles and machinations of the leading Demagogues of a faction; and keeping up that delusion by inflammatory publications in their newspaper; perversely misrepresenting the true state of things, this colony may be said to be under the baneful and illegal influence of a political Junto, who, to cherish and continue their illiberal prejudices against the advancement of the privileges of the free people of colour, in these Islands, and to obstruct the amelioration of the condition of the slave population, would not stop short of the destruction of the Colony."[36] That is essentially what the confrontation was about, improvement in the condition of blacks and coloreds, slave and free, in the Bahamas. Free people of color in Andros and Turks Island also drafted petitions supporting the governor but theirs were less fiery.[37] The first signature on the Andros petition belonged to Simon Evans, a slaveholding planter. The New Providence petition contained the names of George Watkins Sr., Timothy Cox, and Stephen Dillet—all slaveholders—which suggests that black and colored slaveholders in the Bahamas did not share their white counterparts opinion of Governor Smyth.

The Colonial Office did not accede to the wishes of the assembly. Lord Viscount Goderich sent a message in which he praised the governor, and this was followed by a dispatch informing him that petitions asking for his removal had been dismissed.[38] The assembly expected to be called into session because the government could not operate without money, which it alone could appropriate. Much to its surprise, however, Governor Smyth was able to run the government without reconvening the assembly because its ill-conceived plan to deny the governor funds backfired. The assembly refused to pass a revenue bill, hoping to prevent Governor Smyth from dissolving it again, but assemblymen forgot to pass a law continuing the suspension of the old revenue act, 8th George: 2nd (1735), which automatically became activated upon the expiration of the current revenue act. Thus when the current revenue act expired, after the assembly had been dissolved, the 8th George: 2nd, which granted considerable revenue and placed it at the uncontrolled disposal of the Crown, was activated. The governor used the revenue to pay salaries and provide services at the same level as the assembly had provided, and he used revenue from a more recent act of the assembly, one for which appropriations had not been made, to liquidate one-fourth of the public debt, a lawful use of funds under that act.[39]

Realizing an indefinite continuation of the status quo was undesirable, the Colonial Office reassigned Governor Smyth to British Guiana.[40] Before he left, a majority of the council sent him a laudatory message and the free persons of color of New Providence gave him a silver plate.[41] In June 1833, Blaney Townley (B. T.) Balfour became lieutenant governor, replacing Sir James Carmichael Smyth in the Bahama Islands.[42] John Boyd again wrote a petition on behalf of the free persons of color in New Providence, this time congratulating the new governor on his safe arrival, pledging their loyalty to the Crown, and requesting "protection of their civil and political interests."[43]

The stormy relationship between Governor Sir James Carmichael Smyth and the assembly resulted from a clash of views on race relations: the governor's liberal view versus the assembly's conservative one. He was an unabashed abolitionist governor of a colony that was still struggling to survive economically and whose leaders believed Englishmen did not understand or sympathize with their position. His strong support of free blacks and persons of color and demonstrated concern about the slaves placed in his trust endeared him to blacks and coloreds, free and slave, more so than any other governor. He did not shirk from advancing the humanitarian agenda of the Colonial Office even though it angered the assembly and its white constituency. Politically, therefore, stormy times existed for much of the period.

This political tension did not carry over into the economic arena. Initially, the great economic promise of the early 1780s failed to materialize and economic life was a continuous struggle in the Bahamas, compared with the situation in the sugar-producing colonies. In an 1821 petition to Whitehall, the council and assembly lamented that "goods of every description which formerly found their way thither from the port of Nassau and were afterwards scattered over neighboring province of Spain are now poured in direct abundance from the countries of their growth or manufacture in Europe, America, or Elsewhere."[44] In short, producing nations no longer had to circumvent Spain's prohibition on trade with its colonies because that trade had been opened to other nations. Also, since Spain had ceded the Floridas to the United States, Bahamian seamen were no longer welcomed in waters along the Florida coast where they had made their living turtling and fishing. Cotton production had failed to recover from its long spell of subpar years. The cumulative effect of these, the general assembly complained, was the languishing of commerce, the abandonment of agriculture, the unemployment of the industrious poor, and the flourishing of emigration.[45]

The general assembly may have overstated the seriousness of the economic situation. The commercial treaties Spain had signed with other nations may have changed the flow of goods to its Caribbean colonies, but Bahamian vessels did not stop transporting goods to Spanish colonies. The volume of the traffic merely decreased. Ceding the Floridas (East and West) to the United States in 1819 simply forced Bahamians to become discreet when fishing in waters along the Florida coast. The prospect of America enforcing the ban with a strong naval presence was remote.

If conditions were as bad as depicted in the 1821 petition, this should have been reflected in the 1821 paupers list for Christ Church Parish. The list contained 36 persons, actually 13 fewer than the number in 1811.[46] White females were the largest group on both lists, and free black and colored females were the next. The number of white males on the 1821 list, 8, differs substantially from 1811, when there were only 5. The figure for free black and colored males also increased considerably, moving from 5 to 13. Many persons on the 1821 list were white females over fifty years of age.[47] In spite of increases among males, however, the total number of poor persons had decreased by 1821. So the hardship which the general assembly described was not reflected in the report of the poor.

The total number of persons on the paupers list for the years 1821 to 1825 was 148. Whites composed the largest group (68), followed by free persons of color (45), free blacks (31), and slaves (4). White females (24) on the list outnumbered their free colored (23) and free black (20) counterparts. Whereas white males (40) outnumbered white females on the list and constituted the largest single group of individuals, neither free males of color (11) nor free black males (8) outnumbered their females. The total number of free children of color (11) exceeded that of white (4) and black (3) children combined.[48] The total annual average of all groups was 36. In addition to suggesting that conditions were not as bad as the assembly's depiction (Bahamians were not forced into poverty in any greater number than previously), the list shows that black and colored females (43) tended to suffer greater hardships than their male counterparts (19), and the free persons of color (45) suffered greater than free blacks (31). The situation for the free black and colored females is understandable considering the relative dearth of economic opportunities opened to women compared to those available to men; less clear, however, is the reason why free men of color outnumbered free black males, especially since free black males outnumbered free males of color in the general population.

An 1827 report on the state of the economy was more positive and perhaps more accurate than the gloomy report in 1821. The 1827 report stated that cotton was still raised, but the low prices in London and Liverpool since 1820 and the continued caterpillar and bug attacks tended to dampen enthusiasm for growing the crop. According to the report, Indian corn, or maize, and guinea corn grew on most islands, but the supply seldom met the demands of Nassau. Cuba was now the major provider of corn, although American corn still came into the islands, but it came "circuitously" from neutral ports. Pineapples, once exported in large quantities to the United States, were no longer welcomed there, leaving pineapple growers with a problem of finding new customers for the crop. Many of the Out Islands grew plantains, yams, and sweet potatoes for domestic consumption. Cedars, ship timber, dye wood, the Eleuthera bark, and winter bark sometimes were exported in large quantities. Judging from the report, timber was the most consistently exportable product, and much of the trade was with nearby colonies and countries.[49] Furthermore, commerce with the United States suffered because of trade barriers imposed by the British and Americans. Britain closed the West Indies trade to Americans after the American Revolution, and America reciprocated by closing its ports to certain West Indies produce.

The report showed a diversified economy. New Providence produced cigars from foreign tobacco and it was the shipbuilding center. Turks Island also built ships, and it produced cotton, fishing lines, gloves, and socks. Acklins Island had a small shipbuilding operation. Eleuthera made palmetto plat for hats, arrowroot, and casaba starch. Turks Islands, Crooked Island, Rum Key, Long Island, Exuma, and Ragged Island produced salt. Rum Key (650 acres) and Crooked Island (650 acres) had the largest acres of salt ponds and Ragged Island (42 acres) the smallest.[50] In 1831 the following islands employed at least 100 persons in agriculture: Eleuthera (360), Abaco (250), Saint Salvador (250), New Providence (210), Exuma (200), Caicos (120), Acklins Island (100), Harbour Island (100), Long Island (100), and Turks Islands (100). Eleuthera had the most employed (410) in manufactures. The only other islands with 100 or more persons employed in manufactures were Watlings Island (150), Exuma (120), and Long Island (100). New Providence had more persons employed (245) in commerce than all the other islands combined. In fact, the only other islands with persons employed in commerce were Eleuthera (70), Turks Islands (20) and Andros (10).[51] Surprisingly, Eleuthera, not New Providence, had the most diversified economy in the Bahamas; and more persons in the Bahamas were employed in agriculture than in either commerce or manufacture. Blacks and coloreds dominated agriculture.[52]

Over the years since Lord Dunmore had toured the islands in the 1790s, the economy had not been transformed, but significant changes had occurred. Whereas in the 1790s only Turks Islands produced salt and many islands planted cotton, in 1831 the tables were turned with many islands producing salt while cotton was hardly mentioned. This and the increased manufacturing activity were the most significant changes in the economy, which still had sizable timber and fruit components. Among the Out Islands, Eleuthera seemed to have surpassed the others in its economic development. In spite of the changes, however, the major economic activity of the Bahamas remained agriculture.

The Bahamas was generally sparsely populated. According to government records, only three islands had a population of more than 30 whites per square mile: Turks Islands (86), Harbour Island (48), and New Providence (36). Ragged Island, with 17 persons per square mile, was the only other island with more than 10 persons per square mile. The least sparsely settled islands were Abaco (1), Acklins Island (1), and Saint Salvador (2). Although

Eleuthera had the most diversified economy, it was sparsely populated, containing only 9 whites per square mile, the same number as Watlings Island. Exuma had only 4 per square mile.[53] These figures were consistent with other predominantly agricultural areas with plenty of open space to grow crops. Nevertheless, it would be a mistake to interpret the figures to mean that the population was scattered in isolated farms over the islands, similar to the situation in rural areas of Pennsylvania. Inhabitants in the Bahamas were bunched together in settlements on each island with much of the rest of the island being uninhabited.

Slaves in the Bahamas generally were treated less severely than those in the other British Indies colonies; this is a view shared by historians Michael Craton, William Green, and William Burns, as well as by knowledgeable nineteenth-century contemporaries. Craton stated that conditions in the Bahamas were better than those in other colonies.[54] Similarly, Green said that slaves on the sugar plantations had greater demands placed upon them than those who were producing secondary crops, a category into which the Bahamas fell.[55] Burns concluded that slaves in the Bahamas and Bermuda "were better treated than [slaves] in the rest of the West Indies," but he also said that "slaves in the Bahamas were in many cases only half-clothed and half-fed."[56] An 1820s visitor to the Bahamas wrote that she had "never seen an instance of cruelty to the slaves." She further said, "[T]hey have but little employment, as there are neither sugar nor coffee plantations on the island."[57] In 1830, Governor Smyth, who was not an apologist for slaveholders, said that the slaves in the Bahamas were treated infinitely better than slaves in other parts of the West Indies.[58] Lieutenant Governor B. T. Balfour, Smyth's successor, reported in 1833 that few gangs of slaves were employed in the Bahamas, except on one or two of the Out Islands that had salt ponds.[59] The absence of slave gangs was associated with less demanding work. Having no slave gangs obviated the need for slave drivers, the scourge of slavery. The difference in the treatment of the slaves in the Bahamas and elsewhere in the British West Indies was a matter of degree not of kind. Slavery, of course, was reprehensible regardless of where it was practiced.

As noted earlier, employment did not abound for slaves, but they did work. Higman averred that mechanics in the Bahamas worked "an average 8 to 9 hours per day" during the 1820s.[60] Since work was not plentiful, slaves were often hired out or allowed to hire their own time. Governor Lewis Grant reported in 1826 that "[s]laves of the Bahamas [were] frequently hired by the year to work on plantations" and the annual pay for this work was forty dollars.[61] A profile of the slaves on one of James Moss's plantations reveals a number of interesting things about life on that plantation. Moss was a Nassau merchant who owned 840 slaves and many plantations and at his death in 1820 was the richest person in the Bahamas. The place contained 40 slaves, the most valuable of whom were the carpenter, the captain of the schooner, the head driver, and the cook. These were all vocations with heavy black and colored employment throughout the Bahamas. Strong family ties existed among the slaves on Moss's plantation. John Poor, a manumitted widower, was the patriarch of three generations on the plantation. Daniel, the head driver, and his wife had nine children, ranging in age from three to sixteen. There was a mixed couple—free wife and slave husband—on the plantation. Three slaves had been manumitted and one was scheduled to gain his freedom in 1830. Slaves and free blacks lived together on the plantation often as families. The property was willed to Moss's nephew in England, who transferred most of the prime slaves to Demerara and never came to the Bahamas. So slaves ran the plantation. This plantation reflected the less severe side of slavery: families intact for three generations, occasional manumissions, slaves employed in skilled occupations, absence of white overseers, slaves running the plantation.[62]

The situation on Farquharson's plantation, on Watlings Island, was more severe than that at Moss's plantation. Farquharson continued to grow cotton, but on a small scale. During a two-year period, for instance, only twelve bales were exported. The plantation produced a variety of other crops: guinea corn, pigeon peas, Indian corn, red or cow peas, yams, sweet potatoes, snap beans, castor oil, cabbage, and fodder for cattle. Mules and horses were bred for land transportation and the plantation owned a sloop to transport cattle, fowl, and produce by water. The plantation appears to have produced enough food for its needs; so the slaves should have been well fed.[63] On November 23, 1831, Charles Farquharson, owner of the plantation, wrote in his journal that the men had been employed shipping stock on board his sloop. The next day, many slaves were employed weeding pasture, and the sloop, with its slave crew, headed for Nassau. Each grown woman on the plantation received six yards of cloth for her winter clothing that November. The entry for the following spring contained the seamy side of slavery: "Left Alexander [Alick] in the workhouse [in Nassau] and sends down Mary Ann and her infant child to be sold with Alexander as one of his wives by permission from the Governor."[64]

Farquharson was obviously conversant with the recently passed amelioration acts and he did not want to violate the act that prohibited separation of slave families. His seeking Governor Smyth's permission to sell Alexander, Mary Ann, and her daughter as a family, even though plantation records listed Eliza (Lisey) as Alexander's wife, suggests that (1) Alexander may have been the father of the Mary Ann's baby, (2) Alexander and Eliza may not have taken marriage vows, and (3) Governor Smyth may have been willing to subscribe to the spirit of the amelioration acts in agreeing to accept Farquharson's interpretation of Alexander and Mary Ann's relationship. Farquharson admitted that polygyny was practiced on his plantation with the words "one of his wives." This practice was inconsistent with the values Britain wished to impart among slaves and may have been a major reason why religious instructions were a key provision of amelioration reforms.

The slave population of the Bahamas commenced to decrease early in the 1800s and continued until the Manumission Act (1834) was passed. The primary reason for the decline in the slave population was the ban of African slave trade and transporting of slaves from the Bahamas to other islands. From 1817 to 1834, the rate of decline of the African population was 3 percent annually in much of the British West Indies, but in the Bahamas a relatively high fertility rate resulted in the Creole population outdistancing the African population.[65] Consequently, at the time of manumission the slave population was mainly Creole.[66] Normally, a decrease in the slave population should have resulted in the value of slaves increasing, but this did not happen. According to an 1816 report, slaves just off the ship sold for $300 each in Cuba and seasoned Creole slaves in Jamaica averaged $250 each compared with only $150 each in the Bahama Islands.[67] This supports the assembly's position that the safeguards which Whitehall demanded to ensure enforcement of the Abolition Act were unnecessary. Why would slave traders run the risk of smuggling slaves into the Bahamas when the prices they would receive for the slaves, if indeed they were lucky enough to find buyers, were lower than elsewhere in the region? Why would a slaveholder want to buy more slaves when many he owned were being transported?

The attractive price for slaves in Cuba may have enticed slaveholders to move there. In 1821, Governor Lewis Grant told the Colonial Office that some families had already left for Cuba and others were preparing to go there.[68] The exact number of persons who moved to Cuba is unknown because this violated the law; hence it was done secretly. It was a situation where the governor knew that some had left but could not properly and accurately document how many. Figures are available, however, for those slaves who were transported within the British West Indies. No recorded transporting was done from 1808 to 1815. In 1816, 95 slaves (50 males and 45 females) were transported to Jamaica. The practice quickly escalated in 1817 when 687 slaves were transported from the Bahamas. Between 1816 and 1822, Bahamian slaveholders transported 1,777 slaves (879 males and 898 females) to sister islands in the British West Indies, with a plurality (649) going to Jamaica. Other islands also received large numbers: St. Vincent (543), Trinidad (385), Demerara (102), and Grenada (89). Just 6 were sent to Bermuda; Antigua received 3, and Barbados, 1. [69] In 1824, Governor Grant told Whitehall that in the last three years over 1,000 slaves had been transported from the Bahamas to Demerara, Trinidad, and Jamaica, and a few had "been clandestinely carried to Cuba."[70] In the peak period of the movement, 1815 to 1825, it does not appear that sex or age determined who would be transported. The ratio of 107 males per 100 females transported compared favorably with that of the total slave population: 104 males per 100 females. Only one-third of those transported were prime slaves between the ages twenty and forty-five. Fifteen percent of the 333 slaves transported from the Bahamas in 1821 were African-born.[71]

In his study, David Ellis wrote that over 22,000 slaves were shipped among the British West Indies colonies in the twenty-three years after the slave trade was abolished, and only three colonies had net imports on a significant scale: Demerara, Trinidad, and St. Vincent. The slaves transported to St. Vincent came mainly from the Bahamas. Between January 1, 1815, and February 28, 1825, Bahamian slaveholders transported 3,087 slaves to other British West Indies colonies. Ellis alleges that 5,000 slaves were sent from the Bahamas to Cuba between 1822 and 1825.[72] This is highly improbable. That many could not have gone to Cuba without the slave population showing a much larger decline than it did. Since slaveholding in the Bahamas was not a very profitable venture, the wonder is that more slaves were not transported.

Owning slaves in the Bahamas became an increasingly losing proposition in the aftermath of the abolition of the slave trade and the collapse of many cotton plantations. Did the influx of liberated Africans add to the economic miseries? In other words, could an economy that was experiencing difficulty employing all its slaves find employment for another group of unpaid laborers? Between 1811 and 1828, approximately 1,102 liberated Africans were brought to the Bahamas. The Truck system was introduced, through which liberated Africans were hired out by their masters for a specific salary in return for which they received slave rations. The masters received their wages. Occasionally, holders permitted liberated Africans to find jobs for themselves and compensate their masters for granting them the opportunity. The liberated Africans, who were really indentured servants, received, in return, the nominal slave rations. Some liberated Africans were forced to find their own employment, provide food and clothing, and still pay a specific amount of money to their holders.[73] This was the seamy side of the apprenticeship program to which liberated Africans were subjected before gaining their freedom. Obviously these kinds of practices did not burden the economy because the holders received income from indentured servants in whom they had not made a financial investment. The Truck system worked like the hired-slave practice, but with a major difference, slaveholders had invested money in their slaves whom they subsequently hired out, but the holders did not.

Fortunately, all liberated Africans were not subjected to the Truck system; however, this was not the only downside to the apprenticeship program. Officials expected a significant proportion of the male liberated Africans to be trained as artisans or as pilots, skippers, or navigators of vessels, but few were trained in these skills, although more may have been trained to work on vessels than as mechanics.[74] Interviews of liberated Africans are punctuated with interesting human interest stories. One interviewer described the subject thus: "This African it seems is a most industrious character as will appear from the quantity of provisions he sells." That African paid four dollars a month wages for his wife, a slave, who helped

Early morning in the Nassau Market, 1850.
Courtesy Department of Archives, Nassau, Bahamas.

him farm. A porter was said to have earned an average of twenty shillings weekly and supported himself. Another male started off well, farming a small plot that the collector of customs, the official in charge of liberated Africans, had provided for him, and was able to support himself and his wife, paying her owner four dollars monthly. But he fell upon hard times and was forced to return his wife to her master.[75]

The collector of customs, Charles Poitier, became so concerned about the liberated Africans in his charge that he took unauthorized action to help them. Then, on the other hand, he did not enforce regulations that prohibited females from being employed in agriculture. He was criticized for purchasing land and placing liberated Africans on it without consulting with the governor and for allowing holders to violate the agreement prohibiting female apprentices from working in agriculture. A Mrs. Mitchell was identified as a holder who employed a female apprentice in agriculture.[76] Benebo Berry of Nassau, a free black woman, was one of perhaps many holders who followed the letter of the regulations. She was applauded for treating her female servant well, clothing her properly, and "bringing her up in the manner she ought."[77]

Female liberated Africans generally made a favorable impression and some left an enviable record of industriousness. Governor Smyth was impressed with a group of females who brought the crops produced on their fields to Nassau, a distance of seven miles, twice a day, carrying either a basket of vegetables or a great bundle of wood on their heads.[78] David Bethell sent Irdy, a liberated African apprentice for whom he was the holder, to his plantation on Andros Island; and when he moved his slaves to Turks Islands, Irdy and another apprentice were permitted to remain behind. Working alone, Irdy produced a surplus of ground provisions, loaded these in a boat she had purchased, and transported these to market. She used some of the income from the sale of the produce to purchase other household items, such as chairs, tables, and a good bed.[79] A liberated African female identified only by her tribe, she was an Ibo, supported herself as a washerwoman. Another female of that tribe sold produce, occasionally hired herself out as a washerwoman, and earned about four shillings a week, and she, too, provided for herself.[80]

Although the income generated from their services was modest, these women were success stories. They did not burden the economy because through their own efforts they provided for themselves and simultaneously rendered needed services to the economy. The narrow range and relatively small number of jobs opened to them made their accomplishments more noteworthy than those of the males, who had greater job opportunities. This is not to suggest that liberated African males had a free reign on the types of jobs in which they received training. But their options were greater than those available to their female counterparts. Liberated African females, for instance, did not work in the building trades, serve on vessels, or get recruited into the British West India regiments like liberated African males. The few free black women and women of color who were holders also contributed to the successes of these women by providing positive role models, following the letter of their agreements, and giving the liberated African females proper vocational training.

Did the liberated Africans contribute to racial tensions by exacerbating the black-white racial imbalance? No, they did not. Between 1811 and 1828 the collector of customs admitted 1,102 liberated Africans (females and males) into the Bahama Islands. During almost the same period, in this instance 1815 to 1825, slaveholders transported 3,087 slaves from the Bahamas. Even with the arrival of liberated Africans, the permanent black and colored population, excluding soldiers of the British West India regiments, was declining in the 1820s and 1830s. Since the liberated Africans did not burden the economy and their presence did not increase the black population, they were not real contributors to racial tension.

During the 1820s and 1830s, the government placated whites who objected to the presence of liberated Africans in the Bahamas by establishing several settlements, mainly in New Providence: Headquarters, Grants Town, Adelaide Village, Highborne Cay (on Exuma Island), and Gambier. Headquarters (renamed Carmichael in honor of Governor Sir James Carmichael Smyth) was created in 1825 during the administration of Governor Grant by Charles Poitier, collector of customs. That same year, residents of Headquarters were moved to a site south of Nassau where a settlement was created and named Grants Town in honor of the governor.[81] Also in 1825, the collector of customs reported that liberated Africans wanted to own their own land and were willing to pay one dollar an acre for twenty acres. When the collector approached the owner of the land about selling it, he would only sell the whole tract. The collector described the liberated Africans as orderly and industrious persons who had been so successful growing produce they were "now procuring cattle" to carry to the market.[82] Adelaide Village, named in honor of William IV's queen and located on the South West Bay, was founded in 1831, and Headquarters was reestablished and renamed Carmichael in 1831. The next year, two more settlements were created, one at Highborne Cay and the other named Gambier.[83] Adelaide Village, the settlement at Highborne Cay, and Gambier were created during the administration of Governor Smyth. He was the most sympathetic of the governors to the plight of the liberated Africans, a point which did not escape his detractors in the House. The settlers took great pride in maintaining the settlements: "Cottages are neat and clean and there is an appearance of cheerfulness and industry about the whole African settlement which is gratifying to watch," Governor Smyth once observed.[84]

By the 1820s, three distinct groups of people of African origin inhabited the Bahamas: slaves, liberated Africans, and free blacks and persons of color. The Bahamas probably had more liberated Africans than any other British West Indies colony, and the American South did not have any. The term *liberated Africans* does not appear in African-American history. Liberated Africans occupied the middle ground between slavery and freedom, but they did not create a burden on the economy. Similarly, free blacks and persons of color did not place a burden on the economy, as the following discussion will reveal. In fact, William Vesey Munnings, chief justice of the Supreme Court who was interim governor on several occasions, said that free blacks and persons of color were an asset to the economy. Though not an abolitionist, in 1819 Munnings portrayed free blacks and persons of color as having among themselves "many expert and skillful handicraft and mechanics" who contributed to the support of the government by paying taxes equal to those of whites and in some instances paying higher taxes than the whites.[85]

Gambier residence, 1987. *Courtesy Department of Archives, Nassau, Bahamas.*

Photograph of an African hut from *Starks's History and Guide to the Bahamas* by James H. Stark. *Courtesy Bahamas Department of Archives, Nassau, Bahamas.*

Munnings made the point while arguing unsuccessfully for passage of legislation that would have allowed the introduction of evidence from free blacks and persons of color in trials involving whites, a practice which Jamaica had legalized several years earlier and which Dominica had approved in 1818.[86] Munnings was not alone in his positive assessment of the economic skills and financial status of free blacks and persons of color. Enemies of Governor Smyth, no less, admitted that the colored population included persons of means, some of whom even owned slaves.[87] Such compliments were intended to convince affluent free blacks and persons of color that their destinies were tied to Smyth's opponents. Supporting the governor, they argued, was detrimental to the interests of all slaveholders, not just the white ones.

In the British West Indies colonies, black and colored slaveholders were heavily concentrated in the towns, they seldom owned more than ten slaves, and females outnumbered males.[88] Much of this was also true in the American South where free African-American women composed a larger proportion of the black slaveholders and property owners than their male counterparts.[89] Since in some years the Register of Slaves does not identify slaveholders by race, accurately measuring the number of free blacks and persons of color who owned slaves presents a major problem. Using the baptism record of Christ Church Parish facilitates identification of some of these persons, perhaps even a majority, since many slaveholders baptized their slaves and this was recorded in the register. In addition to the name, color, sex, residence, and, in some instances, vocation of the slaveholder, the register contains the name, color, date of baptism, sex, and many times the date of birth of the slave. On May 12, 1812, for instance, Stephen Rogers of Nassau, a free black man, had his slave boy, George, born April 12, 1812, baptized. Similarly, George Watkins of Nassau, a free black man, had three slaves baptized on January 30, 1814: eighteen-month-old Nancy, a black girl; four-year-old John Portroyal, a black boy; and Price, a black boy born on December 21, 1813. Watkins was perhaps a faithful Anglican because he had a daughter and two sons baptized. The youngest child, Joseph Gould Watkins, born November 19, 1795, who became a religious leader and leading educator in Nassau, will be discussed later in this chapter. John Collie of Crooked Island, a free man of color, tended to baptize his slaves after they had passed infancy. Fanny, a colored slave girl born on January 10, 1803, was not baptized until December 3, 1815, and Rachel, a black slave girl about ten years old, was baptized on June 23, 1816. Murray Farquharson of Acklins Island, a free man of color, followed a similar practice. The practice of late baptisms, however, was not subscribed to by all of Out Islands black and colored slaveholders. Simon Evans of Andros Island, a free man of color, baptized Timothy, a black slave boy born on November 7, 1816, on September 25, 1817. Addelle Jourdan of Long Island, a free woman of color, baptized Sarah, a black slave girl born on November 18, 1821, on April 27, 1822. In both instances the slaves were not yet a year old.[90]

Christ Church Register of Baptisms and to a lesser extent Saint Matthew's Parish Register of Births and Baptisms are virtual gold mines of information on black and colored slaveholders in the Bahamas. The mere fact that the registers give the complexion of these individuals is important in itself, but other useful information is contained in these registers. For instance, the Christ Church register reveals that female slaveholders (53) outnumbered their male counterparts (35) and mulattoes (52) outnumbered blacks (33), even when those who could not be identified by color (3) were included. It was a different story, however, in Saint Matthew's Anglican Church where 34 free black and color slaveholders baptized their slaves. In that parish, males (21) and blacks (19) outnumbered females(13) and mulattoes (15), respectively. Some of these persons baptized slaves in both parishes, most notably John A. Collie, Simon Evans, and Timothy Cox.[91] The nonwhite slaveholders resided on New Providence and on most of the Out Islands. The median number of slaves baptized was 1 and no slaveholder baptized more than 8. These figures may not have reflected the actual number of slaves which these persons owned, and it certainly does not support a conclusion that no black and colored slaveholder owned more than 8 slaves.[92]

George Watkins Sr., a free black carpenter, baptized more slaves at Christ Church than any other free black or colored slaveholder in New Providence. No biographical information is available on Watkins. He received a grant of land from Lord Dunmore in the late eighteenth century.[93] He died in the 1860s, well after the Manumission Act (1834). He was a carpenter who acquired real estate and slaves, an indication that he operated a successful small business. Watkins was married to Sarah in 1794 and to Elizabeth in 1818, but may have survived both wives because neither appears in the will, neither does his daughter Grace, his oldest child.

Watkins had two sons: George Jr. and Joseph Gould. In Britain, under primogeniture laws, the oldest son of an aristocrat inherited the father's title and wealth, forcing the younger son(s) to seek a career in the military, the church, or government service. Since this practice did not operate in the Bahamas, Watkins divided his property equally between his two sons, the older of whom, his namesake, became like him, a carpenter, and the younger chose to pursue the learned professions, religion and education, rather than work as a ship carpenter, the trade for which he had been trained. George Jr. and Joseph were to enjoy the property during their lifetime, after which it was to be passed on to their children; this suggests that the elder Watkins was a family-oriented patriarch who loved his grandchildren and wanted them to enjoy the fruits of his labor.[94] He could not bequeath slaves to his heirs because they were manumitted in 1838. George Watkins Sr., an illiterate free black carpenter who could neither vote, hold public office, nor give evidence against whites in criminal cases, provided his children with the best education the islands offered (they attended Bray's Associates School) and used his influence to get Joseph hired as a lay reader in St. Paul's Chapel. Watkins did well by his sons and grandchildren. His was truly a Bahamas' success story.

Timothy Cox Jr. of Nassau, a free man of color, was a contemporary of the elder Watkins and, like him, worked in the building trades, but Cox built vessels. He married Hannah London in Christ Church in March 1794. Between 1798 and the early 1830s, he had five slaves (three boys and two girls) baptized in Christ Church.[95] In 1817, he was a party to a lawsuit in the general court over repairs to a boat which he had promised to restore to its original state.[96] In the 1820s, his house was one of several destroyed by fire; the government was required to tear down these homes and compensate the owners.[97] By 1835 he owned a lot, inherited from his father, in the

Western District, 240 acres in Blue Hill in New Providence, a lot in the Eastern District of New Providence on which his residence and the shipyard were located, and over 300 acres in Andros.[98] Cox was one of those free persons of color to whom Leonidas alluded in his article in the *Bahama Argus;* a portion of that article introduces this chapter.[99]

In addition to living on many of the islands, black and colored slaveholders pursued many different occupations. They were planters and butchers, artisans and tailors, skippers of vessels and shipbuilders, shopkeepers and overseers, ordnance workers and sextons, washerwomen and sellers of small wares. Murray Farquharson and Simon Evans were just two of the many Out Islands planters who owned many slaves. A case in point, John Collie, an Acklins planter, owned twenty-seven slaves.[100] Most of the black/colored slaveholders, however, lived on New Providence Island. Henry Franks, a stone mason, owned ten slaves.[101] Stephen Rogers rented a dwelling to a French slave who was later implicated in the French Negroes Plot. Rogers owned other buildings and ten slaves, worked for the Royal Ordnance for forty years, and formerly was a popular musician in Nassau. The newspaper reported that over two hundred people attended his funeral. He was one of few blacks and coloreds whose obituary appeared in the newspaper.[102] John Patrick Dean, who was among the first three nonwhites to sit in the assembly (in 1834), owned sixteen slaves; and Samuel King owned eighteen. Anthony Wallace, a house carpenter, owned nineteen slaves, real estate, and a vessel which executors of his will were authorized to sell if it became too costly to maintain.[103] Conversely, the tailor Stephen Dillet owned one slave, like most free black and colored slaveholders.[104] Dillet's grandson, James Weldon Johnson, a leading early-twentieth-century black civil rights advocate and NAACP official, proudly alluded to his grandfather in his autobiography, *Along This Way,* without mentioning that he was a slaveholder, doubtless because he was not aware of this.[105] Turning to some of the female slaveholders, Benebo Berry of Nassau owned a house and lot with outbuildings on West Street and thirteen slaves, seven of whom were baptized in Christ Church; this was the largest number of baptisms by a free black or colored female recorded in the register.[106] Some of the other free black and colored female slaveholders who owned many slaves were Mary Mason (of New Providence) and Harriet Young (of New Providence), with sixteen slaves each; Elizabeth Collie Bowe (sister of John Collie) and Caroline Elizabeth Thurston (of Saint Salvador), with thirty slaves each; Victoria Hannah (of Acklins Islands), with thirty-two slaves; and Margaret Clark (of Exuma), with fifty-eight slaves. Margaret Clark also owned 2,544 acres of land.[107] The above persons are just a sampling of the free black and colored slaveholders in the Bahamas where the typical nonwhite slaveholder was a free female who owned one slave.

The reason why so many free blacks and persons of color opted to own slaves is difficult to determine because the wills they left are generally the extent of written records expressing their state of mind. There was no single reason, however, why free blacks and persons of color owned slaves. Although many of these slaveholders manumitted their slaves in their wills, effective after the death of the wife or the husband, whichever one survived the other, suggesting that black and colored slaveholders often were not interested in fostering perpetual slavery, most probably owned their slaves for economic reasons. The frequency with which manumission clauses appeared in wills and the consistency with which they baptized slaves show that black and colored slaveholders thought of their slaves as persons. In the American South, manumitted slaves were often required by law to leave the state; hence, it was not unusual to have the handful of free African American slaveholders there own their own relatives, whom they had purchased but could not manumit without separating the family. Since Bahamas law did not require manumitted slaves to leave the colony, the motivation for free black and colored Bahamian slaveholders to own slaves was perhaps different than that for free African-American slaveholders.

Free blacks and persons of color acquired their slaves through purchases from private individuals (whites and nonwhites) and estates, as gifts, inheritances, and bequests, through purchases from slave traders, and as a result of their slaves giving birth.[108] The depressed slave market, which made slaves affordable to free blacks and persons of color of modest means, probably did not play a major part in the practice of nonwhite slaveholding; it perhaps increased the number but not signficantly. Settling liberated Africans in the Bahamas contributed to depressed prices for slaves, as did the failure of the cotton plantations. Slaveholders complained that the presence of liberated Africans depressed slave prices and forced them to sell more of their slaves to pay debts to British creditors.[109] This doubtless affected the size of their holdings. Owning slaves helped nonwhites in a business, reduced the workload, increased the output of the operation, and could result in increased income by hiring out the slaves.[110] While these may be similar to the reasons whites owned slaves, since most of the free black and colored slaveholders lived in New Providence and had only one slave to manage, their slaves were probably treated better than slaves of white slaveholders, most of whom lived on the Out Islands and owned a larger number of slaves.

Further evidence that economics was the driving force behind the ownership of slaves among free blacks and persons of color is evident in the 1834 Register of Slaves, which required slaveholders to state where and how their slaves were employed. In addition to employing slaves in small businesses, they were employed in a wide range of occupations. It was not uncommon to see females employed in the fields, or children as young as five years of age and adults in their seventies working full-time. The compensation returns also shed light on the subject by attaching a value to the skills the slaves possessed. Henry Franks (a stone mason) owned a head tradesman valued at sixty-five pounds sterling and three inferior tradesmen. Obviously, the presence of tradesmen among Franks's holdings is indicative of his using them in his business. Since Frank did not baptize any of his slaves he could not be identified as a slaveholder from perusing church registers. Timothy Cox, who owned twenty-seven slaves at one time, had reduced his holdings to six in 1834. He owned a head tradesman, but the five other slaves were domestics. James Rutherford, overseer of the Wylly plantations, employed his three slaves (two males and one female), the total value of whom was fifty-seven pounds sterling, as field hands. They thus were valued at less than Franks's slave artisan.[111]

In addition to being slaveholders, blacks and persons of color were overseers and drivers. James Rutherford was overseer of the Clifton, Waterloo, and Tusculum plantations, which contained a total of forty-three slaves. After inspecting the grounds in 1818, Rutherford reported that the Negro grounds at Clifton were in good order and well-planted with potatoes, yams, peas, eddies, corn, and beans. A total of sixty acres was under crop.[112] Joseph Rumer, a forty-two-year-old black, supervised two hundred slaves while he himself was a slave. After gaining his freedom in the early 1820s he continued to supervise slaves; this time the number was much smaller, eight. It was not long after becoming a freeman that Rumer began to prosper economically, so much so that he was able to purchase the freedom of his son and in 1834 owned twenty-one slaves.[113] In 1833, Jock, a slave overseer, and Linas, a slave driver, were tried for flogging Charlotte, a slave mother of six. Linas flogged her on orders from Jock.[114] They were convicted for committing the same offense that Governor Smyth could not get an indictment against John Wildgoos for committing.

In 1827, the Home Office conducted a census of former slaves (females and males) who had been manumitted during the last seven years to ascertain how well they were coping with their freedom. The return solicited the name, color, age, occupation as a slave and as a free person, and the present economic status of 260 females and 146 males. Only 63 females had occupations listed beside their names. The most frequently listed occupations for the females were domestic (24), and huckster (14). Of the total of twelve occupations listed, none of the others had more than 7 females. Twenty-two of the females were described as doing well and 4 as doing very well—1 domestic and 3 hucksters. Moreover, 12 had left the colony: 2 had moved to England, 7 had moved to Cuba, 2 to Key West, and 1 to Tortola.[115]

The females compared favorably with free African-American females in Charleston, South Carolina, who also were employed in twelve occupations, but compared unfavorably with those in Savannah, who were employed in twenty occupations. Seamstress, fruiterer, and washerwoman were the leading occupations of Charleston's females. Most of the other occupations were similar to those in the Bahamas. Washerwoman, seamstress, seller of small wares, housekeeper, and nurse were the leading occupations of the Savannah females, who also generally practiced the same occupations as the other two groups of females.[116] Seamstresses were in greater demand in Charleston and Savannah than in the Bahamas where only one female listed that occupation. The dearth of seamstresses in the Bahamas may have resulted from women buying their garments in England because this was deemed more fashionable; it may also have been a matter of a shortage of cloth to make garments. The paucity of carders, spinners, and weavers among Bahamian females, free and slave, occupations essential to making cloth, tends to support this conclusion.

The male return contained fewer names than the female one, but more than twice as many occupations (twenty-seven), and more names (seventy-nine) had occupations beside them.[117] The Bahamian males, like their female counterparts, were employed in the same number of occupations (twenty-seven) as the Charleston males and more than Savannah's (eighteen).[118] The most frequently listed occupations were domestic (eleven), sailor (eleven), and carpenter (eleven). Sixteen of the males were described as doing well and seven as doing extremely well. Among those with very favorable situations were Thomas Symns, a black fisherman; Sandy Cunningham, a black pilot; Ben Rolle, a mulatto skipper of a vessel; Toby McKinnen, a mulatto carpenter and sponge collector; Joseph Rumer and George Clark, slaveholders; Charles Bain, a mulatto harness maker who was described as making a fortune; and Pepper Simkins, a black cigar maker who was described as getting rich. The males, furthermore, were employed in some of the same occupations as the females: domestic, cook, huckster, and planter. Only one of the former slaves practiced tailoring.[119] The reason for this may have been the same as for the females.

The job market in the Bahamas was divided primarily along gender lines, with females and males usually working in different occupations. To a lesser extent, the job market was also divided along racial lines. Whites, for example, were not employed as agricultural laborers, common laborers, porters, warehouse laborers, caulkers, or shoemakers. Jobs in which both white and nonwhite males were employed sometimes paid whites over three times as much as blacks, coloreds, and liberated Africans. White carpenters and masons, for example, received £81.2s annually while black, colored, and liberated African ones received £25.4s. Although the difference in pay sometimes was not that large, it was nonetheless revealing; white sailmakers and tailors, for instance, received £42 annually while black, colored, and liberated African sailmakers received £28 and tailors received £25.4s.[120] The difference in the rate of compensation did not result from superior skills of white males. It resulted instead from prejudice, which ran rampant in the job market, depriving free blacks and persons of color of equal pay for the same level of service. Similarly, sexism permeated the economy, barring women from working in certain occupations. Free black and colored males subscribed to this practice with the same fervor as white males, but the situation was not unique to the Bahamas.

Prior to 1834, the Bahamas did not have any university-trained black or colored professionals. Outside of the successful artisans, businessmen, and planters, the free blacks and persons of color drawing the highest compensation were two public servants: the clerk of visitors of the King's School and the reader for St. Paul's Chapel. John Boyd held the highly regarded position, for a free person of color, of clerk of visitors of the King's School, an appointment he received from Governor Smyth. Commenting on the beautiful penmanship of Boyd, a self-taught man of color, Governor Smyth proudly told the Colonial Office "[I]f your Lordship has time to look at the minutes herewith enclosed; your Lordship will not look at them with less interest for their being in the handwriting of a free black man of the name Boyd whom I have appointed clerk of the Visitors."[121] John Boyd's penmanship was the equal of any in the Bahamas and it graced the numerous petitions of free persons of color in New Providence submitted to the governor and written to newspapers in the 1830s. The Board of Visitors was the governing body of the King's School, a secondary school, and its clerk had the following responsibilities: "It will be the business of the clerk to receive the orders of the Senior visitor residing at Nassau as to the summoning a Board. The Clerk will keep a Journal of the Proceeding of the Board of visitors, and it will be his business to prepare, under the authority and direction of the Board of Visitors whatever rules and Regulations they may sanction, or what communications, they may be desirous of making either to the Master, or any other person."[122] Built at the urging of Governor Smyth, the King's School was opened to all free children regardless of color or gender, but the enrollment was capped at one hundred pupils.[123] Boyd received £50 annually from the public coffer, and in 1834 he was paid an additional £37.18s.4d.when he was appointed messenger to the council.[124] He probably could have purchased a slave but did not own any.

Joseph Gould Watkins was the only nonwhite who received higher compensation from the government than John Boyd, and, like Boyd, he had a beautiful handwriting. He was born free in Nassau and married one of James Moss's mulatto slaves on December 21,1820, after she had given birth to two of his children. His wife, Ann, was manumitted that same year; consequently, the five children baptized after their marriage were born free.[125] Unlike his slaveholding father, Joseph Watkins never owned a slave, not even his wife, although he was financially able to purchase one. This may have endeared him and Boyd to Governor Smyth, who spoke highly of both men and gave them good appointments. Watkins was appointed teacher of children of liberated Africans. It was said of Watkins that he read the liturgy better than most curates in England. He received £100 for being reader at St. Paul's Chapel, £25 for teaching at its school, and £18 for teaching at Bray's Associates School.[126] He was involved in the issues of the day and signed petitions which Boyd drafted. Since his wife and two of his children were former slaves, Watkins was probably very supportive of Governor Smyth's efforts in behalf of amelioration reforms. He lived to see all slaves manumitted, dying in 1870 long after this event had occurred in the Bahamas.[127]

Joseph G. Watkins and John Boyd were among the most highly respected free blacks and persons of color of their generation. The generation before theirs, that of George Watkins Sr. and Timothy Cox Jr., were blue-collar workers who made a comfortable living working with their hands while Joseph Watkins and Boyd were white-collar workers who earned a livelihood through their intellect. Boyd's positions as clerk of visitors of the King's School and messenger for the council gave him access to the rich and powerful men who sat on those bodies. Watkin's positions as the leading nonwhite in the Anglican Church, by virtue of his position as reader of St. Paul's Chapel, and as the leading educator, by virtue of his position as schoolmaster, earned for him the respect of the governor and influential persons in the established church. After civil liberties gains enabled free blacks and persons of color to vote and hold elective office, these two were eclipsed by persons with political savvy, but during the amelioration period of 1823 to 1833 they were the leading nonwhite public figures in the Bahamas, especially during the Smyth administration.

Boyd, Watkins, and other free blacks and persons of color in the Bahamas tended to fare better than their counterparts in the American South. Boyd could not have functioned in the positions he held if he were in the American South, and Watkins would not have been allowed to operate a school that was opened to free black and colored children and funded by the government with the blessing of the established church. Understandably, a group of thirty-two blacks and coloreds who fled Florida to avoid capture by Andrew Jackson headed for the Bahamas rather than for either Savannah or Charleston. Risking their lives on the high seas in rickety boats and vessels, these persons crossed the Gulf before being rescued by wrecking vessels and brought to Andros Island. They built a community at a place called Red Daye. Many of those settlers became prosperous by cutting trees and dye woods, gathering sponges, and salvaging wrecks. They were able to engage in wrecking after several settlers had saved sufficient funds to purchase vessels. They also supported themselves by gathering fish, conch, and crabs and growing Indian corn, plantains, yams, potatoes, and peas. One of the group became the owner of several slaves.[128] Similarly, Ann Davis, a free black woman, Simon Evans, and Castleton Evans were all slaveholders on Andros.[129] The Andros settlers built a church but could not find a preacher to conduct worship services. About the same time that the collector of customs was approving the Andros group's freedom petition in the late 1820s, Prince Clear, a free black man from New Providence, purchased a one-hundred-acre tract of waterfront property on Grand Bahama Island for eight shillings and four pence. Clear, a sailor and former slave who was manumitted in perhaps the early 1820s, must have been very successful because besides purchasing the large acreage he bought the freedom of his two sons.[130]

Prince Clear's purchase of that choice waterfront property symbolized the continued economic advancement of free blacks and persons of color in spite of the stormy political climate that descended upon the Bahamas at times. The House of Assembly, with the enthusiastic support of most whites, balked at passing an acceptable slave registration act and all the amelioration reforms, even at the risk of causing a constitutional crisis that would lead to the governor dissolving the House. White voters for their part endorsed the unruly behavior of their elected officials by returning them to office, thus frustrating governors' efforts to fill the assembly with more cooperative persons. That body, moreover, made a mockery of the justice system by failing to indict John Wildgoos for twice ordering his female slave flogged while simultaneously supporting the conviction of a slave overseer and the slave driver whom he ordered to flog a female slave. Sir James Carmichael Smyth was a determined and sincere advocate of amelioration reforms and the granting of civil liberties to free blacks and persons of color. He created a sanguine climate that encouraged free blacks and persons of color to demand their rights. They even belittled the House for opposing him. The political tension did not adversely affect the economic advances of blacks and coloreds, however, many of whom fared well economically. Free blacks and persons of color, females and males, enjoyed opportunities equal to those in Savannah and Charleston in some instances and better in others. No free black in Charleston could match the extensive real estate holdings of Timothy Cox Jr., who owned over 540 acres of land in New Providence and Andros. Murray Farquharson of Acklins Island did not have an equal in Savannah. Since it is difficult to get an accurate and complete count of free black and colored property holdings, the total value of property owned by the group cannot be computed. Contemporaries of that period continuously tell us that the holdings were extensive. Maybe we should believe them.

CHAPTER V

Blacks and Coloreds: The World in Which They Lived, 1816–1834

Education is certainly gaining ground in the Island of New Providence, especially among the Coloured People of free condition.
—Lewis Grant, March 29, 1828

The social, educational, and religious life of free blacks and coloreds continued to improve as their numbers increased and the number of slaves decreased, as more schools were established and the number of black and colored children attending them increased, and as religious life was enriched with the founding of more black and colored churches. Besides retaining certain African practices, blacks and coloreds started civic and fraternal organizations. Thus, by 1834 there was a world of difference between the Bahamas that greeted the Loyalists in 1784 and the one in which former slaves would begin their lives as free persons upon manumission. A color bias still existed between blacks and coloreds. Blacks commingled with blacks, coloreds with coloreds, and liberated Africans with liberated Africans; seldom did the social lines among these groups cross.

The number of free blacks and persons of color increased during the several decades leading up to the Manumission Act (1834), mainly owing to increased manumissions, the influx of liberated Africans, and a significant increase in births over deaths. Conversely, the white population decreased because of emigration and, to a lesser extent, an excess of deaths over births.

The slave population also decreased, but this was the result of transportation to other islands in the British West Indies. In 1819, the slave population of 11,155 consisted of 8,589 Creoles and 2,566 African-born slaves. Creole females outnumbered males, 4,441 to 4,148. Most of the Creole slaves in both sexes fell into the thirteen to sixty age group, and surprisingly there was almost an equal number of males and females in that group, 72 males and 73 females. Most of the African-born slaves were also in the thirteen to sixty age group, but the males outnumbered the females. The African-born slaves above the age of sixty outnumbered the Creoles in that age group even though the Creoles outnumbered them nearly 4 to 1 in the general population. In short, the African-born slaves were living longer than the Creoles.[1]

In December 1822, the total slave population had decreased to 10,649.[2] The decrease occurred both for males and females, Creoles and the African-born. The disparity between the male and female Creoles was not as great as in 1819, but it remained the same among the African-born slaves. By 1834, the slave population was down to 10,001.[3] Thus, from 1819 to 1834 the Bahamas had a net loss of 1,154 slaves. When the total slave population is considered, it gives the misleading impression that slavery was dying in the Bahamas because decade after decade the population declined; however, the slave population on most of the Out Islands increased during those years. A sizable decrease occurred in New Providence, where between 1822 and 1834 the slave population declined from 2,935 to 2,250, contributing to the net decrease for the islands.[4] The slight increase on the Out Islands resulted from natural causes, not from smuggling or transportation from elsewhere.

Although decreases in population appear among both the males and females, between January 1, 1822, and January 1, 1825, the male population showed particular decline. Fewer males were born than females (302 males and 350 females), more males died than females (229 males and 138 females), and more males ran away than females (73 males and 62 females).[5] Even though comparable numbers of males and females were transported, the combined totals from deaths and runaways, besides the smaller number of births, account for the greater loss of male slaves. How did the slave population trend in the Bahamas compare with that in Jamaica? From 1817 to 1829 Jamaica experienced a decrease in its slave population in spite of receiving transported slaves from the Bahamas. In 1817, Jamaica had a total of 346,150 slaves (173,319 males and 172,831 females), but in 1823 the number had dropped to 336,253 (166,595 males and 169,658 females). The number of slave deaths that year, 26,351 (14,030 males 12,321 and females), exceeded births by 3,102.[6] In the Bahamas in 1823 the 203 births (91 males and 112 females) exceeded deaths by 60 percent. Deaths among Jamaican slaves were consistently greater than births, just the opposite of the Bahamian situation. Both colonies suffered decreases in their slave population, but for different reasons: excessive mortalities in Jamaica, transportation in the Bahamas. Sugar was a profitable export, but producing it came at a heavy toll in slave lives.

Manumissions concomitantly helped decrease the slave population and increase the free black and colored population; mainly it was blacks who were freed. Little, if any, official action was taken to discourage manumissions. No tax nor fine was imposed on the parties and the only expense was about five shillings (seventy-one cents), the charge for recording the manumission. The small amount charged to record the transaction was nonetheless more than many could afford; as a result, many manumissions went unrecorded. To encourage manumissions, Samuel Nesbitt, secretary of the colony, advertised in the newspaper and had clergy in churches with large numbers of black and colored worshipers announce from their pulpits that the manumission fee would be waived for all manumissions issued before December 31, 1831.[7] Manumissions also were encouraged by not forcing those who received them to leave the islands, unlike the general practice in the American South. Furthermore, the relatively large number of free blacks and persons of color, reaching nearly 3,000 in 1831, was a stimulus for additional manumissions. Throughout the British West Indies manumissions were highest in colonies with relatively large numbers of freedmen. Two hundred and seven slaves (84 males and 123 females) purchased their freedom from January 1, 1817, to December 31, 1830, and another 461 (228 males and 233 females) were given their freedom. The total manumitted was 668.[8] By comparison, only 680 slaves were manumitted in the seventy-three-year period between 1742 and 1815.[9] The upswing resulted from slaveholders becoming increasingly receptive to freeing their slaves; the improved economic condition of blacks and coloreds, which allowed more of them to meet the purchase price of slaveholders; and increased government action. From January 1, 1808, to November 1, 1822, for example, 790 slaves gained their freedom through being escheated (to the Crown) and then manumitted. Understandably, with its relatively large number of manumissions, the Bahamas had the highest rate of manumissions in the British West Indies.[10]

A Bahamian official reported in 1822, "[N]o correct census of the Free People of the Bahamas has ever been taken nor is it scarcely possible to do it, as it is so fluctuating."[11] The official probably overlooked the rapid increase that resulted from manumissions in the free black and colored population in the 1820s and the influx of liberated Africans. In the year of the report

(1822), the free black and colored population rose to 2,034 (794 males and 1,240 females).[12] The census taker realized, however, that there may have been an undercount of the males, many of whom were engaged in marine occupations and spent much time at sea. This was a perennial problem in attempting to get an accurate count of the males. Even if an accurate count of that population could have been taken, it may not have changed the imbalance in the sexes. In the two-year span from 1823 to 1825, males increased by only 3 (from 804 to 807), but the females increased by 94 (from 1,258 to 1,352).[13] The failure to divide the census return by color prevents giving a clearer picture of how the increases were driven. Without this information an educated guess would place more of the increase among the blacks than the coloreds, not because black women were more fertile or because the genes of blacks predominated in mixed-color partners, but because the slave population was mainly black and more of that color were manumitted. Furthermore, liberated Africans, with maybe rare exceptions, were also black. Governor Grant estimated that 800 liberated Africans were in the islands.[14] The Turks Islands population breakdown in 1825 showed 456 whites (249 males and 207 females), 148 free blacks and persons of color (68 males and 80 females), and 1,361 slaves (709 males and 652 females).[15] Throughout the British West Indies colonies free black and colored females generally outnumbered males, except in Barbados where the males had a slight majority, 2,609 to 2,537.[16]

The health figures for blacks and coloreds, free and slave, tended to be more favorable than those for whites. In 1824, the ratio of deaths among whites was 1 to 78; for free blacks and persons of color it was 1 to 81; and for slaves, 1 to 486. Whites thus had a higher portion of deaths than the rest of the population. The next two years free blacks and persons of color had the highest ratio, 1 to 27 and 1 to 59, respectively, but the following year whites again had the highest ratio, 1 to 61. In each of those four years (1824–1827), slaves consistently had the lowest ratio, and in each instance it was well below those of the free groups. Free black and colored females tended to be more fertile than females from the other two groups. In 1824 the white female population (2,272) gave birth to 57 babies, the slave females (8,629) gave birth to but 128, and the free black and colored females (1,332) gave birth to 75. The figure for free black and colored females was larger in actual number and proportionately than that for the whites, and it was larger proportionately than the number for the slaves. The same thing happened in 1826 when the population of white females (2,291) gave birth to 77 babies, the population of slave females (4,594) gave birth to 123, and the population of free black and colored females (1,362) gave birth to 112. During that span of years births among white females never reached 80; on at least two occasions, on the other hand, births among free black and colored females were more than 100, although their population never reached 1,400.[17]

Juxtaposing figures for deaths and births gives a clearer picture of why free blacks and persons of color increased in number and what contributed to the decrease in the number of whites, but does not help with the slave situation. In 1824 whites suffered 58 deaths and enjoyed 57 births, slaves had 35 deaths and 128 births, and free blacks and persons of color had 27 deaths and 75 births. In 1825, both free groups had more deaths than births: whites had 79 deaths and 70 births and free blacks and persons of color had 79 deaths and 74 births. Conversely, slaves had 24 deaths and 117 births. Only in 1826 did the number of white births exceed deaths, 77 births and 66 deaths; and the excess for free blacks and persons of color was greater, 56 births only 19 deaths. In 1827 whites had 74 deaths and 71 births, slaves had 48 deaths and 136 births, and free blacks and persons of color had 34 deaths and 107 births.[18] While the number of deaths among whites exceeded the number of the births, the opposite was true among free blacks and persons of color, where births exceeded deaths by 161.

The excess of births over deaths is another reason for the steady increase of free blacks and persons of color, although the increase was smaller than that from manumissions. Slaves enjoyed an even larger excess of births over deaths, but transportation and manumissions negated it. The difference between births and deaths among whites was not significant. So the major reason for the decline in their population was emigration. Robert Montgomery Martin raved about the 1826 mortality figures, bragging that "the proportion of deaths to the population in 1826 was only 1 in 45 that is less than the mortality of England."[19] Martin used an aberration as a norm; the year he chose was a time when the deaths compared favorably with the births. The tropical climate and general unsanitary conditions in the Bahamas were less conducive to the survival of the British than the conditions in Great Britain. Less clear is why slaves had proportionately lower deaths than free blacks and persons of color. If the figures for blacks and coloreds were separated, one could discern whether blacks or coloreds had the more favorable statistics for births versus deaths. If the blacks had the better numbers, then biological factors were probably involved. Conventional wisdom in the American South had it that mulatto slaves could not endure the heat as well as their black brothers and sisters. If the coloreds had the better numbers, then dietary factors were involved. Turks Islands mortality figures separated free blacks and persons of color, for the period 1822–1826, when the thirteen burials consisted of nine blacks and four coloreds.[20] Since the entire return was not divided by color, determining how these figures relate proportionately is impossible.

In 1829, the Royal College of Physicians in London asked whether any remarkable instances of longevity were present in the Bahamas? The answer was yes: "A few of the Blacks have lived to the age of 100 and upwards. As for whites, they seldom reached 80."[21] This information supports the mortality figures. Blacks and coloreds lived longer than whites, but who lived longer among the free blacks and persons of color, males or females? In 1826, males and females had the same number of deaths (nineteen), and the next year more males (eighteen) died than females (sixteen).[22] Since the females exceeded males in the general population by almost five hundred, the male deaths per one hundred were greater in both years. In spite of the dangers associated with childbearing, females tended to live longer than males. Medical records are not available to provide the causes of deaths among the different groups; this leaves us groping for the reason the disparity was so great between the free black/colored males and their female counterparts.

Blacks and coloreds continued to observe the African customs practiced in the earlier years. Although not called Junkanoo at the time, the most widely acknowledged precursor of the present Junkanoo observance occurred during Christmastide in 1832 on the Farquharson plantation on Watlings Island. On Christmas Eve a 120-pound hog and a young 260-pound heifer were slaughtered. The master divided all the hog and one-half of the heifer among the slaves, with each adult receiving four pounds. Each child received one-half cup of sugar, and each adult, a bottle of rum, a large cup of sugar, and clothing. These were the Christmas presents. On the evening of December 26 the slaves "had a grand dance" that lasted until almost daylight the next day.[23] This festivity is often perceived as a form of Junkanoo celebration. Christmastide was thus a time when slaves ate, drank, and made merry, a marked contrast to the normal routine. The Africans also retained the practice of spacing babies. The lactation period of from two to three years survived. Slave women in the West Indies breast-fed their babies for a minimum of two years, whereas their North American counterparts breast-fed theirs for one year.[24] This was perhaps a reason why slave women in the British West Indies generally were less fertile than those in North America and would explain the small number of births among slave women in the Bahamas. As stated earlier, in 1825 the female population was 4,594; nevertheless only 117 babies were born; this was lower proportionately than the number for the free females of all colors.[25]

There are no extant records of social and civic organizations, but some probably existed. The Youraba Societies that had their official beginning in 1836 were perhaps the outgrowth of earlier groups that may not have had that name.[26] The name itself is as close an approximation of Yoruba, the tribe in West Africa, as the spelling of asu(e) is to that of esusu, the West African practice from which asu(e) was derived. They also joined Friendly Societies and Lodges. Church, however, was perhaps their main outlet.[27] The Bahamas doubtless also had a Masonic order. The flap that arose in 1825 over Stephen Dillet's application to participate in a procession that the white Masons had scheduled is the most compelling evidence we have of this. The *Bahama Argus,* the organ of the anti-Smyth faction, mistakenly wrote that Dillet had presumed to apply for admission into the white Masonic order on the islands when in fact he had responded to a public call from that group for all master masons to join in the procession.[28] The *Royal Gazette,* the pro-Smyth paper that published the Masons' advertisement, rejected its rival's account, stating that the advertisement said "all master masons were invited" to participate in the procession. If Dillet responded to a call for all master masons to join in the procession, then he must have been one himself. If the whites in Nassau did not know this, then he must not have belonged to their lodge. This raises the question, How did he become a master mason?

Did the free blacks and persons of color in New Providence do as African Americans in Boston, Massachusetts, did when they were rebuffed by the white Masonic order? There they applied to the Grand Lodge in England for a charter. Prince Hall, a West Indian, spearheaded the move to organize a black lodge. After receiving the charter in 1787, Hall and his followers organized African Lodge No. 459, the first black Masonic order in North America. He subsequently assisted African Americans whom the local white lodges had rebuffed in other northern cities, Philadelphia and New York, to mention two.[29] Dillet could have appealed to the black lodge which Prince Hall and his followers had started in Boston, or to an offshoot of that lodge, especially the ones in either Philadelphia or New York City. Moreover, he could have joined the Bienfaisance Society in Jamaica, a freemason lodge founded in 1819.[30] Not knowing how Dillet became a Mason hinders learning when he became one. What is nonetheless certain is that he was one. It is improbable that he could have become a master mason without being a member of a lodge.

The dearth of social and civic organizations did not cause free blacks, free persons of color, and liberated Africans to spend their leisure time in unlawful pursuits. Liberated Africans as a group had almost no criminal records. Between 1820 and 1827 only one liberated African was incarcerated for committing a crime, and it was only a misdemeanor. Liberated African females had a spotless criminal record. One white female was incarcerated for committing a misdemeanor and three free black and colored females were jailed—one for grand larceny and two for committing misdemeanors. These women's records nevertheless were not as bad as the men's; men committed more crimes and they were usually more serious. Free black and colored males were incarcerated for allegedly committing two murders, two grand larcenies, and one felony, whereas white males, who had the worst criminal record of any group, were arrested for allegedly committing two murders, two grand larcenies, two felonies, and four misdemeanors.[31] The number of white inmates was equal to that of all the other nonslave inmates. They therefore committed a disproportionate number of the crimes. All wrongdoers were not incarcerated together. "Females were separated from males, blacks[coloreds] from whites, debtors from criminals, and the convicted from the accused." A year following publication of the return, Governor Smyth created the Board for the Superintendence of the Jails and Places of Confinement to address the issue of whether the different categories of inmates were indeed separated.[32]

The figures did not include slaves who also may have been incarcerated. Slaveholders probably handled the vast majority of slave infractions, administering on the spot punishment rather than confining slaves in jail with the resultant loss of work. The jail records do not identify the victims, where there were victims, which prevents determining whether the murders, for instance, were white on white and black on black, or another combination. One cannot determine, moreover, where the crimes were committed. It would be interesting to learn whether Eleuthera and Turks Islands, or the Out Islands generally, were crime free. The total number of arrests (twenty) during the seven years was relatively low, which suggests that Bahamians tended to be law-abiding subjects.

The low instances of criminal activity were consistent with a literate society, and this appears to have been the situation in the Bahamas, well-stocked with schools for the size of its population. Shirley C. Gordon did not perceive the islands in this light, however, because her study of West Indian education overlooks the Bahamas. In describing education in the British West Indies before emancipation she writes, "The pre-emancipation society was therefore, not in any sense an educational one." She continues "[A]t no stage was there much thought of aim or standard. It was not in fact a system either in thought or practice."[33] Addressing an enquiry concerning the education of free children of color in the Bahamas, Theodore George Alexander wrote that he knew of no "refusal to admit them to vacancies" in the poor schools. Then Alexander made an interesting, but incorrect, remark; he said that parents of free children of color preferred to keep their children home to help them work rather than have them in school.[34] This was not true. Alexander was correct, however, when he said that there were not restrictions "against the admission of the children of free people of colour."

Throughout the period, the prevailing mood favored educating free black and colored children. Financial considerations caused whatever opposition that surfaced against education. Derogatory remarks against educating free black and colored children were not voiced in high places. Some whites may have objected to integrated schools and discriminated in their admissions policies, but this did not dampen the enthusiasm for learning or adversely affect academic progress because blacks and coloreds emphasized education and believed it was the primary reason whites were better situated than they. Acquiring an education would lead to parity with whites in all endeavors of life, they believed; and it was most assuredly the key to power and wealth. Consequently, blacks and coloreds, free and slave, craved education. When the King's School opened in 1833 with accommodations for one hundred scholars, seventy-five of the scholars selected were black and colored and many others were among the unsuccessful applicants. Unfortunately, slave children were not allowed to attend.[35] The Bahamas schools stopped at the grade level that today is called junior high school, or middle school. When children completed that schooling, they were well prepared in writing, reading, and arithmetic and could function in Bahamian society. If they wanted professional training, however, they had to go abroad.

In 1815, Bray's Associates proposed to John Stephen, rector of Christ Church, that their school in New Providence should adopt the Madras, or Bell, System. Stephen was elated over the proposal, but he believed it would be necessary to import someone to introduce the system because no one in the islands was capable, and this would incur an expense which the assembly should assume. Stephen then approached influential assemblymen and received warm support for the proposal, with an eye toward extending the "benefits of that System of Education to the white population" throughout the colony after it had been tried successfully in the Bray's Associates School.[36] The assembly funded the proposal as expected but with the understanding that the white schoolmasters would receive training with Watkins, master of

Bray's Associates School, and nonwhite scholars would be excluded from the previously integrated public schools of New Providence.[37] So the assembly used a proposal to introduce the latest pedagogy into the school for black and colored children as an opportunity to introduce racial segregation into public education in the Bahamas.

In January 1817 Bray's Associates School closed for six months to allow its headmaster, Joseph G. Watkins, to observe the Madras System, a new method of instruction, at a newly built school to which only white children were admitted. Three white headmasters joined Watkins in observing the new system. The Madras System, later called the monitorial system, was popularized by two Englishmen, Andrew Bell and Joseph Lancaster, who developed the system in different educational settings without knowledge of what each was doing or that others were using it. In 1787, Bell went to India and while there one of the many positions he held was at the Military Male Orphan Asylum in Madras. At the asylum a situation developed that resulted in Bell using an eight-year-old boy to assist him in teaching, and with good results. The boy taught the lower classes. The experiment was continued by putting other boys (monitors) in charge of lower classes and making the first monitor superintendent. Meanwhile, in England Lancaster, who had opened a school in the Borough Road, saw enrollment increase from the original figure of one hundred to over five hundred boys. In order to handle the large enrollment, Lancaster turned to teaching some of the older boys who were subsequently assigned to teach others. Although Bell and Lancaster did not invent the system, their success led others to try it since England had a teacher shortage and evinced little interest in spending much money to educate the poor. The teacher shortage in the Bahamas was even more acute than in England, so Watkins and his white counterparts benefited from observing the system in practice. In 1823, the House of Assembly, in a budget-tightening move, suspended the education acts passed in 1816, 1821, and 1822 and replaced these with the Education Act, which created only one school, the New Central School in Nassau, capacity eighty-six children, that the rector and wardens of Christ Church administered. In 1828, the government reestablished the school at Caicos, and the following year schools were reestablished at Harbour Island, Rock Sound, and Green Turtle Cay.[38]

As a result of the assembly's expressed desire to have nonwhite students excluded from the public schools, the policy of opening schools to children of all colors instituted early in the nineteenth century was abandoned. In 1824, Governor Grant informed Whitehall that the legislature had provided funds only for the public school in New Providence and it was opened to white children only. Besides the public school, white children also attended two "tolerably good" private schools. Free black and colored children in New Providence attended a separate school, the one established by the late Dr. Thomas Bray, Bray's Associates School. Turks Islands operated two private schools with about thirty children each, but residents on the Out Islands generally were apathetic toward education. By the early 1820s most of the free children in New Providence, Turks Islands, Harbour Island, and a sizable number on Eleuthera and Abaco, had learned to read and write. Even with the relatively large number of schools, the governor estimated that two hundred free and two thousand slave children under the age of fourteen may have been uneducated. The Wesleyan Methodist missionaries made considerable headway in operating schools for Bahamian children. Building upon the foundation that William Turton had laid in 1803, Wesleyan Methodist missionaries ran Sunday schools throughout the Bahamas and gave slaves the little training they received.[39]

During the late 1820s, the educational situation for free black and colored children continued to improve. Governor Grant reported to Whitehall, "Education is certainly gaining ground in the Island of New Providence especially among the coloured people of Free Condition." He said that prosperous free blacks and persons of color in New Providence were educating their children but that residents on the Out Islands did not show the same good judgment.[40] In 1827, children of both sexes attended the two schools operated by Joseph G. Watkins, with girls (98) constituting most of the 182 children. Scholars at Bray's Associates School were taught reading, writing, and arithmetic, and children at the Sunday school were probably taught to read and spell. Total enrollment in the two schools dropped to 166 the following year when an equal number of boys and girls attended.[41]

The next decade (the 1830s) began with a show of the same strong interest in education. The 1830 Blue Book of Statistics incorrectly stated that the 94 children in the public school included 53 free black and colored children and 41 white. While it is true that the enrollment in the public school was 94 scholars, all were white, as was the headmaster, John Malcolm. The Sunday school Watkins operated had the same number of children (94) as the public school, but they were all black and colored. Watkins added to his teaching responsibility by accepting a position at the recently built Headquarters School for children of liberated Africans. After the assembly had rejected his request for funds to build the school at Headquarters, Governor Smyth funded the school's construction, at a cost of one thousand dollars, from his personal account. Free black and colored children attended the Sunday school in St. Matthew's Parish in east Nassau along with white children. The Sunday school at St. Andrew's in Christ Church Parish, however, was for whites only. The Wesleyan Methodist Sunday schools in Nassau had black and colored children, both free and slave. The Wesleyan Methodist Chapel in Nassau enrolled from 120 to 150 children and their chapel "to the eastward" enrolled "mostly children of slaves." Volunteers of the Wesleyan Methodist Society taught children to read and write and the school ran for about two and a half hours each Sunday morning and two hours each afternoon while the public school and Bray's Associates School operated from nine to two, Monday through Friday.[42] Almost without exception, when the term *chapel* was associated with a facility in Nassau it was for blacks and coloreds. Both the Anglicans and Wesleyan Methodists used the term in that context, but not the Baptists.

In 1830, the total number of children enrolled in school, excluding the ones of the Wesleyan Society, was 833. Most of these children (588) went to school in New Providence, and of these 188 were black and colored. It is unknown whether the public schools in the Out Islands admitted free black and colored children. Since the language of the legislation establishing them did not state that the purpose was to teach white children only, a small number of Out Islands free black and colored children, mainly from affluent families, may have attended these. St. John's Parish on Harbour Island, with 35 boys and 44 girls, and St. Peter's Parish on Abaco Island, with 26 boys and 27 girls, both operated schools in which girls constituted a majority of the children; in St. Thomas's Parish on Turks Islands, with 27 boys and 20 girls, and St. Patrick's Parish on Eleuthera Island, with 33 boys and 31 girls, boys were in the majority.[43] In New Providence boys were usually in the majority in the Sunday schools, except at St. Paul's Chapel.

Schools in Christ Church Parish segregated whites from blacks and coloreds, and the white headmaster was paid much more than Watkins. In 1831, John Malcolm, an Englishman, received an annual salary of £216.31s.4d. for teaching 79 scholars, 43 boys, and 36 girls. Watkins taught 96 children (52 girls and 44 boys) in his Sunday school and 65 scholars (35 boys and 30 girls) in the day school which Bray's Associates funded. Watkins received a combined salary of fifty pounds sterling from the two positions.[44]

Admission practice and compensation policy were discriminatory. When the public school first opened in the 1790s, the intent was to have a color-blind admission policy, and initially the admission practice was consistent with the intent of the legislation, if answers submitted to an inquiry were truthful; but over time the rector of Christ Church obviously strayed from the policy. Free black and colored children were steered to the all-black and colored St. Paul's Chapel Sunday school and the Bray's Associates day school while white children attended the public school. Whenever Christ Church was associated with a school, racial separation was practiced. In addition to public school, Christ Church operated a school at Kirk that had between 80 and 100 children and all were white. On the other hand, St. Matthew's Parish, which did not operate a public school, did not discriminate in its admission practice. The 150 children in its Sunday school were of all colors.[45]

The difference in the compensation paid to Malcolm and Watkins was a clear manifestation of discrimination. Watkins had more scholars than Malcolm and the two used the same teaching method; nevertheless, Malcolm received almost twice as much money for teaching one school as Watkins did for teaching two. Even when Watkins' reader's salary at St. Paul's Chapel was combined with his teaching salary, the total compensation was about 60 percent of that paid Malcolm. Earlier in this study it was shown that white blue-collar workers received higher wages than their black and colored counterparts. Consequently, at all levels in the Bahamas whites were paid higher compensation than blacks and coloreds.

The Wesleyan Methodist Society had surpassed the established church in providing educational opportunities for black and colored children by the time of the Manumission Act (1834), and its admission policy was not discriminatory. The two Sunday schools the society operated in Nassau in 1832 contained 24 white and 281 black/colored children and adults. Wesleyan Methodists also had two weekly catechetical schools that had about 150 black and colored children. The society's missionaries taught catechetical schools and 11 whites and 18 free blacks and persons of color taught the Sunday school. Wesleyan Methodists, moreover, operated ten Sunday schools in the Out Islands where about 630 children of all colors were taught to read and spell. [46]

In March 1832, the House of Assembly neglected to provide funding for the salary of the headmaster of the public school in an apparent move to intimidate Governor Smyth, but he refused to bend to the pressure. The assembly, which had irreconcilable differences with the governor, was subsequently dissolved and he ran the colony without it. Rather than permit the school to close, or call the assembly into session to appropriate the funds, Governor Smyth provided money to operate the school, which he renamed the King's School. His decision was not driven by a desire to send the assembly a message, but by a belief that every British West Indies colony should have at least one school under the immediate control of the government "in which children may be taught to fear God and honour the King; instead of imbibing the American predilection in favor of Republicanism and Infidelity."[47] The governor did not say that the government should control education in the Bahamas but that the government should operate at least one school in which it determined the curriculum. He worried little about American public education, which was practically nonexistent, but greatly about the American political system, which had shown the world that a republic could indeed survive in conditions other than those of Greek republics of Socrates' day.

The King's School was under authority of the Board of Visitors, which the governor appointed. John Boyd was clerk of that board. The Board of Visitors adopted strict rules supporting church and state, but they were liberal regarding admission policy. In a major change of admission policy, reversing the one that had been practiced since 1817, all poor free boys and girls, whatever color, between the ages of six and fourteen for boys and six and twelve for girls, were eligible to attend the King's School. No reason was given for the unequal number of years allotted to boys and girls, but it was perhaps the result of a belief that six years of schooling were sufficient for girls and a desire to separate boys and girls at that crucial developmental period of a female's life. School, which began and ended with prayers, was held Monday through Friday from nine to two. Scholars were required to attend one of the established Sunday schools, and Anglicans were expected to attend "Divine Service" every Sunday. The King's School was required to teach the curriculum produced by the National Society (of England) for Promoting the Education of the Poor in the Principles of the Established Church, which was formed in 1811 and assumed much of the work previously done by the Society for Promoting Christian Knowledge (S.P.C.K.). The headmaster was required to report all rule violations to the Board of Visitors, and the board was required to inspect the school the first Wednesday of each month.[48]

The major differences between the King's School and its predecessors were the administrative structure and the religious requirements. The Board of Visitors replaced the rector, wardens, and vestry of Christ Church Parish as the governing body of the school and all scholars were required to attend Anglican Sunday schools. Governor Smyth sent a strong message when he appointed John Boyd as clerk of the board. Since this freeman of color had the governor's ear, the board was not inclined to disregard the admission policy and discriminate against free black and colored children. The religious requirement could have worked against Baptists, all of whom were blacks and coloreds. Those children had to attend Anglican Sunday schools. Although the rules did not require scholars to attend Anglican "Divine Service," it is improbable that attending Baptist service would have been acceptable, considering the low regard in which Baptists were held. Furthermore, if the governor was concerned about the spread of "republicanism," he did not look favorably upon scholars worshiping in the Baptist faith, even though Bahamians did not have ties with their American counterparts.

In addition to using unappropriated funds to establish the King's School, the governor used them to build a school at Headquarters for children of liberated Africans, then persuaded their parents to build a road leading to it. He was not disappointed with the assembly's negative vote on money for the project, noting that the assembly had been assured it would not be encumbered with expenses associated with liberated Africans since it had objected to the policy. The school was built in 1830 and Watkins was appointed its first headmaster.[49] The governor then appealed to Whitehall for financial assistance, and in May 1831 the Colonial Office granted 400 pounds sterling to build the school and house for the teacher; another 150 pounds sterling were given for the headmaster's salary. To ensure the permanent operation of the school, the Colonial Office promised to ask Parliament to appropriate money for the school.[50]

Headquarters School needed a road built to it; parents had promised to construct it to show their appreciation to the governor for underwriting construction costs, but they reconsidered. Whites in Nassau poisoned the minds of the liberated Africans who were building the road by telling them that the governor had lied about paying for the school because money had been appropriated for it, money that he had used for other purposes. In short, whites claimed that the governor was exploiting them. Liberated Africans then refused to donate free labor and demanded to be paid for building the road. They became surly with the governor, whom they previously used to greet cheerfully. Governor Smyth was taken aback by this behavior and told Watkins to assemble the workers. At the meeting, the governor explained the situation and gave them a choice: they could either honor their pledge and build the road free of charge to the government or accept wages for the work. If they accepted compensation, they would lose claim to the school building and he could do whatever he wished with it, including selling it.[51] After the governor left, the men stayed behind for a meeting with Watkins, who told them how the whites were trying to manipulate them and did not have their best interests at heart. He then asked if they would risk losing Governor Smyth's favor for the few dollars they would receive for building the road. The workers agreed that they should honor their promise.[52]

Watkins shared highlights of the meeting between him and liberated Africans with Governor Smyth, who was so impressed with the report that he sent Watkins' letter detailing the meeting to the Colonial Office. In the cover letter, Governor Smyth lauded Watkins saying, "The part of his letter in which he describes his having paused to see the effect of his statement upon his audience before he went on to explain to them my proposition shows a degree of tact and of judgement not always to be met with amongst orators much more known to fame than this humble black man."[53] The governor was not the only person in high places who respected Watkins. In replying to an Englishman, Munnings once said, "From the charge of being uneducated, I would except the black School Master Joseph G. Watkins."[54] This black man was tactful, astute, and educated, but these traits were not good enough to qualify him to receive the 150 pounds sterling appropriated for the teacher at Headquarters. He received £27.1s.18d. the first year of the school's operation,[55] but in 1831 when the 150 pounds sterling were available, Tom Rigby, a white, received it.[56]

The school at Headquarters was just another example of how educational opportunities for blacks and coloreds continued to expand over time. School enrollment slipped slightly from 1827 to 1832, dropping from 182 children to 161 in the two schools where Watkins taught. This was not indicative of diminished interest in education because in addition to the number of schools increasing between 1815 and 1830 the quality of education improved.[57] Since the vast majority of free black and colored children lived on New Providence Island, and the education acts generally included them under their umbrella, they were not adversely affected by the general lack of schools and interest in education on the Out Islands. Consequently, prior to emancipation a considerable percentage of free black and colored children received some form of education, either in day schools or Sunday schools. This would change, however, after emancipation because all blacks and coloreds would be free and then the Out Islands, where most of the black and colored population lived, would lack schools for the children.

Joseph G. Watkins deserves praise for the caliber of education he provided for free black and colored children. Even though he was highly regarded, Watkins did not teach white children in Nassau. Whites were agreeable to opening schools and admitting free black and colored children to these, and there was not an apparent outcry against white children attending school with black and colored children, but whites were not ready in the early nineteenth century to entrust their children's education to a black man, no matter how highly regarded he was. This does not diminish the contributions Watkins made to education in the Bahamas. He was without doubt the premier black/colored educator of his generation.

In spite of the discrimination, the educational climate for blacks and coloreds was much more sanguine in the Bahamas than it was in the American South, especially the Lower South. In the 1820s, the state of Georgia prohibited teaching slave children to read and write, fearing this would make them ungovernable.[58] A small group of black children there nevertheless received an education because private schools operated clandestinely, disregarding the proscriptive laws. Similarly, in the 1830s, South Carolina passed a law prohibiting "the operation of schools to teach free blacks and/or slaves." Some of the black schools closed and others went underground like they did in Savannah. Although African Americans in these and other states of the Lower South continued to operate private schools despite the prohibitory laws, they did so at their own peril.[59]

Educational and religious institutions were closely associated in the Bahama Islands, as reflected in the fact that the two dominant religious denominations operated most of the schools on the islands. Teachers were mainly clergymen and missionaries. The religious community was predominantly Protestant, just as it was in Great Britain, but the established church was not as strong in the Bahamas as it was in Britain. Much of the blame for this falls at the feet of the Anglican Church for failing to train enough priests to meet the needs of an expanding empire and for lacking the vision to recruit and train local residents to provide religious services for Bahamians. The Anglican Church, moreover, catered to the literate and affluent while neglecting to reach out to the masses. Universities in Great Britain did not train their theology graduates to proselytize among black and colored subjects. Furthermore, Anglicans had an arrogance that prevented them from respecting evangelical churches, and the Anglican Church in the Bahamas appears to have raised that arrogance to a higher level. The contents of an 1817 act entitled "An Act for preventing the profanation of religious Rites" showed this arrogance at its worst. Some of the expressions found in the act were "[f]alse worshipping, pretense of preaching, illiterate, ignorant, ill-dispose persons."[60] Small wonder it was disallowed.[61] It was said that the Reverend William Strachan, rector of St. Matthew's Church (1826–1843), would cross the street to avoid meeting a dissenter.[62] If Anglicans could not respect dissenters, they probably would not be receptive to learning from them. Wesleyan Methodists and Baptists obviously had the best track record among the black and colored majority on the islands, and hence had much to offer other Christian denominations concerning how to proselytize among them.

This is not to argue that the Anglican Church did not attract any blacks and coloreds. Rather, the point is that ignorance of where the masses of blacks and coloreds stood on the religious spectrum hindered efforts to increase the number of black and colored worshipers attracted over the years. The year 1817, for instance, was good for the Anglican Church when it baptized 52 slaves (43 children and 9 adults), and the next year the number swelled to 94 (74 children and 20 adults), but baptisms declined in the years that followed. The number dropped from 75 in 1819 to a low of 34 in 1821. Most of the 320 slaves baptized between 1817 and 1821 were children; only 64 were adults, which was consistent with the church's policy of baptizing infants.[63]

The most active churches in the Bahamas were the Wesleyan Methodist, Presbyterian, Anglican, and Baptist Churches. Wesleyan Methodists showed a greater desire to convert blacks and coloreds than any other religious denomination, except the Baptists. Presbyterians had only one minister in the Bahamas in 1823, whereas Wesleyan Methodists had five "indefatigable missionaries," among whom was William Turton, a freeman of color. There were four other licensed black and colored preachers on the islands, three of whom were Baptists and the other was the reader at St. Paul's Anglican Chapel.[64] It is interesting that Watkins was listed as a preacher in the Colonial Office when in fact his formal title was reader. The governor issued his license. Normally, the bishop issues a lay reader's license. A license authorized readers to conduct services and deliver sermons, but they could not administer the two sacraments of the church, Eucharist and baptism, nor officiate at weddings. The Anglican Church in the Bahamas was under the jurisdiction of the bishop of Jamaica. The three Baptist preachers were associated with churches which did not have ties outside the Bahamas until 1833 when an English missionary was sent to the islands. For the first forty years of its history, therefore, the Baptist Church in the Bahamas was completely black and colored, in the pulpit, choir, and pews.

An 1824 report is quite revealing about the churchgoing habits of Bahamian slaves. Only a total of 150 slaves worshiped in the Anglican and Presbyterian Churches, with the Anglican Church having most of these. This shows that either Anglican slaveholders were not devoted churchgoers, they did not force their slaves to attend church, Anglican clergymen were apathetic, or perhaps all of these reasons. Wesleyan Methodists had 260 slave worshipers and Baptists had more than 300. If these 1824 figures are accurate, less than 800 slaves, out of a total of more than 10,000, were worshipers in the Bahamian churches. Thus, slaves in the Bahamas were not devout churchgoers and they attended worship service less frequently than free blacks and persons of color. The Baptist worship service, the favorite of slaves, was usually depicted as highly emotional with loud shouting and "amen" resounding in the edifice. This scene is different from the one Governor Grant witnessed. He said that the worshipers "comport[ed] themselves in a very creditable manner when attending worship." He envisaged bringing Baptist preachers into either the Anglican Church or the Wesleyan Methodist Society. The governor was realistic about the prospect of this occurring and cautioned against trying to force immediate compliance, instead advising that it should be done gradually over the long term.[65]

Some whites believed the major obstacle to the Anglican Church attracting many free blacks and persons of color was not the worship service itself—the high level of literacy required to understand and enjoy the liturgy—but its uncomfortable accommodations for these persons. Governor Grant recommended that Christ Church provide more and better seating for blacks and coloreds, free and slave, to lure them away from the "fanciful Meeting Houses" with their "ignorant Black preachers."[66] Just about a week after receiving the letter containing this advice from Governor Grant, who was on leave, Acting Governor William Vesey Munnings wrote to Whitehall to inform it of how work was proceeding on repairing the steeple of Christ Church; and he used the opportunity to inform his superiors of a proposal to add seating to accommodate free blacks/coloreds and slaves. Munnings echoed Governor's Grant's belief that an enlarged Christ Church would improve its perception among blacks and coloreds. Munnings singled out Frank Spence, a licensed Baptist preacher, for special attention, noting that his large chapel had a seating capacity of from nine hundred to one thousand; and he lamented that black preachers, including Spence, were not trained in the Holy Orders.[67] Similarly, the rector of Christ Church, who had been on an extended leave of absence in England, believed that lack of space was the major reason many blacks and coloreds, free and slave, did not worship in Christ Church.[68]

Lack of space was a problem the Anglican Church had to resolve if it was serious about attracting many black and colored worshipers, but this alone was insufficient. The lack of space was symptomatic of the major problem the Anglican Church had to deal with: indifference and inability to relate to blacks and coloreds. Governor Balfour was correct when he said that Anglican clergymen by birth, connection, habit, and means socialized with slaveholders and through this identified with that group. To avoid offending slaveholders, the Anglican clergy maintained a safe distance from slaves and sided with slaveholders against them. The governor said that Wesleyan Methodists, on the other hand, mixed with slaves and because of this slaves were attracted to Methodism to a greater degree than to Anglicanism.[69] The Anglican clergy's close association with slaveholders spoke louder than their sermons. Slaves rejected entrusting their salvation to apologists of their oppressors.

It is no big mystery why Governor Grant, Munnings, and the Reverend William Hepworth did not see the problem as clearly as Governor Balfour; and this is not intended to belittle Governor Grant, who was a decent man. Governor Grant did not see free persons of color in the same negative light as most whites. He had a close relationship with Susan Sherman, a free woman of color by whom he had a baby girl; and he consented to Charlotte Dillet, a free woman of color, being the godmother of his daughter. He saw a few prosperous free blacks and persons of color worshiping in Christ Church, some even had slaves baptized there, and he truly believed more would come if there was space for them. Munnings lived in the Bahamas long enough to know that space was not the main problem. He was therefore in a state of denial, and so was the Reverend Hepworth. Christ Church showed little interest in blacks and coloreds; the wardens and vestry, a group of slaveholders, consistently discriminated against black and colored children who applied for admission to the public school, which they administered jointly with the Reverend Hepworth. Governor Balfour brought fresh eyes to the issue. He had just arrived and saw the situation as it really was, no romanticizing, no denials, just the truth, as ugly as it was.

The Anglican Church had not made enlarging Christ Church a high priority over the years because it was content to channel blacks and coloreds to St. Paul's Anglican Chapel. The relationship between Christ Church and the chapel dated to the days of the Paul family. The elder Paul, Joseph Sr., built the chapel, and his younger son, William, switched from Methodist to Anglican and converted the chapel into an Anglican edifice. Upon William Paul's death, Joseph G. Watkins was appointed as reader at the chapel. When Watkins assumed the position, he was young, educated, and inexperienced.[70] He grew into the position over the years and reached a point where he conducted the Anglican service almost flawlessly. Governor Smyth was moved to say the following about him, "[H]e reads the service infinitely better than three fourths of our curates in England."[71] Smyth probably had not observed all the curates in England conducting service. The point he wanted to make was that Watkins ably conducted the Anglican service. A very bright and articulate man, Watkins kept the Anglican cause alive among blacks and coloreds in New Providence. To the shame of the Anglican Church, it did not reward his loyalty and devotion by training him for either the priesthood or diaconate.

The ordination of blacks and coloreds was one area in which the Anglican Church in the Bahama Islands lagged behind the Episcopal Church in the United States, where its first African-American priest, Absalom Jones of Philadelphia, Pennsylvania, was ordained in 1804. The events leading to the ordination were unusual. In 1794, a group of free African Americans, who two years earlier had broken with the Methodist Episcopal Church over an incident that had occurred at St. George's in Philadelphia, subsequently built an African church, and the majority decided to affiliate with the Episcopalians. Absalom Jones agreed to be their leader even though he preferred to remain a Methodist. As part of the agreement that brought the African church into the Episcopal fold, the Convention of the Diocese of Pennsylvania, upon the request of its bishop, the Right Reverend William White, accepted Jones as the leader of the church and waived the knowledge of Latin and Greek required of all clergymen. Worshipers of the African church, in return, agreed not to send delegates to the diocesan convention, the governing body of the diocese. The African church was subsequently renamed St. Thomas African Episcopal Church. Jones was ordained to the diaconate in 1795 and nearly ten years later was ordained to the priesthood.[72] He was therefore the first person of African origin in the Western Hemisphere to be ordained a priest in the Anglican Communion. In 1825, William Leavington, an African American, was ordained in St. Thomas African Episcopal Church; and two years later he founded the first black Episcopal Church in the American South, St. James' Episcopal in Baltimore, Maryland.[73] Neither Jones nor Leavington was as well trained as Joseph G. Watkins, lay reader of Saint Paul's Anglican Chapel.

The situation at the African church in Philadelphia was somewhat similar to that at the chapel in Nassau. The blacks in both places came from Methodist backgrounds, built their own edifices, and agreed to switch to the Anglican Communion. African Americans apparently got the better deal for their leader. Unfortunately for Watkins and his predecessors, blacks and coloreds pressed harder to remove civil disabilities than they did to remove disabilities that existed in the established church. As a result, the Bahamas would have its first black and colored members of the House of Assembly before it got its first black or colored Anglican priest.

In spite of the glass ceiling, so to speak, that stymied his elevation in the Anglican Church, Watkins did very well with St. Paul's Chapel. In 1827 the usual attendance at "Divine Service" was 150, and this increased in 1831 to 250.[74] His chapel grew at a faster pace than Christ Church, even though his task was much more challenging and his resources more limited. Whites in Britain were reared in the Anglican faith long before Britain established a presence in the Bahamas. Worshiping in the Anglican Church was natural, therefore, for whites in the Bahamas. Blacks and coloreds did not form a natural constituency for the Anglican Church because it had not made significant inroads into West Africa by the early nineteenth century. Consequently, blacks and coloreds had to be nurtured in the faith. Watkins ably nurtured them. Moreover, he brought stability to the chapel, his ministry there lasting well beyond emancipation. He alone was indispensable among the religious leaders in the Bahamas. The Anglican priests, Presbyterian ministers, Wesleyan Methodist missionaries, and Baptist preachers all could be, and were, replaced between 1816 and 1834; but who was there to replace Watkins? He was unique.

This was evident with the situation at Headquarters where an Anglican chapel was built primarily for liberated Africans. Watkins was reader there the year he ran the school. The small chapel with a seating capacity of 100 usually had about 40 worshipers at "Divine Service." The seating capacity was doubled in 1831 and there was a commensurate increase at the worship service with 100 persons attending.[75] The Anglican Church never really caught hold, however, among liberated Africans. Disappointed local officials asked liberated Africans why they did not worship at the chapel and were told that the Baptist worship service had greater appeal.[76] Recall how Watkins had talked with them over the road construction issue; he could relate to them better than Rigby, who assumed both duties—at the school and chapel.

Although Wesleyan Methodists did not fare much better than Anglicans among liberated Africans, Methodists made impressive gains among whites, blacks, and coloreds. According to one source, the Wesleyan Methodists had 1,134 worshipers in 1817, a slight majority of whom (597) were blacks and coloreds. The strongest following of blacks and coloreds (335) was in New Providence, which was also an island where the society was relatively weak among whites, with only 73 worshipers. Conversely, on the Out Islands Methodism was generally stronger among whites than among blacks and coloreds. The strongholds of Methodism on the Out Islands were Eleuthera, with 265 white and 54 black/colored worshipers, and Harbour Island, with

211 white and 189 black/colored worshipers. The other Out Islands with Wesleyan Methodist chapels, Abaco (with 12 white and 2 black/colored worshipers) and Long Island (with 1 white and 4 black/colored worshipers), had struggling chapels. Methodism grew stronger between 1817 and 1831, when nearly 950 new members were accepted. The Wesleyan Methodists had sixteen chapels in 1831, only two of which were found on New Providence. The median size of a Wesleyan Methodist congregation in 1831 was 60 worshipers. Nassau and Harbour Island (with 450 worshipers each) had the largest chapels, and Eleuthera had the most chapels, six. Although New Providence did not have many chapels, the two it had were solid; the smaller one had 190 worshipers. Abaco Island had two solid chapels and one that was weak: Green Turtle Key (with 200 worshipers), Cherokee Sound (with 100), and Great Harbour (with 50).[77] Turks Islands, with 100 Wesleyan Methodist worshipers, was the other Out Island with a chapel. William Turton, the lone colored Wesleyan Methodist missionary, although he was sickly, continued his forceful witnessing until he died on Turks Islands in 1825.[78]

The Baptist Church also continued to grow between 1815 and the passage of the Manumission Act (1834). Baptists had three preachers, all black/colored, in 1818.[79] This does not mean that each preacher had a church, because there were two Baptist churches at the most in 1818, if Frank Spence's chapel was organized then. The governor licensed Baptist preachers and he could also revoke the license. Baptist preachers were not allowed to officiate at weddings. In 1822, Sambo Scriven, the patriarch of Baptist preachers, became too ill to continue in the ministry; and the membership called his assistant, Prince Williams, to become the preacher of the Baptist Society, the name of the church at the time. He apparently then applied and received a license. About three years after Williams became the preacher of the society, he and a majority of the membership seized control of the treasury from the trustees who had maintained tight control over disbursements. The trustees were so stingy that they refused to allocate money to bury their former preacher, Sambo Scriven, who was destitute at the time of his death in 1825. Archibald Parker and a minority of the membership, apparently angry over the turn of events, complained to the acting governor, William Vesey Munnings, saying that Prince Williams was an adulterer. Williams and his wife, Margaret, whom he had married in May 1811, were unable to resolve their marital problems, and he left her in New Providence and moved to Harbour Island.[80] Acceding to the pleading of the membership, including Parker, who led a delegation to Harbour Island to persuade him to return, Williams returned to New Providence. When he returned to Nassau, rather than cohabit with his wife, Williams set up housekeeping alone and hired a housekeeper. The membership, Parker included, approved this arrangement.[81]

Williams claimed that the woman, Hagar, was his housekeeper and that his critics had approved of the arrangement. His critics countered that Hagar was his mistress. This was the ostensible cause of the conflict. It was just a smoke screen, however, for the real issue: Who should control the purse strings? Swayed by the moral issue raised in the conflict, Munnings sided with the minority and revoked Williams' license on December 1, 1825.[82] The next Sunday, Parker, who had the keys to the edifice, refused entry to Williams and his supporters, who wanted to worship in the building. Undeterred by the lockout, Williams and his supporters moved to a nearby house and worshiped.[83] Meanwhile, Parker and the others asked Munnings to issue Sharper Morris a license and this was done. Morris became the new preacher.[84]

The following January (1826), Williams petitioned Munnings, speaking for most of the membership, to order the property returned to the Baptist Society. Williams gave valuable information concerning the early years of the society in his petition before chronicling the events that had led to the lockout. At the request of Williams, Andrew Frazer, a free black butcher and slaveholder, had attempted unsuccessfully to reconcile the quarreling couple. Since Frazer's name does not appear on the petition, he may have been a friend, not a member of the society. The fact that Frazer had his slaves baptized in Christ Church lends additional support to this position. Williams said that Parker had agreed with the decision for him to have a housekeeper and that the only reason he and the others had lodged the complaint against him was because they no longer had "the same influence over the funds of the Society as they had heretofore under that of your Petitioner's predecessor."[85]

Revenge may have motivated Parker and the others more than moral indignation; nevertheless, that did not change the truthfulness of their complaint that Prince Williams was living in adultery, a charge which he did not deny. The agreement was that Williams could have a housekeeper. Unless maid was a euphemism for mistress and all parties understood this, he violated the agreement. The society must have believed that Williams wanted a housekeeper as defined by Samuel Johnson's *Dictionary of the English Language.* For his part, Munnings disregarded a basic tenet of the Baptist faith, the majority rule. Williams claimed he had 350 supporters. The petition contained 424 signatures, many of which appear to have been written by the same person.[86] If the names were authentic and authorized, then Williams had a majority of the society on his side and they were entitled to the property under these conditions. What relief was available to Parker and the others? They were entitled to call a conference of the society, confront Williams with the allegations, and demand his resignation. If he refused, they could appeal to the governor to revoke his license, as they did. If the majority had decided to leave the association in protest, dismissal letters could have been given to all who requested these. The lockout would have been prevented, and the minority would have been entitled to the name and property of the society. Parker's group compromised its case, however, by not following the conference route.

They did not resolve the dispute until March 1832 when Sharper Morris's congregation, which much later took the name Bethel Baptist Church, paid the Baptist Society £70.16.0d.,which was used to buy land near the former church. The compensation was much lower than the $245 the society had paid in 1801 for the two lots on which the edifice was built, not to mention materials for the church and furnishings. A new trustee was James Rutherford, overseer of Clifton and the other plantations belonging to the Wylly family.[87] Much later, the society took the name St. John's Particular Church of Native Baptists Society.[88]

The Anabaptists and Bethel Baptist Church.
Courtesy Department of Archives, Nassau, Bahamas.

Little is known about the third Baptist church in New Providence—Frank Spence's Chapel—other than that it was a relatively large place, seating from nine hundred to one thousand worshipers.[89] Spence owned the land and the edifice, so he literally owned the church. Spence was a former slave who came to the Bahamas with a group of American Loyalists in the 1780s and settled on Long Island. His wife, who had been left behind in Florida, came to the Bahamas after Spence purchased her freedom. Earlier, he had purchased his own freedom. They moved to New Providence, living first in what was formerly the Eastern District, where he bought a lot in 1806. He later moved to the southern suburbs where in 1827 and 1830 he bought land on a lane beside the chapel that bore his name.[90]

The schism within the Baptist Society was civil and did not encumber evangelization. About 1830, Sharper Morris visited Turks Islands to assist slaves in obtaining the privilege of conducting independent worship services. He led fund-raising activities and collected enough money to buy land upon which a house donated by an old lady was placed. Because of Morris's efforts, slaves on Turks Islands were not molested in their public worship where formerly this was unthinkable and they were forced to worship clandestinely to avoid punishment.[91] The persecution of those slaves resulted in part from slaveholders' disdain of the dissenters' theology that the slaves had embraced rather than from a desire to keep them ignorant of Christianity. This was a marked difference from why slaves in the antebellum American South created the "invisible institution." Southern slaveholders perceived religion and slave worshipers as an undesirable mix because slaves construed the brotherhood and sisterhood of humankind of which Christianity preached to mean that they were equal to their masters. The Americans who had escaped to Andros Island to avoid Andrew Jackson also joined the Baptist fold and built an edifice where they could congregate on Sundays or at any other time.[92] The Baptist Church kept spreading to the Out Islands. Unlike the Wesleyan Methodist Society, however, it was identified as a church for blacks and coloreds. So that is what the Baptist Church became in the Bahamas.

From its inception until 1833 Bahamian Baptists were not associated with mainline Baptists either in America or in Great Britain, although in the 1790s Brother Amos corresponded with George Liele in Jamaica. This isolation resulted in Baptists on the islands engaging in membership practices inconsistent with those in the mainline churches. The situation changed in 1833 when the Baptist Missionary Society (BMS) in London sent Joseph Burton to the Bahamas. Although he came mainly because his wife's poor health dictated the move to a warm climate, the BMS was presented with an opportunity to carry out a plan to send a missionary. The Burtons arrived in January 1833 to a welcome from governmental officials, the Anglican clergy, Wesleyan Methodist groups, and the Baptists, an unprecedented welcome for dissenters. After meeting with Burton, Morris and Williams agreed to subscribe to mainline Baptists policies and practices on admitting new members. In July 1833, Morris proposed that the BMS should assume control of his congregation and its property, and the BMS accepted it. Williams and his congregation refused to follow this path and parted with the BMS.[93] It is both interesting and unusual that the black and colored Baptists voluntarily surrendered their autonomy and property to the BMS since Baptists prided themselves in congregationalism. The move showed weak leadership and ignorance of the organizational structure of the Baptist Church. The Williams congregation wisely refused to surrender its autonomy.

The spread of Protestant churches, expanded educational opportunities, an increased free black and colored presence, survival of African customs, and the birth of black Masonry and civic organizations characterized the world in which blacks and coloreds lived. The Baptists continued to grow in New Providence and spread to the Out Islands. A school and chapel were built for liberated Africans. The slave population continued to decrease and the free black and colored population continued its upward spiral. The educational climate for blacks and coloreds, free and slave, was more sanguine than it was for African Americans in the Lower South, and slaves had a less abusive and intrusive situation than their brothers and sisters in bondage on the sugar plantations. Even though the word *African* was affixed to many black institutions in the United States, retention of Africanisms was less successful there than in the Bahamas. Moreover, Bahamian slaves attended church and school in significantly lower percentages than free blacks and persons of color and they were not eligible to join such organizations as the Masons. So, besides the legal handicaps associated with their status, their social world was more circumscribed than that of free blacks and persons of color, especially in New Providence. Yet the accelerated pace of manumissions in the 1820s and 1830s brightened prospects of freedom. However imperfect the world in which blacks and coloreds lived may have been, it was a significant improvement over what it was at any other time since 1784.

CHAPTER VI

Race Relations, 1816–1834: A Time Full of Promise

The Laws of the year are distinguished by one conferring on free-coloured persons all the rights which white people enjoy . . . the condition of the Colony is full of prosperous promise.

—Blue Book of Statistics, 1833

From 1816 to 1834, race relations took a decided turn toward favoring blacks and coloreds. The Haitian Revolution, with its attendant tension in the Bahamas, had run its course, the Royal Navy continued to intercept slave ships as they attempted to carry their human cargo to slave markets in the Caribbean colonies, and a chorus of dissenting voices against this policy no longer echoed in the chambers of the assembly. Although whites in the Bahamas, including the remaining Loyalists, had become accustomed to blacks and coloreds in roles other than those associated with slaves, they protested long and loudly when confronted with demands to relieve free blacks and persons of color of their civil disabilities and grant them the franchise. These were nonetheless accomplished by 1833, resulting in free blacks and persons of color serving on grand and petty juries and voting. This was indeed a period of promise. Ironically, just as slave societies throughout the British West Indies were giving blacks and coloreds privileges formerly reserved for whites, the United States was beginning to close the window of opportunity to slaves and free African Americans. In America, the promising years were ending.[1]

Between 1811 and 1827, six slave ships were intercepted and brought to the Bahamas. The smallest number of slaves liberated from a ship was 93, the largest was 221, and the total was 849. Liberated African women gave birth to 253 offspring. In 1811, three slave ships were captured and 439 Africans were liberated and brought to the Bahamas. Adjusting to the new environment evidently was very difficult because in 1828 only 243 of those 439 liberated Africans brought to the Bahamas were still alive. In 1811, the *Rosa* was captured with 221 Africans aboard, only 152 of whom were still alive in 1828. The *Royal* was seized in 1818 with 94 Africans aboard, only 66 of whom were still alive in 1828. Most Africans taken from the *Rosa* and the *Royal* were scheduled to have completed their apprenticeship by 1828. In 1827, the *Bethel* was seized and its 93 Africans were all apprenticed in New Providence where the conditions were much better than on the Out Islands. This was expected to result in fewer African deaths. The *Rosa* and *Hebe* were captured in 1831 and 1832, respectively, with a total of 558 Africans on board. The removal of 401 from the *Hebe* was the largest single seizure of Africans. By 1832, the number of Africans rescued was 1,407, and while many had died, 1,460 babies had been born.[2] Births among Africans exceeded deaths. In 1827, when Governor Grant estimated that the number of liberated Africans in the Bahamas was about 800, the figure was low and misleading.[3] If the figure referred to the number of liberated Africans brought to the Bahamas to date, he underestimated the total. If he referred to the number of the group that was still alive, he overestimated.

Liberated Africans suffered many deaths, and only a part of these could be blamed on the seasoning process. The percentages of Africans liberated in 1811, 1816, and 1818 who were still alive in 1828 were 55, 69, and 70 percent, respectively. The highest percentage of deaths occurred among the group that had been in the Bahamas the longest (seventeen years) and the lowest was among the group that had been in the islands the shortest time (ten years). The condition, age, and sex of the Africans were not given in the statistics. Nevertheless, the general health must have been good and the ages must have fallen in the prime category, or how else does one explain the high fertility rate of the females? This is especially meaningful since the women retained the lactation period practiced in Africa. They breast-fed their babies for two years or longer and spaced childbearing accordingly. The statistics do not say, moreover, whether the Out Islands had a proportionately higher percentage of deaths. The statistics also fail to show whether placing Africans in isolated settlements reduced the percentage of deaths.

Settlements were begun in 1825 with the creation of Headquarters outside Nassau.[4] It was announced in 1828 that Africans complained of abuses every day, showing clearly that life was not easy for these Africans. One woman complained that she had been turned away from the property where her children's father was a slave and where she had been an apprentice for fifteen years, and she did not have means to feed herself and her children.[5] The complaints were lodged against individuals, not against the government, which tried hard to accommodate liberated Africans. This probably reduced the pain. The government bought four hundred acres of good farmland at the request of liberated Africans and formed settlements where they could live to themselves.[6] It also formed a militia company among them, confidently declaring that they could be depended upon to do as commanded whatever the situation, whether it involved going against unruly whites or rebellious slaves.[7] So despite the exorbitantly high number of deaths, liberated Africans owed a debt of gratitude to the sponsors of the Abolition of the Slave Trade Act and the team of naval and customs officials in the Bahamas who enforced the act.

Liberated Africans were not the only group of captives that benefited from strict enforcement of the Abolition Act. In July 1825, the Colonial Office made a critical decision that may have gone beyond the original intent of the Abolition Act. The Home Office ruled that under provisions of the Consolidated Act (1824) relating to the slave trade "persons arriving in any of His Majesty's colonies from any foreign island or state where they were lawfully held in slavery [could] not be sent back thither nor dealt with as slaves and must therefore be dealt with in the same manner as the aliens of African birth or decent."[8] In short, any slave brought to the Bahamas from outside the British West Indies would be manumitted. This ruling had grave consequences for slaveholders in Cuba and the American South. American slaveholders fared better under Lord Mansfield's ruling in *Somerset v. Stewart* (Great Britain, 1772), when he released an American slave brought to England, stating that the country had no positive law regarding slavery, than they did under the July 1825 edict from the Colonial Office. The Somerset ruling was ambiguous, the United States Supreme Court refused to accept it as a precedent, and no American slave, except James Somerset, is known to have been freed under it. Things were different, however, with the Colonial Office ruling.

Almost 300 American slaves were freed under this ruling. These were slaves who either had escaped to the Bahamas from the United States or had been aboard ships that wrecked in Bahamian waters. Before the ruling, American owners of slaves aboard wrecked vessels were allowed to repossess their human cargo. For example, in the spring of 1818 an American vessel transporting 101 slaves left Virginia for New Orleans but ran aground in

Bahamian waters. The vessel and slaves were brought to Nassau where William Vesey Munnings, acting governor and chief justice of the Bahamas Supreme Court, permitted the acting customs collector to authorize the transfer of the 101 slaves to another American vessel that transported them to New Orleans. Munnings approved this action without seeking the counsel of Bahamian law officers. The decision was an aberration.[9]

After the 1818 decision, foreign slaves aboard ships that ventured into Bahamian waters and were subsequently seized by the Royal Navy and runaway slaves who reached the Bahamas were manumitted. Two groups of foreign slaves—one numbering 32, and the other, 97—that reached Andros Island from Florida in 1828 were granted their freedom rather than surrendered to their American owners. The Colonial Office instructed Governor Grant to give the slaves "a certain declaratory of the fact that within" the Bahamas they were entitled to their freedom.[10] This was a limited grant of freedom in that it did not protect them outside the British West Indies; nevertheless, they were free. In January 1831, another American slave ship bound from Virginia to New Orleans wrecked in Bahamian waters. The 165 slaves aboard the ship were brought to Nassau and the court of vice admiralty of the Bahamas declared that they were free.[11] Criticisms from American presidents beginning with Thomas Jefferson notwithstanding, Haiti actually caused less grief to American slaveholders than the Bahamas. If Haiti had invoked a ruling similar to that of the Colonial Office, the United States probably would have taken military action against the island nation, in light of its action against Haiti for staging a revolution to gain its independence.

American slaveholders were not the only group to suffer losses of slaves from the 1825 ruling. In 1831, Francisco Monitt, a slave cook belonging to Don Manuel Monitt, a Cuban merchant, escaped from a Spanish schooner anchored in Nassau Harbor.[12] The schooner's master, Santiago Pasos, asked Bahamian officials to return the slave and he was told: "[I]f you should meet or discover the said Francisco Monitt yourself, you must not attempt to seize him as a runaway slave, or take him by force on board your vessel. Whatever he may formerly have been [he] is now a free man, and any attempt to proceed against him forcibly would be an illegal act for which the person committing it would be liable to be prosecuted—The British Government recognizes no person in a state of slavery in these Islands but those whose names are entered into the Slave Registry."[13]

Thus while attempting to enforce the Abolition Act the British government made its West Indies colonies a potential haven for runaway slaves of other nations and its navy the regional police force for enforcing similar laws that other nations had passed. The irony of the Francisco Monitt case was that Cuba had earlier provided sanctuary for runaway slaves from the British West Indies colonies. In 1787, Cuba refused to release six runaway slaves from Jamaica, claiming that since the slaves had converted to Catholicism Cuban law mandated that the government should provide sanctuary for them.[14] The Monitt case was therefore an unintentional payback.

The British commitment to abolition of the African slave trade must have sent tremors through Caribbean slave societies outside the British West Indies. Foreign powers permitted the Royal Navy to intercept slave ships with illegal human cargo. The British formulated a policy that placed American slaves in transit from one American port to another in the category of illegal cargo if perchance the vessels entered the British West Indies waters. Bahamian officials were encouraged to forego the expenditure of funds for a trial to decide whether the slaves were in Bahamian waters illegally and to operate instead on the premise that foreign slaves represented an unsuccessful smuggling effort. It did not matter whether the slaves arrived in the colony in a ship that inadvertently strayed or was blown off course and ran aground off the coast, or whether they came in boats destined for the Bahamas to seek refuge, or whether they came in schooners that were there on legitimate business. All were treated as if they were illegal human cargo. Neither the British nor their colonial officials in the Bahamas wavered in enforcing the July 25 ruling.

Similarly, the British did not waver on their policy to garrison units of the British West India regiments in the Bahamas. The dire predictions of the policy's critics did not materialize, and critics soon stopped making them. Whites nevertheless were not comfortable with the situation. In the back of their minds was the thought that the black troops were a ticking time bomb, a disaster waiting to happen. In 1816, those latent fears were stoked following a mild protest by troops of the Second West India Regiment. The troops were issued two flannel shirts at the beginning of winter, but unlike in years past when the expense was deducted from the regimental hospital fund, this time the cost was deducted in a lump sum from the December pay of the soldiers, leaving them penniless at Christmas, the most important season of the year. The soldiers complained about the exorbitant cost of the shirts, the manner in which the payment was obtained, and the timing for satisfying that debt. Christmas was their only "season of festivity throughout the year." Although the whole regiment was unhappy with the situation, only four to six soldiers crossed the line expressing their unhappiness. They told inhabitants of Nassau that the regiment had delegated them to warn that the town would be torched if their grievances were not addressed. The regimental officers placed the six soldiers in confinement, and the other soldiers disputed their allegation that the regiment had delegated them to threaten the town.[15]

The civilian committee appointed to investigate the matter reached sound conclusions about the cause of the protest, but its recommendation did not address that issue. The committee concluded that officers of the regiment did not properly handle the payment for the flannel shirts. In fact, the soldiers were not told that the money would be deducted from their pay. Instead of taking the full amount owed at once, the debt should have been liquidated in installments, especially since the December pay was so important to the soldiers. Christmas was the biggest event of the year, yet most of the soldiers were not paid for December. The committee praised the Second West India Regiment for its behavior during the long tour of duty—it had been in the colony since 1809—which had been uneventful until the recent incident. Their behavior was far more acceptable than that of the white soldiers who preceded them. Those soldiers were known for "their riots pilfering and the like." The committee believed, however, that the actual misconduct of the white soldiers was inconsequential when compared with the potential threat of insurrection that the black ones had posed. The committee therefore recommended that an equal number of white and black troops should be assigned to the colony, or that the size of the black unit should be reduced to a number "as may leave the country nothing to fear from them."[16]

The committee unfortunately used the protest of the Second West India Regiment over a purely personal matter that did not involve civilians as an opportunity to lobby for a policy change. The unit's size was irrelevant to the issue; it was the size of the soldiers' December pay that caused the protest. The regiment had more than one thousand soldiers, six of whom, all privates, presumed to speak for the majority and threatened the town. The committee concluded that the six acted alone. It nonetheless impugned the professionalism of the regiment by questioning its commitment to discharge duties properly, though its record strongly showed its commitment. The committee was willing to have businesses pilfered and streets blocked with unruly white soldiers, or have the colony's defenses weakened making it vulnerable to an invasion, rather than have a full force of well-behaved black troops. Being disappointed with the situation was normal for the soldiers; their high expectations had been dashed. They consequently reacted to their disappointment by complaining. They were soldiers, but they were still human beings with the full range of emotions that civilians in Nassau had. In spite of the deep disappointment, the soldiers were restrained, not rowdy, a sign that they were well-disciplined. In failing to offer recommendations that addressed the issue that had caused the protest, the committee missed an opportunity to ensure that the possibility of an insurrection of black troops would become even more remote. The Colonial Office partially endorsed the committee's low regard for what the soldiers considered was a serious injustice. The Second West India Regiment was transferred to Jamaica and all promotions and favors for its officers were suspended until their conduct had been investigated fully. This action was appropriate but the timing was not. Since the regiment had been in the colony for seven years, a very long tour of duty, a change of duty station was long overdue.

Transferring the unit immediately after the incident, however, may have sent a signal that the six soldiers were telling the truth and whites' fears were well-founded. The regiment's British officers had not exercised good judgment in approving the high price of the flannel shirts and authorizing the deductions from the soldiers' pay, so their conduct should have been investigated. As for the whites in the colony, changing one black unit for another was not what they wanted. They wanted a change in the color of the soldiers.

The Colonial Office pretended to persist, but its subsequent move showed that it was having second thoughts about keeping a large contingent of black troops in the Bahamas. About 1,000 soldiers from the Fifth Regiment were designated to replace the Second West India Regiment.[17] The Fifth Regiment was in the colony less than a year before it was disbanded and two garrison companies were formed from it.[18] Meanwhile, the Second West India Regiment was not assigned to the Bahamas until September 1827 when a small detachment of 130 privates from Africa with their wives (22) and children (9) arrived in Nassau.[19] The Colonial Office may have reduced the size of the black garrison to placate whites, believing this did not endanger the colony since it was peacetime. It perhaps had second thoughts because later the unit's size was increased, but not to the 1,000 level.

The British did not have a bad experience with the West India regiments. The soldiers did not "pilfer or riot," hesitate when ordered to present a show of force against unruly slaves, or train their weapons on whites. Those soldiers often married black females, especially liberated Africans, and became heads of households. For their part, whites did not allow their apprehension concerning the reliability of black soldiers to overwhelm them, and they neither harassed nor taunted the troops, if the records are accurate, during the period 1816–1834. The records do not reveal, moreover, that slaves became surly after the colony became garrisoned by black troops. The British West India regiments were thus a successful experiment in race relations.

Having the colony garrisoned with troops of the Royal Army did not preclude the need for a militia, a considerable portion of which consisted of free blacks and persons of color. From the early 1800s, the black and colored males formed separate militia units and provided their own uniforms. Munnings, who was once an officer in a "Black Company" that " then and ever since consisted of free blacks only," said that the blacks in his unit did not complain about the arrangement.[20] Since schools, churches, and occupations did not evince this practice, the reason for it in the militia is difficult to discern. The militiamen could have taken their cue from the British West India regiments, composed either entirely or almost entirely of blacks. New Orleans had a brown militia company composed of mulattoes, and in Haiti mulattoes and blacks had fighting forces that eventually trained their guns on each other with resultant high casualties. Since in the Bahamas the black militiamen—the Black Company—and the colored militiamen—the Brown Rangers—both had white officers, forming separate companies did not give either an advantage over the other.

Since the law did not mandate separation of blacks and coloreds from each other, the Black Company and the Brown Rangers probably happened the same way that color endogamous marriages did. While this lends support to a perception that a color bias existed between free blacks and persons of color, the distinctions that the two groups made between each other should not blind us to an important fact, blacks and coloreds did not form separate castes. Most important, blacks and coloreds had the same legal status and they cooperated to close the privilege gap that existed between themselves and whites. Separate militia units probably did not result then from an animosity between free black and colored males. Free black males outnumbered free mulatto males in the population and they had larger militia units. In fact, during the 1820s, the Black Company was usually the largest militia company in the colony. In 1824, the Black Company (with 90 men) and the Brown Company (with 70) composed 40 percent of the colonial militia.[21] In 1828, the Black Company had grown to 120 men, and it continued to be the largest militia company. That year, the Brown Rangers had a slight increase to 74.[22] Both companies suffered losses in the early 1830s and the Black Company was no longer the largest militia company.[23]

Speaking of the colonial militia, Governor James Carmichael Smyth took an unusual step and was on the verge of taking another one when he was transferred to another colony. He formed a militia company of liberated Africans.[24] In the past, liberated Africans had been recruited for the British West India regiments, but none had been organized into militia units. So this was a first for the colony. Governor Smyth had planned a more significant break with the past, but he was transferred before getting it done. He had anticipated proposing to the House of Assembly amending the Militia Act to allow the commissioning of three or four of the "most respectable of the Coloured People," whom he would later "invite to dinner at the Government House on the King's Birthday."[25] This would have been a far-reaching move and a significant step toward closing the existing gap between whites and blacks/coloreds. Governor Smyth was familiar with free blacks and coloreds' history of local service to the Crown and believed that this should be rewarded, especially since the group had qualified leaders to fill the militia positions.

The primary responsibility of the liberated African militia company was to suppress slave uprisings. The Bahama Islands was fortunate in that it had not experienced a serious slave uprising during the period 1816 to 1834, although there were several personal altercations between slaves and their masters, unruly acts, and work stoppages. The nature of these acts was less threatening than the ostensible goal of the "French Negroes Plot" of the 1790s and the rebellions that occurred in other British West Indies colonies. On April 14, 1816, an insurrection occurred at Codrington in Barbados where slaves burned and pillaged a considerable part of the island. Whites believed that the rebellion occurred when literate freedmen and slaves, who read English newspapers, misconstrued the intent of the Registry Bill and spread rumors that the Crown had freed slaves but slaveholders had refused to comply with its wishes.[26] Demerara (in 1823) and Jamaica (1831–32) also had major slave rebellions, which a desire for freedom spurred.[27] The Jamaican rebellion erupted on Christmas in 1831, and before it had run its course sugar estates in western parishes had been burned and pillaged, forcing whites in droves to flee to the coastal ports.[28]

In the Bahamas, however, something personal that had happened to a slave, or slaves, or unhappiness with changes in the status quo, changes that threatened their accustomed autonomy, usually caused the disturbances. For instance, the disturbance on the Rolle plantation in Exuma resulted from slaves' reaction to rumors that they were going to be moved to Trinidad, thus stopping their autonomy. The slaves responded by refusing to work and displaying firearms. This was the so-called "Pompey rebellion." The disturbances on the Joseph Hunter plantation (in 1831) on Cat Island and the Farquharson plantation (in 1832) on Watlings Island were not aimed at overthrowing slavery. On Hunter's plantation, a slave named Dick disagreed with his master and fired a gun at him. Six slaves came to his assistance.

Similarly, on the Farquharson plantation the disturbance stemmed from a personal disagreement, this time between the slaveholder's mulatto son, James Farquharson, and a slave named Alick, who objected to the manner in which his wife and brother had been treated.[29] When the younger Farquharson attempted to beat Alick for his insubordination, the slave fought back; and soon other slaves, armed with clubs and sticks, supported him. Farquharson appealed to his neighbors for help, one of whom, Prince Storr, a free black overseer, brought some of his trusted slaves to prevent the situation from escalating. The disturbance on William Johnson's plantation in Eleuthera (in 1833) appeared to have resulted from a refusal of slaves to work, but only after the governor had dispatched troops from a British West India regiment to the uprising was it revealed that the slaves were unhappy over the lack of food and clothing.[30]

The Bahamas' disturbances mentioned above do not fall under the rubric of either a rebellion or a revolt. There were no deaths nor property destruction and the causes were usually not deliberate attempts to defy authority. The defiant behavior was an outgrowth of slaves reacting to their grievances, or to what they perceived as broken promises, and each was directed toward a particular act of the slaveholder, not against the institution of slavery. Thus, the Bahamas, like the other marginal colonies in the British West Indies, did not have a major slave uprising in the years immediately preceding emancipation.[31]

A major reason the Bahamas escaped the kinds of slave uprisings that occurred in Jamaica and Barbados was because conditions for slaves were not as bad in the Bahamas as they were in those colonies. Another positive for the Bahamas was the leadership of governors such as the four who served during the years 1816–1834: Charles Cameron, Lewis Grant, Sir James Carmichael Smyth, and B. T. Balfour. These governors conveyed to blacks and coloreds, free and slave, the message that the Crown was concerned about their welfare and was actively working to improve conditions. So blacks and coloreds were loyal to the Crown and patiently waited for implementation of reforms. Governor Grant did not waver in liberating slaves brought to the Bahamas off slave ships. Governor Cameron showed concern by tackling the issue of slave marriages. According to conventional wisdom, marriage freed the slave from bondage. It was revealed that most slaves were not married, which some found appalling.[32]

Governor Cameron raised the issue of slave marriage by posing a question concerning the legality of slave marriages to the attorney general, the solicitor general, and the rector of Christ Church. The question had surfaced from a situation involving the marriage of a male slave to a free woman. The owner had consented to the marriage in writing and had also given orders to publish the banns, but he stopped publication of the banns after the second one, when a lawyer told him that consent to the marriage would be construed as a declaration of emancipation. The marriage was then canceled. This incident happened in 1814 and Governor Cameron visited it then. He revisited it in 1816 perhaps at the urging of Downing Street. When the incident arose originally, Governor Cameron had asked two questions: "Whether the marriage of a slave is or is not conformable to the principles of our [Bahamas] laws?" and "Whether a slave, if married with his owner's consent, could on proof of that circumstances ground a claim for his liberty?"[33] Responding to queries dated January 26, 1814, Wylly declared that marriages were considered civil contracts in Bahamas law. Contracts were valid only if contracting parties had "sufficient legal ability." The very nature of slavery precluded slaves from entering into valid contracts. A marriage between a slave and a free person, declared Wylly, was therefore a "mere nullity." If the owner consented, however, the situation was altered and "if sufficiently evidenced, may probably be considered as amounting to an emancipation."[34] Wylly, who did not have formal legal training, gave this interpretation of Bahamas law in his capacity as a law officer of the islands.

The thoughtful response of Reverend John Stephen, rector of Christ Church, to the first question showed why he was perhaps the best rector that Christ Church had during the period covered in this study. The rector said that marriage was more than a civil contract; "it [was] also a religious contract founded on an Institution of God. Since the matrimonial law was as much a part of English law as the civil law, argued the rector, the latter alone could not answer the question." The priest then alluded to an issue with which the Church wrestled in the eighteenth century: baptism of slaves. The rector said that it was supposed a baptized slave would immediately be freed if taken to England, whereas an unbaptized slave would not. Slaveholders in the West Indies, unfamiliar with the law, transferred the principle to the British settlements and concluded that a slave baptized in the colonies would be equally entitled to his freedom. The rector argued that Blackstone refuted this interpretation of the law in his *Commentaries of the Law of England.* After alluding to the analogy, the Reverend Stephen said that "the present obstruction" could be removed easily by passing a law allowing slaves to marry with the consent of their owners, "but securing the owners' property in them as well after marriage as before."[35]

Governor Cameron sent Stephen's letter to Bahamian law officers for their reaction. After reading it, Wylly did not change his position. He said, "I adhere in all respect to the opinion which I had the honor to give your Excellency on the 26th January 1814."[36] William Martin, the solicitor general, assumed a position similar to Wylly's. Martin said that "from the Nature of slavery any contract entered into by them (without the consent of their owner or owners) should be void, parties in that state being rendered by law incapable of entering into any contract whatever."[37] Martin failed to respond to two key queries. The first was the question that the governor asked earlier about whether the owner's consent to the marriage freed his slave, and the second one grew out of Stephen's letter: Did it provide an acceptable way around the problem?

The governor sent Wylly's and Martin's responses to Stephen, who again took a pen to hand and expressed his thoughts in a way that displayed a superior grasp of the issue, compared with that of the colony's law officers. The cleric said that Wylly and Martin "seem[ed] both to admit indirectly at least that the marriage of a slave with the consent of his owner would be legally valid." Wylly's position was that a slave was incompetent to make a contract even with his owner's permission. Following this line of reasoning, in order for a marriage (which was a civil contract) between a slave and a free person to be considered legal, therefore, the letter of consent must be construed as a letter of manumission. Consequently, because of the freedom gained from the letter, the slave would become eligible to enter a contract. Thus, the marriage then became legal. Stephen appears to have contradicted himself when later in his response he claimed that Wylly did not respond to the question of whether the owner's consent to a marriage would be construed as a grant of manumission, unless the rector did not understand the connection between the owner's consent and the legality of a marriage based upon it. Stephen correctly concluded that Martin did not give an opinion. Concerned lest his position on the subject should be interpreted as a veiled attempt to manumit slaves, the rector stated that his reason for advocating legalizing slave marriages was to keep slaves from wallowing in the cesspool of immorality. Through legalizing those marriages virtue would replace vice.[38] In short, he believed that slaves blamed their promiscuous behavior on an inability to marry.

Downing Street turned its attention to the issue in 1816. The Colonial Office, to whom a copy of Stephen's letter had been sent, said that ecclesiastical law allowed slaves to marry either slaves or free persons without the consent of their owners, whose property rights would not be affected unless

Bahamian law, custom, or judicial decision stated otherwise. Expressing a desire to end the debate, the Colonial Office requested a statement giving the existing law of the Bahamas on the subject, as derived from "legislative or judicial authorities."[39] Wylly first answered the request by noting, "[O]ur colonial laws are silent upon the subject of marriage of slaves and there being no Spiritual courts in the colonies we are of course but little versant in the Ecclesiastical Law except so far as it has been adopted by statute."[40] Following this, he retreated from his January 26, 1814, letter, claiming it "was merely that of a common lawyer." After attempting to cover his tracks by making light of a position he had taken earlier, Wylly then presented the results of his research on the subject. He said that (1) the acts of the assembly were silent on the subject; (2) only three acts of Parliament concerning marriage were in force in the Bahamas; (3) the common law of England, where it had not been altered, was in force in the Bahamas; consequently, any part of the common law which related to marriage was in force in the Bahamas; and (4) marriages were solemnized in the Bahamas by persons of holy orders, in or out of church, either after publication of banns or by license from the ordinary.[41] Martin's response did not clarify the question, as he rambled and skirted the issue.[42]

Enough thoughtful attention had finally been given to the issue to eradicate the ignorance concerning it. Wylly had been forced to retreat from his position that slaveholders surrendered their property rights whenever they consented to their slaves marriage; he had earlier equated the letter of consent with manumission. Wylly's research of the issue had yielded information that contradicted the conventional wisdom upon which his initial answer to the question was based, thus shedding light on an area where previously darkness dwelled. Governor Cameron and Stephen, two Englishmen, aided in getting the subject addressed. The governor raised the issue and guided the debate, soliciting information from individuals and sending the Colonial Office the learned opinion of Stephen. The rector of Christ Church made several significant contributions. His analogy concerning the controversy over slave baptisms was relevant and placed the issue in the proper perspective. In the seventeenth century, conventional wisdom held that baptizing slaves was tantamount to manumitting them because Christians could not enslave other Christians, but the bishop of London subsequently ruled that baptism freed slaves' souls only and did not affect their labor obligations to their masters. Similarly, Stephen believed that conventional wisdom concerning masters allowing slaves to marry was as inaccurate as that concerning baptism. His statement that marriage was more than a civil contract showed that the church was not going to surrender something as important as marriage to the state. Moreover, his manner of circumventing the obstacle created by conventional wisdom's interpretation of owners' consent to their slaves' marriages was consistent with Downing Street's understanding of the law. As the premier religious leader in the colony, Stephen showed genuine concern about the moral well-being of slaves. Realizing that some slaves used the dashed hopes of ever getting married as a crutch to prop their moral depravity, he was determined to hold such individuals morally accountable. In the end, the legality of slaves marriage was proclaimed. The Bahamas thus joined St. Vincent as the only British West Indies colonies that recognized slave marriages.[43]

The nonwhite leaders of the movement to remove civil disabilities from free blacks and persons of color were more concerned about serving on juries, testifying against whites, voting for the assembly, and sitting in that body than they were about slaves taking a trip to the altar. Their situation was similar to that of free blacks and persons of color in the other British West Indies colonies where in 1816 none permitted free blacks and persons of color to vote, hold elective office, or sit on juries. Most, moreover, did not allow nonwhites to give evidence against whites, except in certain civil cases.[44]

Governors of the Bahamas generally supported Downing Street's efforts to rid the islands of discriminatory laws and practices, but sometimes when the monetary costs of such action were considered too great, a governor would ask to have the reform delayed. Such was the case when the British Privy Council disallowed "An Act for the Building and Repairing of Churches and for the Support of the Poor" in 1827. The act was disallowed because it excluded free blacks and persons of color from voting for vestrymen and serving on the vestry, although the vestry taxed them for parochial purposes. This was taxation without representation because free blacks and persons of color could neither vote for the persons who taxed them nor sit in the body that made the decision. The Privy Council instructed Governor Grant to reject a revised version of the bill if it contained a similar provision. The governor appealed to his superiors to allow the act to stand since it did not explicitly exclude free blacks and persons of color from the vestry. Suspending the act, the governor pleaded, would create a hardship on the "poor of all colours" because it contained the main funding for their support. Extending the scope of the franchise, the governor reasoned, could achieve the Privy Council's objective to give free blacks and persons of color voice and vote in vestry matters. Meanwhile, the act in question was of short duration and would come up for renewal shortly, when the desired changes could be added.[45]

Was Governor Grant compromising his principles for the sake of keeping afloat his program for the needy of the colony? No, he was not foregoing granting the franchise to free black and colored males, but he opted to achieve this through another piece of legislation rather than sacrificing the needs of the poor. So this was not a matter of selecting between the franchise for free black and colored males and food for the poor. Both could be achieved, the governor contended, without hurting either. To get a sense of the assembly's feelings about enfranchising free black and colored males, Governor Grant had asked several conservative members of that body their thoughts on the issue; and they seemed receptive to the reform, provided these persons met the property, residence, and age qualifications. The assembly did not object, moreover, to free black and colored males serving on juries when parties in the cases were the same color.[46] The governor's willingness to accept a limited jury role for free nonwhite males showed, however, that he was not cut from the same cloth as his successor, Governor James Carmichael Smyth, a forceful advocate for the removal of civil disabilities that degraded and humiliated free blacks and persons of color.

After hearing lectures from governors over the years on the appropriateness of treating slaves humanely and granting free blacks and persons of color civil liberties, the assembly began to act on legislation concerning these matters in the mid 1820s; and by 1830 significant legislation in this regard had been passed. In January 1824, "An Act for Granting a Further Extension of Privileges to Certain Free Persons of Colour in Certain Cases" was passed. Provision 1 of that act allowed freeborn blacks and persons of color who were born in the Bahama Islands and their counterparts from other countries who met a five-year residence requirement to give evidence in court. Provision 2 extended the same privilege to manumitted Christian Creoles who had been free for five years. The privilege was not extended, however, to manumitted natives of Africa.[47] Denial of the privilege to natives of Africa continued an earlier practice based on the presumption that Africans were culturally inferior individuals who did not have the maturation necessary to understand the importance of the privilege and so might abuse it.

In April 1830, Governor Smyth reported to Whitehall on the Consolidated Slave Act and a piece of significant civil rights legislation. The 1830 act deleted odious provisions of an earlier version that punished free blacks and persons of color for not showing proper deference to whites and required manumitted free blacks and persons of color accused of crimes to be tried in a slave court. The assembly also passed an act that permitted free blacks and persons of color who met the property requirement to vote for members of the House of Assembly. Earlier, the assembly had passed a more restricted act that had granted the franchise to only one person, Murray G. Farquharson, a free man of color and Crooked Island planter.[48] The later act broadened the scope to include all free black and colored males who met the qualifications. The heart of this legislation was provision 3, which stipulated suffrage qualifications. To vote, one was required to be a male owner of "an estate, real and personal, or personal property valued at two hundred pounds," or fifty acres of unencumbered land under active cultivation or improvement. Provision 4 stated that the portions of the law enfranchising free black and colored males should not be construed "to include enfranchisement in the election of vestrymen or the privilege of being chosen to the vestry of any parish in the Bahamas."[49] This provision cast a shadow over the proposal that Governor Grant had offered to circumvent unacceptable provisions of the Church Building and Repair Act of 1827 and effectively closed the back door on efforts to extend voice and vote privileges to nonwhites in vestry matters.

By enfranchising free black and colored males, the Bahamas joined the list of British West Indies colonies that followed Grenada in this matter. Grenada's act in 1823 did not have the high property qualifications found in that of the Bahamas, neither did it permit free blacks and persons of color to sit in the legislature.[50] The "brown privilege bill," which Barbados passed in 1832, enfranchised free black and colored males and removed all disabilities imposed upon blacks and coloreds. The act set a double standard for voter qualification, however, by increasing the property qualifications to ownership of ten or more acres of land or ownership of a town house, or houses, whose annual taxable value was at least thirty sterling but exempting previous voters—all of whom were white—from the new requirement.[51] The property qualification in Barbados was still lower than that in the Bahamas, but this was misleading. Ten acres of land in land-scarce Barbados were more difficult to get than fifty acres in the Bahamas where land was more plentiful.

Once free blacks and persons of color gained the privileges of giving evidence against whites and voting, the battle shifted to gaining jury privileges. Governor Smyth's position on this issue was more enlightened than that of his predecessor, who apparently would have restricted nonwhites to testifying against other nonwhites. In an 1831 address, Governor Smyth told the legislature, "With respect to our juries—the common Law which obtains in all cases not specially provided for by statute, acknowledges no difference in the colour of a man's skin as a reason for debarring him from the free exercise of his civil rights. The free people of Colour in these Islands are consequently . . . As eligible by law at this moment to sit both of Grand and petty juries, as any other inhabitants . . . to the exclusion of ignorant or incapable people, You may regulate the amount of the qualification by a colonial act for either jury—the law however must be impartial and equally affect all persons without any reference to colour."[52]

This was indeed a remarkable statement on race relations. The governor realized that all free blacks and persons of color were not qualified to render the kinds of judgment expected of jurors; and in such cases they should be disqualified, but whites should be held to the same standard. The major flaw in the existing policy, he seemed to argue, was that it presumed whites alone were capable of serving on juries.

The House of Assembly had made jury qualifications sufficiently difficult to ensure none but the rich would serve on the grand jury, and the petty jury's qualifications were only a little less imposing. Grand jurors were required to be male, residents of New Providence, between the ages of twenty-one and sixty, and owners of either a minimum of five hundred acres of land or property valued at one hundred pounds sterling. Petty jurors were required to be male, British subjects, between the ages of twenty-one and sixty, and owners of property valued at a minimum of forty pounds sterling.[53] The governor probably believed that the qualifications were sufficiently stringent to disqualify the riffraff of all colors, thus obviating the necessity to subscribe to discrimination. This may have contributed to his disgust with the current discriminatory policy.

The year 1832 brought an end to color discrimination in the grand jury selection process. That year, the provost marshal, William Vesey Munnings, selected grand jurors in the regular manner and sent the list to the governor, who rejected it and reprimanded Munnings for not selecting qualified free black and colored jurors. Samuel Nesbitt, colonial secretary, acting on orders from the governor, informed Munnings, "The Governor has directed me to acknowledge the receipt of jurors summoned for the present term. . . . It is evident that not one single coloured person was summoned as a Grand Juror and . . . not more than eight coloured people are summoned to serve as petit jurors."[54] The provost marshal was told that the policy of barring free black and colored males from the grand jury must be discontinued and "at least eight of the most respectable and wealthy of the colored population must be added to the grand jury list." Moreover, Munning was ordered to stop delegating the selecting of jurors to his deputy.[55]

Munnings complied with the governor's orders almost to the letter. The grand jury list was amended immediately by adding the names of eight free black and colored males.[56] A month later another name, Joseph G. Watkins, was added, bringing the total to nine. The provost marshal may not have included him in the first group because of economic reasons. When the governor saw that Watkins had been excluded, however, he may have ordered a change. Nesbitt announced in the *Royal Gazette,* "Mr. Joseph Watkins whose respectability of character and conduct fully entitle him to be a Grand Juror has been placed by the Provost Marshal on the Grand Jury List."[57] Since the announcement did not allude to Watkins' economic standing, his sterling character must have qualified him. When the grand jury was summoned the following January, Stephen Dillet, Frederick Fowler, David G. Cox, Henry Franks, and John Patrick Dean were among the grand jurors seated.[58] These men thus became the first nonwhite grand jurors in the islands' history. Furthermore, the number of nonwhites on the petty jury was increased to about twenty-eight, including George Watkins Sr. and George Watkins Jr.[59]

"The Committee of Free People of Colour Established in this Island [New Providence]" (CFPC), which spearheaded the drive to attain civil liberties, had nine members appointed to the grand jury and two to the petty jury.[60] John Boyd, Stephen Dillet, Robert Price, Joseph Watkins, and other members of the CFPC enthusiastically supported Governor Smyth and urged him to remove the civil disabilities. Boyd wrote at least three petitions after free blacks and persons of color had agreed upon their contents. The petitions usually bore the names of hundreds of the free black and colored males, including Joseph G. Watkins, Prince Williams, and Sharper Morris, three religious leaders in New Providence. Frank Spence, a Baptist preacher, did not sign the petitions, but James Rutherford, a trustee of the Baptist Society, Williams's church, did.

Free blacks and persons of color in the Bahamas, especially those in New Providence where most lived, organized to combat discrimination. The relatively good educational opportunities available to black and colored inhabitants and the strong nonwhite churches that produced religious leaders who could rally the troops, so to speak, were instrumental in the success of this effort. Whites had tried unsuccessfully to polarize nonwhites by appealing to the affluent among them to be passive onlookers in the unfolding drama. Writing in the anti-Smyth newspaper, the *Bahama Argus,* one white went as far as to tell affluent free blacks and persons of color to stop signing petitions and stated that they were being duped by rabble rousers. Responding to this condescending letter, an unidentified free man of color, who may have been a member of the CFPC and delegated by it to respond to the letter, said that persons whose names appeared on petitions were party to drafting the language of those petitions.[61] The letter from the unidentified free man of color is an example of how open access to schools came into play. This letter was just one of several that free blacks and coloreds had published in the newspaper, countering those that whites wrote. Moreover, the well-written petitions that they drafted were the results of good schooling. Throughout the struggle, free blacks and persons of color articulated their grievances clearly, forcefully, and publicly.

Unfortunately, we do not know much about the eleven individuals on the CFPC. We know more about Watkins than anyone else. Little is known, for instance, about Stephen Dillet, who came into prominence at this time. We learn from his grandson, who became a leader in African Americans' struggle to end Jim Crow, that Dillet was born in Haiti and came to the Bahamas during the Haitian Revolution. Dillet advertised in the local newspaper and apparently was a successful tailor.[62] In 1834, he and John Patrick Dean, a free man of color and butcher, were among the first three nonwhites elected to the assembly. Dillet, moreover, emerged as the leading nonwhite politician in the post manumission period. Henry Franks and Frederick Fowler were stonemasons, both of whom advertised their businesses in the local newspaper.[63] Robert Price and Edward Bridgewater were mariners, and David G. Cox (son of Timothy Cox Jr.) was a ship carpenter. The vocations of Edward P. Laroda, William Cooper, and James Minns are unknown, but they were probably businessmen.

CPFC members were property owners, but the absence of property tax rolls prevents determining the extent of their holdings. Inventories and wills are useful in determining the worth of free blacks and persons of color only if the persons died during or shortly after the period under study, but none in this group did. Most were Anglicans, native born, and literate. Similarly, the majority were slaveholders, with Dean owning the most, sixteen. Beyond this, there is precious little else that is known about this first group of free black and colored community leaders in the Bahamas.

Many white grand jurors protested against the appointment of nonwhite jurors. Their petition criticized those free black and colored males on the grand jury list and characterized them as "ignorant individuals who had been drawn indiscriminately with white inhabitants." The petitioners threatened to boycott the grand jury and contended that the status quo on the grand jury should be maintained until the legislature passed a law defining jury qualifications.[64] John Wildgoos and the others of his ilk who signed

The Committee of Free People of Colour
Free Black and Coloured Jurors (1833)

1 William Bain	P	14 John P. Dean	CG	26 Samuel Minns	CG
2 Juva Baldwin	P	15 Stephen Dillet	CG	27 James Minns	CG
3 William W. Baldwin	P	16 Simon Evans	P	28 Thomas Perpall	P
4 John Baptiste	P	17 Frederick Fowler	CG	29 Robert Price	P
5 Joseph Bosfield	P	18 Henry Franks	CG	30 James Rutherford	P
6 John Boyd	CG	19 Abraham Garner	P	31 John Sims	P
7 Britain Bridewater	P	20 Joseph Hall	P	32 Gilbert Smith	P
8 Edward Bridgewater	CP	21 Peter Johnson	P	33 John Smith	P
9 Edward Brister	P	22 William Johnson	P	34 George Watkins, Sr.	P
10 John Brown	P	23 Benjamin Lightborn	P	35 George Watkins, Jr.	P
11 William Cooper	CP	24 Edinburgh Love	P	36 Joseph G. Watkins	CG
12 David G. Cox	CG	25 Scotland Love	P	37 Samuel Watkins	P
13 Joseph G. Cox	P				

C=Commitee of Free People of Colour G=Grand Jury P=Petite Jury

the petition either did not know the free black and colored grand jurors, which is hard to believe since all grand jurors, white and nonwhite, came from New Providence, or they had little regard for the truth, which is probably more accurate. The provost marshal did as ordered and selected nine highly qualified and respected free black and colored men. Dillet and Dean would later become assemblymen, Boyd had written a book of poems, Watkins was a respected schoolmaster and lay reader in the Anglican church, and Henry Franks was a successful owner of a lime business whose advertisements had appeared in the local newspaper. These men were not ignorant. Since the legislature was all-white and generally shared Wildgoos' feelings on race relations, relying on it to correct the wrong was unrealistic. Wildgoos, a whiskey storekeeper, symbolized the backward thinking of the white small shopkeepers who dominated the assembly and shaped the debate over race relations.

The white petitioners did not prevail on the jury issue and, as result, juries in the Bahama Islands stopped being all-white. Indeed, the courthouse scene changed, for, in addition to free black and colored men sitting on juries that deliberated the fate of whites, blacks and coloreds of both sexes appeared on the witness stand to give testimony against whites. In November 1831, a free black woman named Phoebe Watkins gave sworn testimony in a case involving an officer in the Royal Army.[65] Furthermore, Phoebe Watkins served on an unusual jury of "matrons" whom the court appointed in an unusual case. Hannah Harris was indicted and subsequently convicted on a larceny charge, but upon hearing her death sentence, Hannah said that she was pregnant. The judge impaneled a jury of twelve matrons composed of eight whites and four nonwhites—Phoebe Bowles, Celey Lord, Phoebe Wallace, and Watkins—to find out if Harris was pregnant. They concluded that she was not.[66] This may have been the first all-woman jury in the Bahamas, and it contained free blacks and women of color. Another first for the criminal justice system was Governor Smyth's appointment of Joseph G. Watkins as a constable in the Western District of New Providence; he was excused from duty on Sundays, however, to avoid interfering with his lay reader responsibilities at the Anglican chapel.[67] The criminal justice system of the Bahamas thus was changed.

While the above changes were important, they did not destroy the old system. At best they were milestones along the path to a more equitable system. Meanwhile, much work needed to be completed before free blacks and persons of color would gain relief from the degrading civil disabilities. To his credit, Governor Smyth tried very hard to eradicate the civil disabilities in his short term at the helm of the government. In an address to the council and assembly, he admonished those bodies to "let every man be esteemed and treated according to his conduct and character and not the colour of his skin."[68] Those words are remarkably close to the ones that Martin Luther King Jr. uttered over a century later in addressing the problem of Jim Crow in American society. In his address, moreover, the governor warned lawmakers that the Crown would not renew discriminatory laws once they had expired. Smyth also said that since distinctions between whites and blacks/coloreds must ultimately cease, lawmakers should end civil disabilities voluntarily. This would both ease tension and gain supporters among free blacks and coloreds.[69]

The assembly neither listened to the governor nor followed his advice. Lawmakers instead petitioned Britain for Smyth's removal in the mistaken notion that a different governor would bring a different message. The assembly succeeded in getting Governor Smyth removed, but the message did not change. This became clear when B. T. Balfour, Smyth's replacement, chastised the rector of Christ Church for his policy of separating whites from worshipers of other colors in divine worship and for following the same policy in the burial of the dead. Lieutenant Governor Balfour told the Reverend William Hepworth of Christ Church, "[A]mong the prejudices which unfortunately still prevail in West India and colonial society there are none more offensive or repugnant to every feeling which the Christian should hold than those distinctions which are allowed to exist between the freemen of different colours during divine service and the disposition of their bodies after death." The lieutenant governor said that he found it impossible to believe human intellect could be so degraded as to attempt by any reasoning process to justify the idea that being buried near a "coloured body" could offend the "dignity of a white corpse." Balfour continued, "Having received His Majesty's instruction . . . to introduce more liberal feeling into the Coloured society, and to check all prejudices which are irritating to any class of His Majesty's subjects, and relying Sir on your cordial cooperation with me in this task . . . I have now to request that for the future no distinction of burial ground be made between white and coloured man. Let us at least have the consolation of feeling that distinctions of pride are lost in the grave."[70] Balfour, moreover, reminded the rector that he alone was the master of the burial ground and ordered him to stand firm against vestry encroachment upon his authority.

Balfour, who had told free blacks and persons of color that he hoped the end to every distinction between freemen was near, brought that goal a step nearer to achievement when he signed "An Act to Relieve His Majesty's Free Coloured and Black Subjects of the Bahama Islands From all Civil Disabilities."[71] This act was among the more significant ones passed during the 1820s and 1830s. Bahamian lawmakers hoped that this action would draw free blacks and persons of color to them, assuring continued white domination of the islands; they did not want free blacks and persons of color to unite with the soon-to-be manumitted slaves.[72] Because of this law, all blacks and coloreds who were born free in the Bahamas, or elsewhere in the Western Hemisphere, were entitled to the same privileges as whites. All Creole slaves were entitled to these privileges after the second anniversary of their manumission, but African natives were ineligible, whatever their status. Free blacks and persons of color were eligible to give testimony in all "courts of civil or criminal jurisdiction" in the Bahamas, but a six-year residential requirement was imposed upon those born in Africa, unless they secured a certificate from an Anglican clergyman declaring that they understood the significance and obligation of oath taking.[73] This act placed a capstone on legislation to give full rights and privileges to free blacks and persons of color, especially the males.

Downing Street was unhappy with restrictions in the Removal of Civil Disabilities Act, especially the two-year waiting period required of manumitted blacks and persons of color who were born in the Bahamas and the total exclusion of natives of Africa from its privileges. A glaring weakness in the act, which Edward G. Stanley detected, was that manumission had to come "by some act of the owner or by the sentence of some court of justice." If that section was interpreted, observed Stanley, "all the negroes and coloured people about to be emancipated under the Act for the Abolition of Slavery would be excluded from the benefit." In spite of his reservations about particular sections of the act, Stanley recommended approval with the expectation that the unacceptable passages would be revised.[74] The Removal of Civil Disabilities Act was thus allowed to stand, creating another milestone along the path toward destroying the old degrading practices. Writing at the end of 1833, a Bahamian official optimistically proclaimed that the present condition of the colony was "full of prosperous promise."[75]

Additional improvements in race relations occurred in 1834 when the first free blacks and persons of color were officially elected to the assembly. Stephen Dillet had been elected to the assembly from Nassau in an 1833 election, but he was barred from taking his seat on a technicality. Balfour called a special election the following year to resolve the controversy, and in that election Dillet and two other members of the CFPC, John Patrick Dean and Edward P. Laroda, won seats in the assembly.[76] Laroda, who had signed at least two Boyd-drafted petitions, was the only one of the three who had not been a grand juror. Although free blacks and coloreds did not constitute most of the eligible voters in the Bahamas, they composed a majority in some districts that sent members to the assembly, and those were the ones where CFPC members were victorious. Dillet was elected from a district in Nassau, Dean from one in the Western District of New Providence, and Lorado from a district in Exuma. The high property qualification required to be eligible for the franchise thus did not adversely affect the political fortune of free blacks and persons of color.

The election of these three men placed the Bahamas in the vanguard of the movement to integrate British West Indies legislatures. Although Jamaica elected nonwhites to its assembly before the Bahamas, a smaller number was elected in the former than in the latter. In 1831, Price Watkis and John Manderson, two men of color, were elected to the forty-five-member assembly of Jamaica. In 1833, St. Kitts elected three freemen of color to its assembly. Barbados did not integrate its assembly, however, until 1843 when Samuel Jackman Prescod, a freeman of color and editor of that island's first freedman newspaper, was elected.[77] In 1834, the twenty-nine-member Assembly of the Bahamas had three freemen of color whereas Jamaica's assembly, which was almost twice as large, had only two and Barbados's did not have any. The larger colonies apparently did not lead the way in changing the color of colonial assemblies.

The assembly and the Colonial Office had different views on race relations. The assembly, whose views on race relations were similar to those of whites generally, and the Colonial Office, whose views were far advanced of those in the Bahamas, often had heated exchanges over the issue; but their differences never reached the boiling point. The major casualty was Governor James Carmichael Smyth, whom the Colonial Office transferred to another colony in the British West Indies though it had praised him highly.[78] The Colonial Office, without admitting as much, in its wisdom decided to acquiesce to the demands of the assembly for Smyth's removal in order to establish a more sanguine legislative atmosphere for passage of the reforms. Without complaining, unlike Lord Dunmore in the 1790s, Governor Smyth sailed to Demerara, his next assignment, with the beautiful silver plate that free blacks and persons of color had given him "as a sincere token of gratitude," confident that the removal of a messenger would not change the message.[79] Governor Smyth's removal allowed the assembly to save face, the small price the Colonial Office reluctantly paid to get its big prize: humanitarian reforms.

Balfour chided the rector of Christ Church for permitting discrimination against persons of a different color to exist in his edifice and the parish's cemetery.[80] He did not say persons of a different race and this made a world of difference. In the American South, where miscegenation laws were widespread, whites referred to themselves and African Americans as belonging to different races, the white and the black. Implicit in Balfour's statement, however, is that there is just one race: the human race. The absence of miscegenation laws in the Bahamas reflected this. The social gap between people of the same race but of different colors was a difference of degree; the gap between people of different races, on the other hand, was a difference of kind. Eliminating prejudices between groups of the same race was less intimidating than eradicating racism. Free blacks and persons of color who now sat as jurors and in the assembly were Bahamians just like those who once had denied these privileges to them; they subscribed to the same ethos as whites and were well situated financially.

Whites in the Bahamas implicitly accepted Balfour's position. In the reform legislation, the assembly did not draw a distinction between blacks and persons of color, a distinction which would have been an indication that its members bought into the race ideology of their American cousins in South Carolina and Louisiana where special privileges were provided for mulattoes because of their close biological association with whites. The key factor in determining who should be granted privileges therefore was not how many generations one was removed from his white ancestors; rather, status at birth and place of birth were the key factors. Accordingly, if one was born free in the Bahamas, he was entitled to the privileges immediately. If one was a Creole slave who had gained free status, he had to wait awhile. If one was born in Africa, however, he was denied the privileges. Thus free blacks and persons of color were placed in three legal categories: (1) free-born, (2) manumitted Creole, and (3) native of Africa.

Race relations in the Bahamas changed rapidly in the 1820s and 1830s. Prejudices still existed, but they generally did not originate in the law. Whites did not take long to adjust to the nonwhite jurors, court witnesses, voters, and assemblymen; they soon realized, moreover, that removing civil disabilities would not cause significant changes in the power structure. Whites still composed most of the free persons on the islands; and with manumission looming on the horizon, delaying reforms any longer could further damage race relations and push free blacks and persons of color into an alliance with the slaves once they were manumitted. Whites concluded that it was better to grant reforms before manumission when they and most wealthy free blacks and persons of color had similar interests. They were slaveholders. After manumission it would be too late because then free blacks and persons of color and the manumitted slaves would have similar interests. They were all nonwhite. Thus in the years between 1816 and 1834 free blacks and persons of color were extended civil privileges in a nonviolent, though at times tense and contentious, transformation of the political and legal systems, paving the way for manumission.

CHAPTER VII

Race Relations, 1816–1834: Emancipation, the Hidden Agenda

After the clear evidence, which exists, that compulsory Manumission was agreed upon by the Government and announced both here and in the colonies as part of the measures to be enforced for carrying into effect the Resolution of 1823 . . .

—William Huskisson to Wilmot Morton Earlham, November 7, 1827

Slavery was abolished in Haiti after a bloody revolution, and blacks gained control of the island. Slavery ended in the United States because the American South misunderstood the intentions of the country's first Republican president, Abraham Lincoln, and seceded from the Union, precipitating the Civil War, the aftermath of which was ratification of the Thirteenth Amendment, which abolished slavery, except as a punishment for crime. The nonviolent emancipation of slaves throughout the British West Indies was sandwiched between these two bloody events. The bell began to toll for slavery in the British West Indies during the second decade of the nineteenth century. After that time, it was not a question of whether slavery would be abolished, but how it would happen. One group of British leaders advocated permitting slavery to follow the path of European serfdom and die gradually, with little probability of violence, whereas another group demanded immediate emancipation. While the two groups debated the issue and courted public opinion, Parliament pursued its secret agenda of emancipation by empowering the Colonial Office to order colonial legislatures to pass strict laws enforcing the ban of importation of African slaves into the colonies and then pressuring those bodies to pass amelioration reforms. The amelioration period, 1823–1833, was expected, in some quarters, to result in the peaceful death of slavery in the colonies. When this did not happen, Parliament passed the Manumission Act (1833), providing for compensated emancipation and ordering colonial legislatures to pass enabling legislation by August 1, 1834. The Bahama Islands, like other colonies in the region, did as directed.

Ironically, the manumission bill had an easier time in the Assembly of the Bahamas than the slave registry bill. Demands to get slaves registered emanated from concerns that planters might attempt to smuggle slaves into the region, thus violating the Abolition Act. James Stephen, legal adviser in the Colonial Office, brother-in-law of William Wilberforce, and a man whom detractors dubbed "king Stephen and Mr. Over-Secretary Stephen," was the driving force behind efforts to get colonial legislatures to pass an acceptable slave registry law.[1] The Colonial Office pressured Governor Cameron to get a slave registry act passed in the legislature. Planters were told that a slave registration act would convince all that they were not trying to smuggle slaves into the colony in violation of the law.[2] Governor Cameron addressed the legislature a year after a December 1816 report by a select committee complained that the Bahamas was being punished for the misdeeds of inhabitants in Trinidad and St. Lucie.[3] The following December, another committee reported its findings concerning alleged illicit slave trading that followed a route from Cuba to Exuma to Jamaica. The committee found "that no illicit import of Africans ha[d] at any time since the abolition of the slave trade taken place therein."[4] Since Bahamian planters were not engaged in smuggling, the committee reasoned, no need existed to enact a law that was intended primarily to curb this practice. The Colonial Office refused to accept this position and demanded that Bahamian lawmakers pass slave registry legislation, just as their counterparts in the other colonies were doing.

Realizing that further attempts to convince Downing Street that a slave registry act, if its intent was to prevent smuggling slaves into the islands, was unnecessary, the assembly passed in 1817 a slave registration bill that required triennial registration of slaves; but the body dissolved before the governor approved the bill.[5] Four years later, the assembly passed another slave registration bill and this one reached Governor Grant's desk. All slaveholders were required to complete a return containing the number of slaves they owned on the first of January (1822), the name, sex, age, color, and place of employment of their slaves, and whether they were Creoles or natives of

Africa. A new position, registrar of slaves, was created to oversee implementation of the act. Every six months customs collectors were required to submit reports of slaves transported to another British West Indies colony and collect six pence for each slave transported. Governor Grant signed the act and sent it to Britain.[6]

Downing Street detected shortcomings in the act and recommended its approval to the Privy Council with reservations. Lord Bathurst, who read the act thoroughly, told Governor Grant that the Bahamian act was less complete than those of other colonies; but he construed its passage as an indication that the legislature had abandoned its objection to slave registration and now embraced it. Most of the shortcomings Lord Bathurst identified were omissions that would normally go unnoticed and did not prevent execution of the act's essential purpose. He mentioned, for instance, that the act did not contain a provision for public inspection of "the Books of Registry," no right of appeal was "given against acts of the Registrar" by aggrieved parties, and no penalty was assessed for holding unregistered slaves or giving false descriptions of slaves. He complimented lawmakers on the section of the act that dealt with transferring slaves from one British colony to another, claiming it was stronger than those in other slave registration acts in the region.[7] This act received a better review than its successor, the Act to Establish Triennial Registration of Slaves in the Bahama Islands (1827). Although Governor Grant also approved that one, the Privy Council disallowed it because it failed to correct shortcomings noted in Lord Bathurst's long 1824 missive concerning the 1821 act.[8]

Lawmakers' failure to draft an acceptable slave registry act was not indicative of a desire to defy Downing Street. Once they decided to accede to orders from Britain, Bahamian lawmakers tried to pass a slave registry act. The Colonial Office demanded policies, however, that may have worked well in Barbados, Jamaica, and Trinidad, but not in the Bahamas where geographical conditions and demand for slave labor were different from those in other colonies. This was an example of one glove size not fitting all hands. Ordering compliance in principle was a reasonable expectation; demanding expenditure of funds to hire officials to carry out the tight surveillance that Downing Street wanted was both burdensome and unnecessary. Bahamian planters showed greater interest in transporting slaves to other British West Indies colonies than in smuggling Africans into the islands. Besides having higher births than deaths among slaves, unlike Jamaica where the opposite occurred, the Bahamas was provided with additional free labor under the apprenticeship program introduced to prepare liberated Africans for freedom.

There was therefore little apparent need to smuggle slave laborers. Downing Street would have been well-advised to spend more time policing its apprenticeship program for liberated Africans, where slaveholders constituted most of the persons to whom liberated Africans were apprenticed, to ensure that slaveholders were not exploiting the apprentices, which they were, and less time badgering lawmakers about passing an airtight slave registration act.

After several unsuccessful attempts to pass an acceptable slave registry act, lawmakers turned their attention to drafting amelioration legislation. Beginning in 1823, the Colonial Office initiated a program to improve conditions for slaves in the colonies, hoping that this would lead to emancipation without Parliament having to pass additional legislation. Giving slaves religious instruction was the linchpin of the program. Among the other important reforms ordered were legal recognition of slave marriages; a ban on separating slave families by sale, using the whip in the field, flogging female slaves, having Sunday markets, and working slaves on Sundays; admission of slave evidence in court under certain conditions; and permission for slaves to own property.[9] Concerned that it violated constitutional rights of West Indians, Parliament opted to allow colonial legislatures to enact amelioration reforms, just as it had done with the slave registry issue. In Crown colonies reform legislation emanated from Parliament.[10]

Under the speakership of Lewis Kerr, the House of Assembly agreed with most of the reforms and stated that many items had been passed in the Bahamas. Bahamian lawmakers agreed with Parliament that promoting correct religious instruction among slaves was important and stated that the islands had "some licensed Negro preachers, one of whom had a small stipend from the country" (they were referring to Joseph G. Watkins). The assembly further gave its support to legal recognition of slave marriages, noting, "[O]n our plantations it has long been the established policy of the country to promote and encourage marriages." Lawmakers responded positively, moreover, to slave manumissions and ownership of private property. They objected, however, to confirming these practices "by legislative enactment," arguing that it was unnecessary and would interpose "the palpable arm of the law between the master and his slave" in matters in which formerly "all ha[d] hitherto tacitly acquiesced in harmony and mutual good will."[11] This was absurd. Slaves did as they were told and masters did whatever they wished. "Mutual good will" and one-sided relationships such as existed between master and slave are incongruous. The major problem that lawmakers had with the proposed amelioration reforms, therefore, was not with the reforms per se, but with granting these as rights to which slaves were entitled. Consequently, lawmakers weakened amelioration acts to ensure that slaveholders' property rights were protected.

Lasting about from 1823 to 1833, the amelioration period was the intermediate step between the abolition of the African slave trade and emancipation. The amelioration period thus was one of the most significant slave-related events in the British West Indies. The first step in achieving the desired reforms was to decrease masters' hold on their slaves. This would allow slaves to enjoy some of the same rights as free persons. Central to the success of the program was the reduction of masters' interference in the lives of slaves, a point Peter Kolchin identified as the reason that southern slavery was "unusually restricted."[12] In January 1824, Bahamian lawmakers passed the first of a trilogy of acts that composed the amelioration reforms: "An Act to amend, consolidate and bring into one, the several Laws relating to Slaves, and for giving them further protection and security, and for suspending several acts, and clauses of acts therein mentioned, and for other purposes" (Consolidated Slave Act of 1824). This act included many provisions of the 1797 Consolidated Slave Act, provisions that granted proper food and clothing, protected aged and infirmed slaves against abandonment, protected all slaves against physical abuse, and permitted slaves to enjoy certain holidays. Besides these provisions, the Consolidated Slave Act of 1824 legalized slave marriages and prohibited separation of slave families.[13]

Slaves' marriages were recognized since there were no laws to the contrary, but now they gained the sanction of the law. Rectors were authorized to marry slave couples or mixed couples (slave and free person), but slaves had to receive permission from their owners. The marriages were legal in the eyes of the law and had to be registered in the common register in the same manner and form as those of free persons. Publication of banns or any dispensating license of marriage or other faculty or license was not required for the slaves.[14] This way encumbrances that often prevented poor free persons from formalizing their relationship, because they could not afford to pay the license fee, were removed. The law was quite clear in stating that the legality of the marriage did not affect masters' right of ownership and authority over their slaves. In a related matter, husbands and wives and their children under fourteen years of age belonging to the same master could not be separated.[15] Although this act did not affect masters' right of ownership, it obviously compromised the authority of masters and limited their ability to interfere in the lives of slaves.

The second statute of the trilogy was passed in 1826. In this act, manumission procedures were discussed in great detail and restrictions placed on whipping slaves, but these were not the most significant provisions of the statute. That honor belonged to section 8, which allowed slaves to give evidence in civil and criminal cases, subject to many exceptions and limitations. This law, like some previous ones, made a distinction between natives of Africa and Creoles, unlike statutes in the American South. Natives of Africa were not allowed to give evidence, but Creole slaves were.[16] A much stronger African cultural presence pervaded the Bahamas than the American South; this may have affected whites' perception of Africans.[17] African customs such as Junkanoo, obeah, *asu(e),* and *wonny* and African foods such as *fufu, acarra, mymy,* and *agedi* were in plain view and may have convinced whites that Africans had not been assimilated and consequently did not understand European ways and were not yet ready to follow traditional British values.[18] Perhaps this is why the right to give evidence was withheld from native Africans, unless they had been in the islands at least five years and were familiar enough with Christianity to understand the significance of taking an oath. Slaves (Creoles and natives of Africa) were not permitted to testify against whites in capital felony cases. By inference, they could testify against whites in all other cases, except in criminal cases involving their masters.[19]

Having extended the right to give evidence in civil and criminal cases only to Creole slaves, the statute then limited this right by excluding the evidence sometimes. Slave evidence was inadmissible in cases involving the claim of another slave for freedom, nor could slaves appear as witnesses to prove the execution of any deed or writing or any will intended for the manumission of a slave or for conveying or bequeathing a slave.[20] Lawmakers may have believed that slaves were incapable of judging the facts on their merit in cases that dealt with slaves obtaining freedom, or they may have believed that since slaves identified so closely with manumission, having them involved in legal decisions on the subject was a conflict of interest.

Section 36 of the 1826 statute legalized a longstanding custom: slave ownership of property. Slaves were permitted to inherit and own real estate and personal property without a limit placed on its value, and they could defend that property in court as if they were free persons. Again, however, a restriction was attached to the right. The court would assign legal defense and regard slaves as if they were "infants under the age of twenty-one." The passage did not negatively affect the ownership provision of the act, hence it did not present a serious problem. The section's last passage stated "that nothing herein contained shall extend or be construed to extend to authorize any slave to acquire or become the owner of a slave or slaves, or of any fire arms, gunpowder or ammunition without the especial permission of their owners, or others having charge of them respectively."[21] This passage did not expressly prohibit slaves from owning either other slaves or firearms, unlike southern statutes; rather, slaves had to receive permission to do so, which was different from an outright prohibition.

Section 37 of the statute allowed slaves to deposit money for safekeeping into a chest deposit controlled by the receiver general and treasurer. Accounts did not accrue interest. Slave depositors instead of earning interest on their accounts had to pay a 3 percent commission upon withdrawing money from their accounts if done within twelve months after the deposit.[22] The commission (which was tantamount to a fine) was probably intended to discourage frequent withdrawals, which happened when one was not disciplined enough to keep money in a savings account and let it work for the depositor. Under the language of the statute, money could not work for the slave depositors if they kept it there indefinitely, which contravened good banking policy. William Huskisson, president of the Board of Trade, pointed this out in his review of the statute.[23] The statute nevertheless had a positive feature. Section 38 permitted slaves to designate persons to whom the account would go in case of the depositor's death, and the decision had the legal standing of a will. Masters thus did not gain automatic control of their slaves' property upon their death, reaffirming that slaves' property was theirs to own and dispose of as they wished.[24]

Several provisions of the 1826 statute contrasted strikingly with laws in the American South. Southern slave codes, for example, posited slaves' property under the ownership of their masters, who could deny slaves control of property that they may have earned by the sweat of their own brow and without any assistance, financial or otherwise, from their masters. Even with the restrictions placed on the admissibility of slave evidence, Bahamian slaves were legally entitled to exercise rights in the eyes of the law, rights which eluded their sisters and brothers in the American South. Bahamian slaves, moreover, were not prohibited absolutely from owning firearms. When coupled with the legal rights granted in the 1824 statute, the provisions of the 1826 act placed Bahamian slaves in a much more advantageous position under the law than Southern bondsmen.

The third statute of the trilogy, the Consolidated Slave Act of 1830, addressed the British Ministry's criticism that the Bahamian legislature had failed to consolidate "the whole of their Slave Codification Act." The Ministry was concerned that adding new progressive legislation to a body of slave codes that included some of the old pre–amelioration period laws which remained on the books created a legal quagmire. To correct the situation, slave codes dating back to George III, codes that had not been repealed in the two earlier acts (1824 and 1826), were inoperative. Moreover, many restrictions placed upon slave evidence were removed, natives of Africa were no longer excluded from giving evidence, residence requirement was removed, and magistrates as well as clergymen could certify slaves, qualifying them to give evidence in civil and criminal cases.[25] Consequently, the 1830 act simplified the slave code and modified requirements for admission of slave evidence, but it did not break new ground.

By 1830, the confusion that surrounded the legal status of slaves and existed because of the plethora of consolidated slave acts passed since the 1780s was clarified. More important, the amelioration period created, in principle, a mini-bill of rights for slaves. Privileges that were once granted at the pleasure of slaveholders, and thus could be withdrawn at their displeasure, were now protected by the law and became rights. As laudable as the reforms were, however, the Bahama Islands fell short of enacting the total package recommended. The general assembly, for instance, did not ban flogging of female slaves and did not remove all the conditions placed on admitting slave evidence in court.

None of the colonial legislatures passed all the mandated reforms, and most complained of interference by the Colonial Office. Barbados and Jamaica, among others, joined the Bahamas in successfully resisting pressure to ban flogging of female slaves. Resistance to recognizing slave marriages and banning whips from the field was widespread.[26] Conversely, Grenada passed a bill that admitted slave evidence without qualifications and Nevis passed a series of slave laws that drew warm praise from Downing Street.[27] In spite of resistance to amelioration, conditions for slaves improved in the British West Indies because of the amelioration program. James Stephen, who was not known for lavishing praise on the colonies, admitted that conditions were better in Jamaica because of the amelioration.[28]

The British West Indies colonies differed significantly in internal economic endeavors and treatment of slaves, but their political and religious institutions tended to be similar. The Bahamas generally did not fare well when compared economically with other colonies. The Bahamas, for example, employed only 54.5 percent of its slave workforce in the field; this was a smaller percentage than that in all the other colonies except British Honduras, which employed only 48.1 percent in the field. Only Anguilla (with 74.9 percent) and Barbuda (with 72.5 percent) had lower percentages of slaves employed than the Bahamas (with 77.2 percent). The Bahamas also ranked near the bottom in the percentage of slave tradesmen (2.7 percent); only Anguilla had a lower percentage of slave tradesmen (1.4 percent). The Bahamas had 31.8 percent of its slave workforce employed as domestics; only one other colony had a higher percentage thus employed, British Honduras with 46.4 percent. Similarly, the Bahama Islands had the highest percentage of slaves working on wharves (10.1 percent).[29]

The Bahamas fared much better in comparisons dealing with health. Whereas slaveholders in the Leeward Islands gave slaves a weekly allowance of nine pints of corn or beans (approximately 1,850 calories daily), Bahamian slaveholders gave slaves one peck or sixteen pints of unground Indian or Guinea corn (approximately 3,275 calories daily). Slaves in Jamaica received 3,000 calories daily. Jamaica's slaves commonly received free time Saturday afternoons and Sundays, however, to work in allotted provision grounds that provided most of their food. Slaves in Barbados were usually not given free time Saturday afternoons since most of their food was provided for them.[30] Further, whereas the slave population in the sugar colonies, such as Jamaica, had an excess of deaths over births, the Bahamas did not.[31]

The above comparisons reveal a mixture of positives and negatives for the Bahamas. Glaring negatives were the low employment of slaves and the small percentage involved in skilled trades. A positive was that slaves generally worked in less demanding occupations, that is, as domestics instead of field hands. Domestic servants and sailors worked long hours because of the nature of their work, but it was not arduous work. Slave mechanics, on the other hand, usually worked between eight and nine hours daily, about the same hours as white mechanics. Plantation slaves and salt rakers were usually employed in the task system, which allowed them to finish their chores and have the rest of the day to work for themselves.[32] The relatively lighter work schedule coupled with being fed better than slaves in other colonies translated into Bahamian slaves having a less burdensome situation than their counterparts in other colonies. Therefore, the Bahamas did not have as much ground to cover in ameliorating the conditions of slaves.

The assembly had completed much of what was asked of it by 1830; and Governor Smyth, who assumed office near the end of the legislative program, believed that the two remaining reforms—further extension of the capabilities of slaves to give evidence and the ban on flogging female slaves—would be enacted in another session or two.[33] Expansion of capabilities of slaves to give evidence occupied the thinking of Charles Nesbitt, deputy secretary of the Bahamas, who theorized to the governor that "the

Crown ha[d] a right to the evidence of all his subjects in criminal cases, for the essential ends of justice." Nesbitt then suggested that Parliament should pass a declaratory act stating that evidence of slaves "[was] and must be considered as admissible before His Majesty's courts of justice."[34] The governor was so intrigued with what Nesbitt had written that he sent it to Lord Goderich, who, in his response to Nesbitt's letter to the governor, said that the idea had also occurred to him some time ago. Lord Goderich shared his thoughts with Sir George Murray, who asked the solicitor general and attorney general if Parliament could pass such a law. Lord Goderich then alluded to laws pending in Parliament: "should they answer the expectations which led to their adoption not only the admission of slave evidence, but many other mitigations of the Slave Code must immediately follow." He asked the governor to treat his letter confidentially.[35]

In spite of the act granting the privilege of introducing evidence in court, little movement occurred in that direction. In February 1833, three years after the act had been passed, Nesbitt complained that only sixty-seven slaves had been certified to give evidence in court. According to the act, certified slaves had to be reported to the clerk.[36] Slowness on this score was not symptomatic of how other reforms were carried out. It just happened that admission of slave evidence and banning flogging of female slaves were the two toughest nuts to crack.

Lawmakers never acceded to the order to ban flogging of female slaves, although they did modify the practice on two separate occasions. In 1824 the practice was modified by requiring female slaves twelve and older to be flogged privately. Then in 1826 another slight change in the practice was enacted. Female slaves could be whipped only in the presence of their owner(s) and the person administering the punishment, no other males.[37] This was as far as lawmakers would go in the matter. So female slaves were still subjected to the painful and humiliating experience of flogging. Having the flogging administered privately to a restricted number of male spectators was a distinction without a difference.

Failure to secure legislation banning flogging of female slaves did not diminish Governor Smyth's resolve to enforce the amelioration reforms that were passed. In early 1833, he sent Captain William McVicar of the Second West India Regiment to Government Harbour on Eleuthera Island because he had received "a number of distressing complaints" about mistreatment of slaves. McVicar was expected to stay on Eleuthera for up to two months.[38] Sending the captain was a clear signal that the Out Islands were not out of reach and that the governor expected compliance with the amelioration reforms throughout the Out Islands. This was very different from previous governors who would send a detachment of troops to the Out Islands to suppress a slave disturbance, but not to protect slaves from cruel masters. It was action of this kind that endeared Governor Smyth to blacks and coloreds, free and slave, and made him unpopular among whites.

Were the rights granted in the amelioration reforms ignored with impunity by whites since lawmakers had granted them grudgingly? They probably were enforced. Colonial governors, who reputedly enforced the slave legislation mandated by the Colonial Office, would not have allowed otherwise. It was unlikely that a situation existed similar to the one in the American South, where slaveholders ignored slave codes with impunity if the violations were not blatant and did not contravene social convention.

The amelioration reforms marked a serious effort to restore humanity to slaves, who continued to have a dual status: they were both property and persons. Now, however, the human aspect of their being predominated. This was significantly different from the principle which governed the slave codes in the American South. Why the difference in temper and tenor of the southern codes? At the very moment in history when the British government acquiesced to pressure from humanitarians and leaned on the Bahamas and other colonies in the British West Indies to inject "humanity and justice" into their slave codes, the national government of the United States was under the control of southern politicians who protected the interests of slaveholders. Except for John Quincy Adams, who abhorred slavery, presidents during the 1820s and early 1830s were slaveholders whose political party, the Republican Party, subscribed to the principle of states' rights. As a result of the 1832 schism among Republicans, Andrew Jackson's supporters formed the Democratic Party, which rested on a southern base but attracted supporters in the North and Midwest. In short, after watching the Northeast use the principle of states' rights in the years preceding the War of 1812 to protest the embargo and nonimportation policies of the Jefferson and Madison administrations, the American South wrapped itself tightly in the mantle of states' rights in the 1820s and 1830s. Interestingly, it was the protective tariff issue that caused traumas in the South then, not slavery. John C. Calhoun wrote the *South Carolina Exposition and Protest* to argue against tariff legislation, not against the Missouri Compromise. Nevertheless, the South was confident that the peculiar institution (slavery) was safe from federal intervention because national leaders, who generally either supported slavery or were sympathetic to it, pursued a laissez-faire policy on the slavery issue.

The situation in the Bahamas was quite different. Humanitarians pushed the British ministry to adopt a policy that was inimical to slavery. Although the Bahamian legislature passed reform acts that were much more progressive than the previous slave codes, the Colonial Office criticized the acts for not going far enough. Downing Street had the following reaction to a provision which legalized slave marriages in the 1824 act: "On the subject of marriage the Legislature of the Bahamas have adopted the suggestions of His Majesty's Government, with the exception that the consent of the Owner is an indispensable condition, and that no Provision is made for the possible case of that consent being withheld from caprice, or improper motives." Concerning the 1826 act, Huskisson similarly feared that exceptions attached to the provision authorizing admission of slave evidence undermined the intended reform; he noted "that numerous exceptions which [were] made by the Act to the admissibility of the Class of Witnesses, have nearly deprived the general Rule itself of its practical value."[39]

By the end of the amelioration period, therefore, London operated at a higher moral plane respecting the slavery issue than Washington, and this was reflected in the slave codes of the British West Indies compared with those of the American South. Granted London had greater political leverage in dealing with its West Indies colonies than Washington had with the South, but different political systems would be a major factor in explaining the difference in the slave codes of the Bahamas and the American South only if both Washington and London were antislavery camps. Then one could argue that the difference in slave codes was because Washington lacked the power to force reforms upon the American South as London had done in the West Indies. Since Washington and London leaders had different views on slavery, however, it did not matter that Washington could not exert the same pressure on the American South that London exerted on its West Indies colonies. Washington did not use its "bully pulpit" to attack the evils of slavery because James Monroe (1817–1825) and Andrew Jackson (1829–1837) did not believe that slavery was evil. Furthermore, Washington was far less forceful than London in enforcing legislation which both capitals had passed, abolition of the slave trade. Washington's record on enforcing that legislation was abysmal, which is the reason the Bahamian liberated Africans did not have American counterparts.

The acts passed during the amelioration period were not revolutionary because they did not reject the principle that slaves were property, but those acts did recognize the humanity of slaves in ways that were previously taboo. As a result of those measures, a real body of rights was conferred upon slaves.

They were entitled by law to sufficient food, proper clothing, and protection in old age. Moreover, they could own property, both real and personal; give evidence against whites in both criminal and civil cases, even if only on a conditional basis; and will property to their heirs. This placed the Bahamian slave codes among the less dehumanizing ones in the English-speaking Western Hemisphere.

The Bahamas probably passed more amelioration legislation than most of the other colonies, but this did not prevent British officials from being disappointed with these reforms. Failure to go further with the legislation than the assembly was willing to go played into the hands of compulsory emancipation advocates, who had gained a large majority in Parliament by the early 1830s.[40] Thus, after ten years of insisting upon reforms to ameliorate the condition of slaves, British leaders concluded that amelioration had failed and embarked upon a scheme of systematic emancipation of slaves in its West Indies colonies.[41]

Emancipation was always the goal of British leaders. The debate was over the manner of achieving it. Serious talk of emancipating slaves began in the 1820s, if not earlier, when the question of compensation had been considered. George Chalmers, colonial agent, probably learned of this and told Bahamian leaders, who responded by writing a pamphlet in 1823 expressing their concern about the proposed abolition of slavery in the West Indies.[42] Wilmot Horton talked of pledging a fund "to supply the excess of price which the Master may and ought to receive in compensation for the loss of his slave."[43] Responding to this idea, Huskisson told Horton that Parliament had agreed upon compulsory manumission. He said, "After the clear evidence, which exists, that compulsory manumission was agreed upon both here and in the colonies as part of the measures to be enforced for carrying into effect the Resolution of 1823, . . . I cannot bring my mind to believe that Parliament will be induce[d] to create any fund for the purpose you mention."[44]

Writing a few years later, Lord Howick also showed that in 1823 Parliament had pledged itself to manumission but that manumission would come gradually: ". . . a course of policy quite at variance with that pointed out in the Resolution of 1823 . . . In the Resolution referred to, and in Mr. Canning's speeches, it was distinctly stated, that the ultimate extinction of slavery was to be attempted, not by any law for the direct liberation of slaves or their children, but by gradually improving their condition and mitigating the severity with which they are now treated, in short, by a process similar to that which in this country and in the greatest part of Europe, without any sudden or violent change, has by degrees converted the serfs and bondsmen of the dark into the free peasantry of modern times."[45] Howick told Thomas F. Buxton, in the strictest confidence, that he and other members of the government would understand if Buxton pushed for immediate emancipation. Howick then asked Buxton to "consider this letter as strictly private and confidential," which suggests that British leaders may have soured on amelioration as early as 1831 and were tacitly encouraging Buxton to move forward with his emancipation plans.[46]

Buxton did introduce an abolition bill in Parliament, but he agreed to withdraw it when the government announced that it would sponsor one.[47] After the new colonial secretary, Edward G. Stanley (Earl of Derby), tried unsuccessfully to draft an abolition bill, the task fell to James Stephen, who drafted the Manumission Act (1833) in forty-eight hours and watched exhausted as it moved through Parliament with only two slight amendments.[48] The Manumission Act ended perpetual slavery, provided twenty million pounds sterling to compensate West Indian slaveholders, and required slaves to undergo a short apprenticeship, beginning August 1, 1834, before gaining complete freedom. The compensation that each colony received was contingent upon the value of its exports to Great Britain. Compensated emancipation was approved because protection of property was the cornerstone of the English constitution.[49] Since Britain recognized slaves as property, though it abhorred the practice, manumission deprived slaveholders of their property, thus entitling them to compensation for this loss. This prevented the act from violating the rights of slaveholders. Priscilla Buxton, daughter of Thomas Buxton, attended the debate on the manumission bill and recalled Stanley giving the "capital speech" and Howick following him with a speech supporting emancipation. At the end of the debate, she remembered her jubilant father saying, "[M]y work in life is done, since I have lived to hear my own doctrines from the Treasury bench. Emancipation is effected. The thing is done."[50]

The colonies would not receive their compensation, however, until their legislatures passed acceptable emancipation acts. Jamaica, which passed an act in December 1833, was the first colony to pass an acceptable act.[51] Most of the other colonies passed emancipation acts in short order, with Antigua and Bermuda conferring immediate freedom of slaves, bypassing the apprenticeship period.[52] The Bahama Islands was the only colony, however, to adopt the entire compulsory manumission program that the Crown had recommended.[53]

Viewed against the background of violence associated with emancipation in Haiti and the United States, Parliament's decision to opt for immediate compulsory emancipation over gradualism and the colonies' swift and nonviolent acceptance of the Manumission Act (1833), in principle, raises a question concerning why emancipation was achieved without violence in those slave societies. West Indian slaveholders never justified slavery on any ground other than that it was unavoidable. Sugar growers were dependent upon slave labor because there was no better known way of growing and harvesting the cane crop.[54] When colonial sugar ceased to be competitive in the world market, this reason for justifying slavery rang hollow and West Indian sugar growers were left bereft of the clout they once had in Parliament. The pace of economic decline in the sugar colonies may be debated, but the fact that it happened, and that this swung the pendulum in favor of the abolitionists, is not debatable.[55] Bahamian slaveholders, who figuratively had been living on life support provided by West Indian sugar growers since the cotton plantations faltered at the turn of the century, had little clout in Parliament. The measuring stick of a colony's value, as seen in the major criterion for determining compensation to colonies (value of exports to Britain), showed unmistakenly why the Bahamas had little clout. Realizing the tide had turned against them, West Indian planters wisely submitted to the inevitable and accepted compulsory emancipation. In short, they took the compensation offered and acquiesced.

Keeping slaves under control posed a greater problem in the Bahamas than getting the assembly to pass an acceptable manumission act. Understanding that misconstrued rumors concerning the Manumission Act (1833) could cause major problems, in July 1833 Lieutenant Governor Balfour addressed slaves in the Bahamas, telling them that Parliament had passed a law freeing slaves but that they would become apprentices for some years to their masters, for whom they would be required to work a certain number of hours daily. He also told them when the apprenticeship would begin and that its duration had not yet been determined. Slaves were admonished to shun rumors concerning manumission.[56] The address effectively filled the void between Parliament's action and the convocation of the assembly to legislate on emancipation.

Bahamian lawmakers did not hesitate nor engage in acrimonious debate over emancipation. In fact, emancipation went more smoothly in the Bahamas than elsewhere.[57] Responding to Lieutenant Governor Balfour's address to the legislature, the council stated that it would "anxiously bestow [its] utmost attention to the details connected with that great measure [the Manumission Act]."[58] These lawmakers probably saw abolition of slavery on the horizon from the time Parliament abolished the African slave trade

(1807). The legislature passed the Manumission Act on February 15, 1834. Beginning on August 1, 1834, slaves six years old and older would become apprenticed laborers for their last owner until August 1, 1838. Slaves were divided into two categories, praedial and non-praedial. Praedials were basically agricultural workers and non-praedials were workers not directly engaged in agriculture.[59] Although slaves did not become free immediately, perpetual slavery ended immediately because children could no longer be born slaves.

Once the legislature passed the Manumission Act, Bahamian slaveholders became eligible for their share of the twenty million pounds sterling that Parliament had provided to compensate slaveholders in the British West Indies. There were 10,001 slaves (valued at a total of £292,135) and 1,108 slaveholders in the Bahamas.[60] Those slaveholders received £128,296 in total compensation for their slaves; this was considerably less than their £292,135 market value because compensation was based upon the value of the goods the islands exported. Moreover, Bahamian slaveholders received an average of £12.14s.6d. per slave; this was the lowest average of all the nineteen colonies. On the other hand, British Guiana averaged £52 per slave; Trinidad, £50; and Jamaica, £20.[61]

To avoid confusion about the manumission act which the legislature of the Bahamas passed, Lieutenant Governor Balfour explained the difference between a slave and an apprentice to freedmen. He told them that a master may whip a slave, but "he may not dare not strike an apprentice, he [would] be punished." A master could place a slave in the workhouse, but he could not imprison an apprentice. A master had absolute control over a slave's labor, but not over that of an apprentice, who could be worked only five days a week and nine hours each day, except sailors and house servants (non-praedial), who could be worked seven days a week and more than nine hours each day. They were entitled to their freedom, however, after four years, whereas those who worked in the fields (praedial) became entirely free after six years.[62]

The end of perpetual slavery came swiftly once the wheels were set in motion. Parliament used a perceived failure of amelioration as a pretext to impose manumission upon the colonies, but amelioration was not given time to work in the Bahamas. Even Governor Smyth, an acknowledged abolitionist, spoke positively about the assembly's reform acts. The assembly passed most of the amelioration reforms demanded and with far less reluctance than it showed toward the policy of garrisoning British West India regiments in the Bahamas. A slave registry was unnecessary in the

Bahamas; nevertheless, the assembly passed two triennial registration acts that the Governor Grant approved, showing that the acts were crafted to address the issue. Downing Street recommended disallowing the second of these acts but had earlier said that the assembly's opposition to the policy was a thing of the past. So perhaps Downing Street should shoulder some of the responsibility for failure of the Bahamas to craft acceptable legislation on these issues. With abolitionists setting the agenda in the Colonial Office, pleasing it on these issues became difficult.

On August 1, 1834, the day perpetual slavery ended in the Bahama Islands, royal officials in the colony reported that the situation was very tranquil and that freedmen went about their work, with few temporary exceptions stemming from misunderstandings between apprentices and their employers.[63] Abaco Island was quiet, as a missionary walked from one end of the island to the other. Similarly, a missionary on Harbour Island said that there was no excitement on that island. Conversely, troops were sent to restrain insubordinate apprentices on Lord Rolle's plantation on Exuma Island.[64] New Providence Island was more lively than Abaco or Harbour Island, but not disorderly like Exuma. Freedmen there rejoiced and held a festive public demonstration. Hundreds of cattle were slaughtered and roasted, and the townspeople and the government gave hundreds of gallons of molasses with a full supply of bread.[65] Thus, the Bahamas was generally subdued on the manumission day.

Epilogue

No rational person will now question the competency of free persons of colour to exercise their inalienable rights as British subjects, on account of the colour of their skin, or of their servile origin.

—C. R. Nesbitt (1834)

C. R. Nesbitt, author of the introduction to John Boyd's *The Vision and Other Poems,* wrote the above statement in his introduction as he commented on how the three free men of color elected to the assembly in January 1834 ably conducted themselves in that body.[1] Nesbitt was among the minority of white Bahamians who believed that free blacks and persons of color were entitled to be treated similarly to whites. Accordingly, in 1832 he introduced a bill to grant them "all the rights, privileges, immunities, and advantages that they would have been entitled to had they been born of, and descended from, white ancestors."[2] The vote against this measure, three yeas and seventeen nays, probably accurately reflected white Bahamians' feelings concerning race relations.

Fortunately for free blacks, persons of color, and slaves, British leaders dictated which path race relations would take and they sent to the islands Crown officials who generally favored their position on race relations. The Colonial Office, the primary agency for implementing the policy, came under the influence of humanitarians and abolitionists during the years after the American Loyalists arrived in the Bahamas; and the Crown officials sent to the islands pressured the legislature of the Bahamas to pass legislation and accept policies that created a sanguine atmosphere for blacks and coloreds. Neither the Loyalists who came to the islands in 1784 nor the Conchs, whom they met there, held views toward blacks and coloreds that were significantly different from those of whites in the United States. Nevertheless, Loyalists and Conchs would be moved over the next fifty years in a direction that was away from the situation in the American South, indeed in the United States generally, and would become the unwilling architects of a transformed society.

From 1784 to 1834 race relations in the Bahamas became increasingly less hostile than in the American South. The Bahama Islands, for example, did not have antimiscegenation laws and encouraged free blacks and coloreds to educate their children. At times, children of all colors attended school together. The Crown paid a free black man to teach school and trained him to use the Madras (monitorial) System. Moreover, the Crown appointed a freeman of color as clerk of the King's School. The black presence in the Bahamas was further heightened by two practices: (1) garrisoning British West India regiments, sometimes numbering over one thousand, in the Bahamas and (2) enforcing the slave trade ban and settling Africans rescued off slave ships in the islands. These practices, together with others, distinguished race relations in the Bahama Islands from those in the American South even before the amelioration reforms were approved and civil disabilities removed.

The Bahamas may well have been among the leaders in race relations in the British West Indies colonies. Although it was not the first to extend voting privileges to free black and colored males, it was the only colony to implement all the manumission requirements. The presence of a strong independent black and colored church provided leadership opportunities and facilitated marshaling black and colored supporters of Crown officials. Furthermore, slaves generally were treated less cruelly in the Bahamas than in the other British West Indies colonies, and the Bahamas had less racial strife than those colonies.

However much white Bahamians may have opposed the race relations measures of the British government, they usually protested in legitimate forums and acted within the law once the measures went into effect. However much free blacks and persons of color chafed under discriminatory civil disabilities, they did not foment civil strife. However much slaves hated servitude, their trust in the Crown was not shaken. In the end, remarkably, there were no slave rebellions or white lynch mobs in the Bahamas. So at the same time that credit is due to British officials for setting a high moral tone on race relations, credit is also due to Bahamians—black, brown, and white—for keeping the peace as the islands moved toward a second turning point within a span of fifty years. In 1784, the American Loyalists introduced plantation slavery in the Bahamas, a turning point in Bahamian history. In 1834, three men of color joined their white brethren in the House of Assembly, heralding the attainment of full political rights for free blacks and persons of color, and 10,001 slaves stood poised to embark upon the preliminary phase of the Manumission Act, which would eventually result in their freedom, marking yet another turning point. The Bahamas, with strong urging from the Colonial Office, thus was transformed nonviolently from a slave to a free society.

Notes

INTRODUCTION

1. D. Gail Saunders, *Slavery in the Bahamas, 1648–1838* (Nassau, 1985), 122.

2. B. W. Higman, *Slave Populations of the British Caribbean, 1807–1834* (Baltimore, 1984), 317–19.

3. Paul Albury, *The Story of the Bahamas* (London, 1975), 123. Jamaica received $6, 220,000. Moreover, slaveholders in Guiana and Trinidad received $52 and $50 per slave, respectively, whereas those in the Bahamas received £12:14s.6d.

4. Michael Craton and Gail Saunders, *Islanders in the Stream: A History of the Bahamian People* 2vols. (Athens, Georgia, 1992–1998); A. Deans Peggs, *A Short History of the Bahamas* (Nassau, Bahamas, 1959); Michael Craton, *A History of the Bahamas* (London, 1962); Paul Albury, *The Story of the Bahamas;* Howard Johnson, *The Bahamas from Slavery to Servitude, 1783–1933* (Gainesville, 1996).

5. James H. Stark, *Stark's History and Guide to the Bahama Islands* (Boston, Massachusetts, 1891), 51; James Stuart Murray Anderson, *The History of the Church of England in the Colonies and Foreign Dependencies* (London, 1845), vol. 1, appendix 3; Peggs, *A History of the Bahamas,* 7.

6. Albury, *The Story of the Bahamas,* 123.

7. Arnold Talbot Bethell, *The Early Settlers of the Bahamas and Colonists of North America,* 3rd. ed. (Norfolk, England, 1937), 83; Albury, *The Story of the Bahamas,* 123.

8. Daniel McKinnen, *A Tour through the British West Indies in the Years 1802 and 1803, Giving a Particular Account of the Bahama Islands* (London, 1804), 235–36; Peggs, *A Short History of the Bahamas,* 7.

9. McKinnen, *A Tour through the British West Indies,* 235–36.

10. Stark, *Stark's History and Guide to the Bahamas,* 130–31; James M. Wright, "History of the Bahama Islands, with a Special Study of the Abolition of Slavery in the Colony," in *The Bahama Islands,* ed. George Burbank Shattuck (Baltimore, Maryland, 1905), 422.

11. "Queries to Captain Phenny Governor of the Bahama Islands, 1723," Colonial Office Papers, Department of Archives, Nassau, Bahamas (hereafter referred to as C.O.), 23/13/98.

12. H. Johnson, *The Bahamas from Slavery to Servitude, 1783–1933* (Gainesville, 1996), 8.

13. Colbert Williams, *The Methodist Contribution to Education in the Bahamas* (Glouster, England, 1782), 24.

14. C.O., 23/22/59

15. C.O., 23/22/59

16. C.O., 23/23/28.

17. C.O., 23/23/28.

18. C.O., 23/23/28.

19. C.O., 23/16/6; C.O., 23/23/28.

20. C.O., 23/10/198; C. F. Pascoe, *Two Hundred Years of The S.P.G.: An Historical Account of the Society for the Propagation of the Gospel in Foreign Parts, 1701–1900* (London, 1901), 219.

21. C.O., 23/24/78.

22. Sandra Riley, *Homeward Bound: A History of the Bahama Islands to 1850, with a Definitive Study of Abaco in the American Loyalist Plantation Period* (Miami, Florida, 1983), 104.

23. Joseph Byrne Lockey, ed., *East Florida, 1783–1785: A File of Documents Assembled, and Many of Them Translated* (Berkeley, 1949), 99, 210.

24. Ibid., 178–79.

25. C.O., 23/26/26.

26. Thelma Peters, "The Loyalists Migration from East Florida to the Bahama Islands," *Florida Historical Quarterly* 40 (October, 1961): 128.

27. Peters, "The Loyalists Migration from East Florida," 137; Peggs, *A Short History of the Bahamas,* 16–17.

28. Lockey, *East Florida, 1783–1785,* 23.

29. Mary Beth Norton, "The Fate of Some Black Loyalists of the American Revolution," *Journal of Negro History* 58, no. 4 (October, 1973): 411.

30. C.O., 23/29/191; Pascoe, *Two Hundred Years of the S.P.G.,* 221.

31. C.O., 23/29/189.

CHAPTER I: POLITICS AND ECONOMICS IN THE COTTON KINGDOM, 1784-1815

1. Higman, *Slave Populations of the British Caribbean,* 43.
2. Williams, *The Methodist Contribution to Education in the Bahamas,* 24.
3. C.O., 23/34/273
4. Craton and Saunders, *Islanders in the Stream,* 154.
5. Ibid.

6. Message of Governor John Maxwell to the Assembly May 10, 1784, C.O., 23/25/195.

7. Lockey, *East Florida, 1783–1785*, 287–88.

8. Wilbert Siebert, "The Legacy of the American Revolution to the British West Indies and Bahamas," *Ohio State University Bulletin* 27 (April, 1913): 25–26.

9. C.O., 23/25/197.

10. Thelma Peters, "The American Loyalists in the Bahama Islands: Who They Were," *Florida Historical Quarterly* 40 (January, 1962): 231–32.

11. Lockey, *East Florida, 1783–1785*, 287–88.

12. Ibid., 746–47.

13. C.O., 23/25/381.

14. At the Council Chamber Whitehall, April 26, 1787, Liverpool Papers, vol. 201, British Museum, London, England.

15. C.O., 23/27/75; C.O., 23/27/78; C.O., 23/28/149.

16. C.O., 23/34/273.

17. The Assembly discussed providing aid to Joseph Eve, who had built a cotton gin on his plantation on Cat Island, and Lord Dunmore did not voice an objection to this effort. The substance of the proposal will be discussed later in this chapter.

18. C.O., 23/32/121.

19. The Humble Address of the General Assembly, 1793 Session, C.O., 23/32/20; Address of Lord Dunmore to the Assembly, 1793 Session, C.O., 23/32/209; C.O., 23/32/163.

20. See Martin Ros, *Night of Fire: The Black Napoleon and the Battle for Haiti*, trans. Karin Ford-Treep (New York, 1994).

21. Craton and Saunders, *Islanders in the Stream*, 1: 202–3.

22. C.O., 23/34/117; George Chalmers to John Wells, April 8, 1797, Correspondence of George Chalmers, vol. 1, 1787–1798, British Museum, London, England; George Chalmers to Committee of Correspondence, April 8, 1797, ibid.

23. George Chalmers to Thomas Roker, April 22, 1797, Correspondence of George Chalmers.

24. C.O., 32/35/92.

25. C.O., 23/35/89.

26. C.O., 23/36/69.

27. C.O., 23/28/31.

28. Consolidated Slave Act of 1797, Laws of the Bahamas (ms. duplicate), December 11, 1795–November 23, 1798, Department of Archives, Nassau, Bahamas.

29. C.O., 23/39/2; C.O., 23/39/144; William to John King, February 1, 1801, C.O., 23/40/9.

30. Robert Hunt to Lord Hobart, January 30, 1802, C.O., 23/41/81.

31. James Halkett to Lord Hobart, September 12, 1802, C.O., 23/42/13.

32. C.O., 23/46/117.

33. C.O., 23/46/116.

34. C.O., 23/44/74.; C.O., 23/45/15; C.O., 23/45/16.

35. H. M. Dyer to Lord Hobart, June 2, 1804, C.O., 23/45/130; Earl of Camden to H. M. Dyer, February 9, 1805, C.O., 23/46/40.

36. H. M. Dyer to Lord Camden, September 26, 1804, C.O., 23/46/39.

37. William Vesey Munnings to Lord Castlereagh, November 14, 1808, C.O., 23/55/1; William Windham to Charles Cameron, February 7, 1807, C.O., 23/50/107; Charles Cameron to William Windham, May 11, 1807, C.O., 23/51/105; Charles Cameron to Edward Poole, January 7, 1808, C.O., 23/53/1.

38. Benjamin Moodie to John Forbes, June 14, 1812, C.O., 23/59/62.

39. William Vesey Munnings to Lord Liverpool, September 14, 1812, C.O., 23/59/70.

40. William Vesey Munnings to Lord Bathurst, December 5, 1812, C.O., 23/59/81.

41. Charles Cameron to Lord Bathurst, December 15, 1812, C.O., 23/59/95.

42. Ibid.

43. Charles Cameron to Lord Bathurst, March 28, 1814, C.O., 23/60/61.

44. Charles Cameron to Lord Bathurst, May 30, 1814, C.O., 23/60/73.

45. Charles Cameron to Lord Bathurst, July 8, 1815, C.O., 23/62/65.

46. C.O., 23/63/24.

47. C.O., 23/63/25.

48. C.O., 23/63/22.

49. Edward Brathwaite, *The Development of Creole Society in Jamaica, 1770–1820* (Oxford, 1971), 170; Mavis Christine Campbell, *The Dynamics of Change in a Slave Society: A Sociopolitical History of the Free Coloreds of Jamaica, 1800–1865* (Rutherford, New Jersey, 1976), 72–73.

50. C.O., 23/54/265; C.O., 23/54/269.

51. C.O., 23/60/20; C.O., 23/60/44; C.O., 23/60/49.

52. C.O., 23/61/107; C.O., 23/61/108

53. C.O., 23/61/108.

54. C.O., 23/61/106; C.O., 23/61/183; C.O., 23/62/4.

55. McKinnen, *A Tour through the British West Indies,* 223.

56. C.O., 23/35/127.

57. Anthony Thompson, *An Economic History of the Bahamas,* (Nassau, Bahamas, 1979), 6–7.

58. Peters, "American Loyalists in the Bahama Islands," 226.

59. Lockey, *East Florida, 1783–1785,* 161.

60. Siebert, "Legacy of the American Revolution to the British West Indies," 18–19.

61. C.O., 23/45/67.

62. William Robertson to the Reverend Dr. Morice, October 6, 1791, Harbour Island, "State of the Population, ect. of the Bahama Islands in June, 1788 . . . ," C.O., 23/29/195. William Robertson, a S.P.G. missionary on Harbour Island, described the old inhabitants as "very ignorant people," whom the governor and council tried to protect from the oppressive new inhabitants, who despised them.

63. Extracts from the Minutes of Council of the 15th and 23rd of July, 1790, C.O., 23/30/238.

64. Howard Johnson, *The Bahamas in Slavery and Freedom,* (Kingston, Jamaica), vi, 2.

65. *A Short Journey in the West Indies in Which Are Interspersed Curious Anecdotes and Characters,* vol. 1 (London, 1790), 119.

66. C.O., 23/26/26.

67. C.O., 23/25/305.

68. C.O., 23/28/31.

68. C.O., 23/16/185.

70. Ibid.

71. McKinnen, *A Tour through the British West Indies,* 216.

72. James Halkett to Lord Hobart, September 12, 1802, C.O., 23/42/13.

73. C.O., 23/25/305.

74. Observations of the Bahama Islands, C.O., 23/31/278.

75. Earl of Dunmore to George Chalmers, December 16, 1793, Correspondence of George Chalmers.

76. Thompson, *An Economic History of the Bahamas,* 11.

77. McKinnen, *A Tour through the British West Indies,* 182; D. Gail Saunders, *Bahamian Loyalists and Their Slaves* (London, 1983), 36–37.

78. William Wylly, *A Short Account of the Bahama Islands* (London, 1789), 3. This work is printed in the Colonial Office Papers. C.O., 23/29/191.

79. H. Johnson, *The Bahamas from Slavery to Servitude,* 8.

80. C.O., 23/18/1.

81. C.O., 23/39/260.

82. C.O., 23/25/329.

83. C.O., 23/25/372

84. *Bahama Gazette,* June 20, 1789.

85. *Bahama Gazette,* October 24, 1789.

86. C.O., 23/28/95.

87. The Humble Petition of the Council and General Assembly of the Bahama Islands, C.O., 23/29/171; C.O., 23/29/167.

88. Report of the Committee to Take into Consideration the State of the Bahama Islands, C.O., 23/29/172.

89. C.O., 23/28/105.

90. D. G. Saunders, *Bahamian Loyalists,* 39; Peters, "The American Loyalists in the Bahama Islands," 237. Patricia E. Krueger, a descendant of Eve's brother and an acknowledged family genealogist, said that Eve's mother was kicked out the Quakers for marrying out of the faith and Joseph Eve was not a Quaker, contrary to popular belief.

91. Observations of the Bahama Islands, C.O., 23/31/278.

92. C.O., 23/34/189; C.O., 23/34/207; C.O., 23/34/223.

93. Peters, "The American Loyalists in the Bahama Islands," 238.

94. Bryan Edwards, *The History Civil and Commercial of the British Colonies of The West Indies,* vol. 2 (London, 1793), 277.

95. Peter Edwards to George Chalmers, January 27, 1798, Correspondence of George Chalmers. Chalmers was the colonial agent for the Bahamas, and Edwards was one of the leading cotton growers.

96. C.O., 23/34/327.

97. Peter Edwards to George Chalmers, January 27, 1798, Correspondence of George Chalmers.

98. Minutes of the Council in Assembly, November 24, 1797, C.O., 23/37/90.

99. Rosita Forbes, *A Unicorn in the Bahamas* (New York, 1940), 72–73; Albury, *The Story of the Bahamas,* 115–17.

100. C.O., 23/38/139.

101. C.O., 23/39/140; C.O., 12/39/142.

102. C.O., 23/39/260.

103. Ibid.

104. Ibid.

105. Ibid.

106. C.O., 23/39/157.

107. Bahama Agriculture Society, *Rules of the Bahama Agriculture Society* (Nassau, Bahamas, 1801), 3.

108. Bahama Agriculture Society, *Different Subjects Addressed to the Bahama Agriculture Society* (Nassau, Bahamas, 1802), 4.

109. Ibid., 5–6.

110. Henry Campbell Wilkinson, *Bermuda from Sail to Steam: The History of the Island from 1784 to 1901*, vol. 1 (London, 1973), 28.

111. C.O., 23/44/10.

112. C.O., 23/44/182

113. C.O., 23/45/67.

114. Peggs, *A Short History of the Bahamas*, 18; Bonham C. Richardson, *Caribbean Migrants: Environment and Human Survival on St. Kitts and Nevis* (Knoxville, Tennessee, 1983), 76.

115. C.O., 23/66/78.

116. Higman, *Slave Populations of the British Caribbean*, 65; H. Johnson, *The Bahamas in Slavery and Freedom*, 34; D. G. Saunders, *Bahamian Loyalists*, 40–44; Albury, *The Story of the Bahamas*, 115–17.

117. H. Johnson, *The Bahamas in Slavery and Freedom*, 17.

118. Ibid., C.O., 23/46/127; C.O., 23/63/20.

119. H. Johnson, *The Bahamas from Slavery to Servitude*, 15.

120. Higman, *Slave Populations of the British Caribbean*, 180.

121. *Letters from the Bahama Islands Written 1823–4* (Philadelphia, 1827), 81–82; Johann David Schoepf, *Travels in the Confederation, 1783–1784*, vol. 2, trans. and ed. Alfred J. Morrison (Baltimore: Lord Baltimore Press, 1911), 301; William Matthieson, *British Slavery and Its Abolition, 1828–1838* (London, 1926), 77–78; Craton, *A History of the Bahamas*, 196; Albury, *The Story of the Bahamas*, 126; Peggs, *A Short History of the Bahamas*, 20; William L. Burns, *Emancipation and Apprenticeship in the British West Indies* (London, 1937), 71 n.

122. Eric E. Williams, *From Columbus to Castro: The History of the Caribbean, 1492–1969* (New York, 1970), 284.

123. Higman, *Slave Populations of the British Caribbean*, 317–19. Higman classifies the following colonies as marginal colonies because they did not produce a major agricultural export staple and "thus they remained marginal to the imperial plantation economy": Anguilla, the Bahamas, Barbuda, British Honduras, and the Cayman Islands, ibid., 43.

124. Richard Sheridan, *Doctors and Slaves: A Medical and Demographic History of Slavery in the British West Indies, 1680–1834* (New York, 1985), 169–71; James Stephen, *Slavery and the British West India Colonies Delineated*, vol. 1 (London, 1824), 465.

125. E. Williams, *From Columbus to Castro*, 284.

126. For an extensive discussion of the self-hire system, see H. Johnson, *The Bahamas in Slavery and Freedom*, 1–14.

127. H. Johnson, *The Bahamas in Slavery and Freedom,* 4; Schoepf, *Travels in the Confederation,* 2: 301. For an in-depth discussion of self-hire, see H. Johnson, *The Bahamas from Slavery to Servitude,* 33–46.

128. Schoepf, *Travels in the Confederation,* II, 301.

129. C.O., 23/46/127.

130. C.O., 23/63/20.

131. C.O., 23/30/216.

132. C.O., 23/30/173

133. List of Plantations Under Cultivation on Crooked Island, C.O., 23/31/228.

134. Plan of the Town of Nassau Virons, Island of New Providence, Surveyed by Order to the General Assembly, 1788, Department of Archives, Nassau, Bahamas.

135. C.O., 23/43/188.

136. Bethell, *The Early Settlers of the Bahama Islands,* 107–8.

137. Riley, *Homeward Bound,* 192.

138. Will of Betty Watkins, March 18, 1803, Department of Archives, Nassau, Bahamas.

139. Will of John Williams, January 20, 1818, Department of Archives, Nassau, Bahamas.

140. Will of John Simms, Black man, October, 1809, Department of Archives, Nassau, Bahamas.

141. Christ Church Record of Baptisms and Marriages, 1753–1805, 21 October; 1733–1843, Department of Archives, Nassau, Bahamas.

142. Ibid.

143. C.O., 23/67/237; C.O., 23/66/197; C.O., 23/66/203.

144. Christ Church Record of Baptisms and Marriages; H. Johnson, *The Bahamas from Slavery to Servitude,* 43–44. Johnson mentions that the slave ran away and reneged on his contract to pay Cox each week; this led to the colored slaveholder offering $20 for his capture and return.

145. C.O., 23/29/189.

146. C.O., 23/63/20; C.O., 23/63/21.

147. C.O., 23/66/78; C.O., 23/62/20; Higman, *Slave Populations of the British Caribbean,* 175.

148. C.O., 23/66/78 ; C.O., 23/41/116.

149. C.O., 23/35/148; C.O., 23/37/56.

150. *Lucayan Royal Herald and Weekly Advertiser,* August 19, 1789.

CHAPTER II: BLACKS AND COLOREDS: THE SOCIETY THEY CREATED, 1784-1815

1. Winthrop D. Jordan, "American Chiaroscuro: The Status and Definition of Mulattoes in the British Colonies," *William and Mary Quarterly* 3rd ser, 19, no. 2 (April, 1962): 195–97.

2. My late mother told me years ago that her grandmother's mother was an African who did not speak English and my father's brother (who is now ninety-nine years old) told me the same thing about his grandfather, a man named Cuffee, but I did not get the connection until I went to the Bahamas to undertake research for this study. Neither my mother nor my uncle referred to their great-grandparents as liberated Africans.

3. "Sketch of a Report... [1790]," the Bahamas, Official Papers of the First Earl of Liverpool, 1790–July 1791, vol. 161, 217–26, British Museum, London, England; C. F. Pascoe, *Two Hundred Years of the S.P.G.: An Historical Account of the Society for the Propagation of the Gospel in Foreign Parts... 1701–1900*, vol. 1 (London, 1901), 221.

4. C.O., 23/29/172.

5. C.O., 23/29/191.

6. Pascoe, *Two Hundred Years of the S.P.G.*, 1: 220.

7. C.O., 23/30/334.

8. McKinnen, *A Tour through the British West Indies*, 232.

9. C.O., 23/40/129.

10. C.O., 23/47/51.

11. Ibid..

12. Whittington B. Johnson, *Black Savannah, 1788–1864* (Fayetteville, Arkansas, 1996), 123.

13. C.O., 23/59/37.

14. Ibid.

15. Blacks composed 31 percent of the free African-American population in Savannah, 25 percent in Charleston, 24 percent in New Orleans, and 9.3 percent in Mobile County, Alabama. U.S. Bureau of the Census, *Preliminary Report on the Eighth Census, 1860*. This is the first census that separates free African Americans by color.

16. Brathwaite, *The Development of Creole Society in Jamaica*, 168.

17. Charles H. Wesley, "The Emancipation of the Free Coloured Population in the British Empire," *Journal of Negro History* 19, no. 2 (April, 1934): 139–40. Another estimate placed the number of free persons of color at 28, 800; see Gad J. Heuman, *Between Black and White: Race, Politics and the Free Coloreds in Jamaica, 1792–1865* (Westport, Connecticut, 1981), 7.

18. Jerome S. Handler, *The Unappropriated People: Freedmen in the Slave Society of Barbados* (Baltimore, 1974), 21.

19. C.O., 23/59/37.

20. Randall Miller and John David Smith, eds., *Dictionary of Afro-American Slavery* (Westport, Connecticut, 1988), 430–32.

21. C.O., 23/48/146.

22. C.O., 23/48/144.

23. C.O., 23/59/37.

24. Commonwealth of the Bahamas, *Aspects of Slavery: A Booklet to Commemorate the 150th Anniversary of the Abolition of Slav*ery, part 2 (Nassau, Bahamas, 1984), 12.

25. C.O., 23/29/282.

26. Ibid.

27. C.O., 23/29/279.

28. Register of Freed Slaves, 18th and 19th Century, Department of Archives, Nassau, Bahamas.

29. C.O., 23/59/40.

30. D. G. Saunders, *Bahamian Loyalists*, 44.

31. John Boyd, *The Vision and Other Poems, in Blank Verse* (London, 1834), iv. Charles Nesbitt, a prominent white Bahamian, wrote the introduction which contains contemporary information concerning race relations.

32. Lowell Joseph Ragatz, *The Fall of the Planter Class in the British Caribbean, 1763–1833* (New York, 1928), 33.

33. C.O., 318/77/71.

34. Christ Church Cathedral, Marriage Register, 1791–1828, Department of Archives, Nassau, Bahamas.

35. For a discussion of this practice, see Willard B. Gatewood Jr. "Aristocrats of Color, South and North: The Black Elite, 1880–1920," *Journal of Southern History* 59, no. 1 (February, 1988): 3–20. The best work on mulattoes in the United States is Joel Williamson, *New People: Miscegenation and Mulattoes in the United States* (New York, 1980).

36. Christ Church Record, Baptisms and Marriages.

37. Ibid.

38. C.O., 23/45/42.

39. Michael C. Symonette and Antonina Canzoneri, *Baptists in the Bahamas: An Historical Review* (El Paso, Texas, 1977), 5; D. G. Saunders, *Bahamian Loyalists,* 63.

40. Minutes of the House of Assembly, December 23, 1803. C.O., 23/45/77.

41. Minutes of the House of Assembly, January 5, 1804. C.O., 23/45/90.

42. Higman, *Slaves Populations of the British Caribbean,* 126–27.

43. Sheridan, *Doctors and Slaves,* 134.

44. Register of Freed Slaves, 18th and 19th Century.

45. Laurie A. Wilkie, "Continuities in African Naming Practices among the Slaves on Wade's Green Plantation, North Caico," *Journal of the Bahamas Historical Society* 15, no. 1 (October, 1993): 32–37.

46. Winthrop D. Jordan, *White over Black: American Attitudes toward the Negro, 1550–1812* (New York, 1968), 3–43. This chapter, entitled "First Impressions," discusses the English formation of prejudices against Africans and how these were later translated into negativisms toward blackness.

47. Sheridan, *Doctors and Slaves,* 172.

48. Keith Gordon Wisdom, "Bahamian Junkanoo: An Act in Modern Social Drama" (Ph.D. diss., University of Georgia, 1985), 15–16, 27; Edward Clement Bethel, "Music in the Bahamas: Its Roots, Development and Personality" (masters thesis, Universtiy of California, Los Angeles, 1978), 203–4.

49. Gerald Hausman and Kelvin Rodriques, *African-American Alphabet: A Celebration of African-American and West Indian Culture, Custom, Myth, and Symbol* (New York, 1996), 91–92. The term *Gombey* is used in Bermuda. See Frank E. Manning, *Black Clubs in Bermuda: Ethnography of a Play World* (Ithaca, 1973), 154–55.

50. *Aspects of Slavery,* 2: 50.

51. Samuel Johnson and O. Johnson, *The History of the Yorubas: From the Earliest Times to the Beginning of the British Protectorate* (Westport, Connecticut, 1970), 119.

52. Whittington B. Johnson, *The Promising Years, 1750–1830: The Emergence of Black Labor and Business* (New York, 1993), 8, 187; *Aspects of Slavery,* 2: 3.

53. Bethel, "Music in the Bahamas," 91, 123.

54. Sheridan, *Doctors and Slaves,* 77.

55. *Aspects of Slavery,* 2: 50.

56. Sheridan, *Doctors and Slaves,* 78.

57. Edwards, *The History Civil and Commercial of the British Colonies,* 88.

58. Riley, *Homeward Bound,* 140; D. G. Saunders, *Bahamian Loyalists,* 60–63.

59. C. Williams, *The Methodist Contribution to Education in the Bahamas,* 47–48; Riley, *Homeward Bound,* 140.

60. C. Williams, *The Methodist Contribution to Education in the Bahamas,* 47–48.

61. John Richards to Philip Lyttle, Nassau, May 14, 1802, Letters of John Richards, 1796–1802, Bray/Bahamas Collection, F2 , Rhodes House Library, Oxford University, Oxford, England.

62. John Stephen to William Parker, Nassau, New Providence, February 10, 1810, Letters of Reverend Dr. John Stephen, 1810–1816, Bray/Bahamas Collection, F5.

63. Richard Roberts to G. A. Hatch, New Providence, October 9, 1806, Letters of Richard Roberts, 1805–1808, Bray/Bahamas Collection, F4.

64. Thomas Coke, *A History of the West Indies Containing the Natural, Civil, and Ecclesiastical History of Each Island,* vol. 3 (London, 1811), 207.

65. C. Williams, *The Methodist Contribution to Education in the Bahamas,* 48; *Aspects of Slavery,* 1: 15; Pascoe, *Two Hundred Years of the S.P.G.,* 1: 223.

66. John Stephen to William Parker, Nassau, New Providence, August 22, 1811.

67. Ibid., March 18, 1812.

68. Ibid., August 27, 1813.

69. Ibid., January 26, 1814; John Stephen to Samuel Wix, Nassau, New Providence, March 30, 1815.

70. John Stephen to William Parker, Nassau, New Providence, January 26, 1814; John Stephen to Samuel Wix, Nassau, New Providence, March 30, 1815; Saunders, *Bahamian Loyalist and Their Slaves,* 59.

71. C.O., 23/63/25; see also C.O., 23/63/24; C.O., 23/63/29; C.O., 23/63/22; C.O., 23/63/23.

72. C.O., 23/63/26.

73. For a discussion on American education, see Lawrence A. Cremin, *American Education: The National Experience, 1783–1876* (New York, 1980).

74. Handler, *The Unappropriated People,* 173, 178, 180; Edward L. Cox, *Free Coloreds in the Slave Societies of St. Kitts and Grenada, 1763–1833* (Knoxville, Tennessee, 1984), 124–31.

75. *Barron v. Baltimore* (1833). In this case, the Supreme Court affirmed that the Bill of Rights was intended to apply to the national government. Chief Justice John Marshall wrote the decision. See Melvin I. Urofsky, *Documents of American Constitution and Legal History* (New York, 1988), 261–64.

76. *Aspects of Slavery,* 2: 16.

77. Johnson, *Black Savannah,* 8.

78. John Rippon, ed., *The Baptist Annual Register, 1790–1793* (London, n.d.), 437.

79. F. A. Cox, *History of the Baptist Missionary Society from 1792 to 1842,* 2 vols. (London, 1842), 2: 12.

80. Rippon, *The Baptist Annual Register,* 437; Albert J. Raboteau, *Slave Religion: The "Invisible Institution" in the Antebellum South* (New York, 1980), 139–40.

81. Rippon, *The Baptist Annual Register,* 541; F. Cox, *History of the Baptist Missinary Society,* 262.

82. Crosbie Garstin, *Samuel Kelly: An Eighteenth Century Seaman* (New York, 1925), 115.

83. John Asplund, ed., *The Universal Annual Register of the Baptist Denomination, in North America, for the Years 1794 and 1795* (Hanover, New Hampshire, 1796), 87; Sylvia Frey and Betty Wood, *Come Shouting to Zion: African American Protestantism in the American South and British Caribbean to 1830* (Chapel Hill, 1998), 131. Citing Asplund, Frey and Wood say that the church was established in 1788, but Asplund does not give a date for its establishment.

84. Rippon, *The Baptist Annual Register,* 336.

85. John Asplund, *The Universal Register of the Baptist Denomination in North America for the Years 1790, 1791, 1792, 1793 and Part of 1794* (Boston, 1794), 87.

86. *Bahama Gazette,* July 23–30, 1785.

87. D. G. Saunders, *Bahamian Loyalists and Their Slaves,* 63–64.

88. James Stephen to Horace Leviss, April 14, 1829. C.O., 23/81/251.

89. *Bahama Gazette,* July 23–30, 1785.

90. Symonette and Canzoneri, *Baptists in the Bahamas,* 11–18.

91. Johnson, *Black Savannah,* 28–31.

92. Raboteau, *Slave Religion.*

93. C.O., 23/81/316.

94. C.O., 23/28/31.

95. D. G. Saunders, *Bahamian Loyalists,* 63–64.

96. Pascoe, *Two Hundred Years of the S.P.G,* 223.

97. Mrs. ——— Smith's Journal, March 17, 1793, Duke University Library, Durham, North Carolina.

98. D. G. Saunders, *Bahamian Loyalists,* 60–63.

99. Methodist Church, Jamaica District, *Forever Beginning: Two Hundred Years of Methodism in the Wesleyan Area* (Kingston, Jamaica, 1960), 15.

100. Pascoe, *Two Hundred Years of the S.P.G.,* I, 222.

101. Coke, *A History of the West Indies,* 200–202; Williams, *The Methodist Contribution to Education in the Bahamas,* 35.

102. John Stephen to William Parker, Nassau, New Providence, April 24, 1810.

103. John Stephen to William Parker, Nassau, New Providence, August 27, 1813; ibid., January 26, 1814.

104. Williams, *The Methodist Contribution to Education in the Bahamas,* 36.

105. *Instructions for Missionaries to the West India Islands* (London, 1795), 3–12.

106. Williams, *The Methodist Contribution to Education in the Bahamas,* 35. Williams says Turton was white but two other sources contradict this: D. G. Saunders, *Bahamian Loyalists*, 63; and Symonette and Canzoneri, *Baptists in theBahamas,* 5. According to those sources, Turton was a mulatto.

107. Coke, *A History of the West Indies,* 28, 202.

108. Ibid., 202–4.

109. Dean Peggs, ed., *A Mission to the West India Islands: Dowson's Journal for 1810–1817* (Nassau, Bahamas, 1960), 62, 64.

110. Peggs, *Dowson's Journal,* 56–57.

111. Ibid., 61; D. G. Saunders, *Bahamian Loyalists,* 34.

112. C.O., 23/59/39.

CHAPTER III: RACE RELATIONS IN AN AGE OF TRANSITION, 1784–1815

1. Ragatz, *The Fall of the Planter Class,* 33.
2. Presentment of the Grand Jury, C.O., 23/29/189.
3. Wylly, *A Short Account of the Bahama Islands,* found in C.O., 23/29/191ff.
4. "Most Secret and Confidential," C.O., 23/28/149.
5. Journal of the General Assembly of the Bahama Islands: Commencing the 5th February and Ending the 26th June 1789, C.O., 23/30/17.
6. C.O., 23/27/75.
7. Wylly, *A Short Account of the Bahama Islands,* C.O., 23/29/191ff.
8. C.O., 23/36/104; C.O., 23/36/119.
9. C.O., .23/36/119.
10. C.O., 23/36/108.
11. C.O., 23/36/108.
12. C.O., 23/36/117.
13. Journal of the Legislative Council, November 21, 1797, C.O., 23/37/75.
14. Christ Church Record, Baptism and Marriages.
15. Ward, *British West Indian Slavery,* 210–11.
16. Sheridan, *Doctors and Slaves,* 115–16.
17. C.O., 23/35/127.
18. C.O., 23/35/127.
19. C.O., 23/40/35.
20. "Memorial of Moses Franks," C.O., 23/46/127.
21. Ibid.
22. H. M. Dyer to Lord Hobart, July 20, 1804, C.O., 23/45/156.
23. Ragatz, *The Fall of the Planter Class,* 32.
24. Ibid.; Roger Norman Buckley, *Slaves in Red Coats: The British West India Regiments, 1795–1815* (New Haven, 1979), 3–4.
25. Peter Edwards to George Chalmers, January 27, 1798, Correspondence of George Chalmers.
26. Governor William Dowdeswell to George Chalmers, November 5, 1800, Correspondence of George Chalmers.
27. Duke of Portland to Governor Dowdeswell, January 6, 1801, C.O., 23/40/3.
28. "Memorial of Moses Franks," C.O., 23/46/127.
29. C.O., 23/46/21.
30. Buckley, *Slaves in Red Coats,* 2–3.
31. Ibid., 12–13.
32. Ibid., 65, 78.
33. Ibid., 67, 69.
34. "Memorial of Moses Franks," C.O., 23/46/127.
35. C.O., 23/39/134.
36. C.O., 23/40/116.
37. Robert Hunt to Lord Portland, May 9, 1801, C.O., 23/39/132.
38. Ibid.
39. C.O., 23/40/33.

40. Robert Hunt to Lord Portland, June 13, 1801, C.O., 23/40/32.

41. (Major) James Cuming to Governor Dowdeswell, June 29, 1801, C.O., 23/40/188.

42. C.O., 23/40/30.

43. C.O., 23/40/58.

44. John Halkett to Lord Hobart, September 12, 1802, C.O., 23/42/13.

45. Lord Hobart to Governor Halkett, January 6, 1803, C.O., 23/42/123.

46. John Halkett to Lord Hobart, April 20, 1803, C.O., 23/43/145.

47. Ibid.

48. John Halkett to Lord Hobart, April 24, 1803, C.O., 23/43/147.

49. John Halkett to Lord Hobart, April 27, 1803, C.O., 23/43/163.

50. John Halkett to Lord Hobart, October 15, 1803, C.O., 23/44/60.

51. C.O., 23/47/79.

52. C.O., 23/51/95.

53. C.O., 23/51/96.

54. Charles Cameron to William Windham, May 11, 1807, C.O., 23/51/94.

55. C.O., 23/51/99.

56. Ros, *Night of Fire,* 21.

57. Charles Cameron to Edward Poole, January 7, 1808, C.O., 23/53/1.

58. Charles Cameron to Edward Cooke, June 13, 1808, C.O., 23/54/1.

59. C.O., 23/39/132; C.O., 23/44/60; C.O., 23/56/3; C.O., 23/56/74. These documents have information on troop arrival, departure, size of the units, and the former and future duty station, for those units entering and leaving the colony, respectively.

60. (Commandant) Alexander Maclean to Governor Cameron, June 19, 1806, C.O., 23/52/146; Charles Cameron to William Windham, December 13, 1806, C.O., 23/50/120.

61. C.O., 23/54/292; Charles Cameron to Edward Cooke, October 11, 1808, C.O., 23/54/290.

62. H. C. Darling to Governor Charles Cameron, July 23, 1806, C.O., 23/50/14.

63. Buckley, *Slaves in Red Coats,* 140–41.

64. David Brion Davis, *The Problem of Slavery in the Age of Revolution, 1770–1823* (Ithaca, New York, 1975), 218.

65. *The Interference of the British Legislature in the Internal Concerns of the West Indies Respecting Their Slaves Deprecated* (London, 1816), 2–3.

66. Dale H. Porter, *The Abolition of the Slave Trade in England 1784–1807* (Hamden, Connecticut, 1970), 15, 143.

67. William Mathieson, *British Slavery and Its Abolition, 1823–1838* (London, 1926), 20.

68. David Northrup, *The Atlantic Slave Trade* (Lexington, Massachusetts, 1994), xv.

69. George Chalmers to the Committee of Corespondence, Office of Trade Whitehall, April 8, 1797, Correspondence of George Chalmers.

70. Extracts from Two Letters of the Colonial Agent Mr. G. Chalmers to the Commissioners of Correspondence at New Providence, C.O., 23/53/85.

71. Davis, *The Problems of Slavery in the Age of Revolution,* 115–16.

72. Mathieson, *British Slavery and Its Abolition,* 20.

73. Averil MacKenzie-Grieve, *The Last Years of the English Slave Trade: Liverpool 1750–1807* (London, 1968), 283; John H. Parry and Philip M. Sherlock, *A Short History of the West Indies* (New York, 1968), 80–81.

74. Charles Cameron to Lord Castlereagh, March 8, 1808 C.O., 23/53/81; C.O., 23/53/50.

75. Charles Cameron to Lord Castlereagh, July 18, 1808, C.O., 23/54/7.

76. C.O., 23/58/35; Forbes, *A Unicorn in the Bahamas*, 74–75.

77. C.O., 23/58/35.

78. C.O., 23/58/63.

79. Humble Petition of the Legislative Council and the House of Assembly of Your Majesty's Bahama Islands . . . , C.O., 23/58/76.

80. C.O., 23/58/79.

CHAPTER IV: CONFRONTATION AND ADVANCEMENT: ECONOMICS AND POLITICS, 1816–1834

1. Robert Montgomery Martin, *Statistics of the Colonies of the British Empire* (London, 1839), 108.

2. Craton and Saunders, *Islanders in the Stream*, 1: 221–23.

3. C.O., 23/64/66.

4. C.O., 23/64/71.

5. C.O., 23/64/112.

6. Peters, "Loyalists in the Bahama Islands," 232.

7. C.O., 23/64/72.

8. Ibid.

9. C.O., 23/64/87.

10. C.O., 23/64/72.

11. C.O., 23/64/87.

12. C.O., 23/64/62.

13. Ibid.

14. C.O., 23/64/103.

15. C.O., 23/64/62.

16. C.O., 23/64/18.

17. Ibid.

18. C.O., 23/75/156.

19. D. H. Simpson, ed., *The Debate on Abolition of Slavery, 1823* (London, 1968), 37.

20. C.O., 23/84/107; Laws of the Bahamas, December 22, 1814, to January 23, 1822 (ms. duplicate), Department of Archives, Nassau, Bahamas; Laws of the Bahamas, January 9, 1826, to February 11, 1831 (ms. duplicate), Department of Archives.

21. C.O., 23/72/10.

22. Whittington B. Johnson, "The Amelioration Acts in the Bahamas, 1823–1833: A Middle Ground between Freedom and Antebellum Slave Codes," *Journal of the Bahamas Historical Society* 18 (October, 1996): 25–27.

23. C.O., 23/73/8.

24. C.O., 23/86/18.

25. C.O., 23/84/211.

26. C.O., 23/84/213.
27. *Bahama Argus,* September 3, 1831.
28. C.O., 23/84/218.
29. C.O., 23/84/223.
30. *West Indian Slave-holders' Lust of Cruelty, The Same Now as Ever,* extracted from the *Dublin Morning Post,* July 28, 1830. This work is found in the British Library, call number 1879c.5.(14).
31. C.O., 23/84/256.
32. C.O., 23/84/253.
33. C.O., 23/86/74.
34. C.O., 23/86/68.
35. *Royal Gazette and Bahama Advertiser,* February 4, 1832; *Bahama Argus,* February 8, 1832.
36. C.O., 23/86/147.
37. C.O., 23/86/250; *Royal Gazette and Bahama Advertiser,* June 30, 1832.
38. C.O., 23/86/262; *Royal Gazette and Bahama Advertiser,* November 3, 1832.
39. C.O., 23/91/150.
40. C.O., 23/88/133.
41. *Royal Gazette and Bahama Advertiser,* May 4, 1833; ibid., May 11, 1833.
42. *Royal Gazette and Bahama Advertiser,* June 1, 1833.
43. C.O., 23/88/192.
44. C.O., 23/70/16.
45. Ibid.
46. C.O., 23/63/21.
47. C.O., 23/75/74.
48. Ibid.
49. William Vesey Munnings to Earl of Bathurst, New Providence, April 21, 1827. C.O., 23/76/228.
50. Blue Book of Statistics, 1830. C.O., 27/28/80.
51. Blue Book of Statistics, 1831. C.O., 27/29/115.
52. C.O., 23/80/534; H. Johnson, *The Bahamas in Slavery and Freedom,* 25.
53. Blue Book of Statistics, 1831. C.O., 27/29/115.
54. Craton, *A History of the Bahamas,* 196.
55. Green, *British Slave Emancipation,* 27–28.
56. William L. Burn, *Emancipation and Apprenticeship in the British West Indies* (London, 1937), 71 n.
57. *Letters from the Bahama Islands Written in 1823–4* (Philadelphia, 1827), 81–82.
58. James Carmichael Smyth to Sir George Murray, Government House Bahamas, February 20, 1830. C.O., 23/82/69.
59. B. T. Balfour to Right Honourable E. G. Stanley, Government House Bahamas, August 5, 1833. C.O., 23/89/12.
60. Higman, *Slave Populations of the British Caribbean,* 187.
61. Lewis Grant to R. Wilmot Horton, Bahamas, April 18, 1826. C.O., 23/75/247.
62. C.O., 23/83/234; Paul Farnsworth, "Archaeological Excavations at Promised Plantation New Providence," *Journal of the Bahamas Historical Society* 16, no. 1 (October, 1994): 21–22.

63. D. G. Saunders, *Bahamian Loyalists,* 30.

64. *A Relic of Slavery: Farquharson's Journal for 1831–32,* Copied from the Original by Ormond J. McDonald (1903), (Nassau, Bahamas, 1957), 44–45, 59, 64. The infant, a baby girl, was born in March, 1832.

65. Higman, *Slave Populations of the British Caribbean,* 123.

66. D. G. Saunders, *Bahamian Loyalists,* 19.

67. C.O., 23/64/22; C.O., 23/66/27.

68. Lewis Grant to Earl of Bathurst, Government House, August 1, 1821. C.O., 23/70/51.

69. C.O., 23/72/3.

70. Lewis Grant to Earl of Bathurst, Government House, July 1, 1824.C.O., 23/73/72.

71. Higman, *Slave Populations of the British Caribbean,* 82.

72. David Ellis, "The Traffic in Slaves between the British Indian Colonies, 1807–1833," *Economic History Review* 2nd ser., 25 (1972): 57–58.

73. *Aspects of Slavery,* 2: 20–21.

74. "Report on the State and Condition of the Liberated Africans," C.O., 23/79/4.

75. C.O., 23/80/166; C.O., 23/80/189.

76. Memorandum to Mr. Villiers, C.O., 23/74/188.

77. C.O., 23/80/459.

78. James Carmichael Smyth to Lord Viscount Goderich, Government House, Bahamas, February 5, 1832, C.O., 23/86/36.

79. H. Johnson, *The Bahamas in Slavery and Freedom,* 23.

80. C.O., 23/80/189.

81. *Aspects of Slavery,* II, 24.

82. C.O., 23/75/251.

83. *Aspects of Slavery,* II, 24.

84. C.O., 23/86/36.

85. *Royal Gazette and Bahama Advertiser,* March 17, 1819. See also C.O., 23/68/261.

86. Simpson, *The Debate on Abolition of Slavery,* 74.

87. *Bahama Argus,* April 9, 1832.

88. Higman, *Slave Populations of the British Caribbean,* 107.

89. Loren Schweninger, *Black Property Owners in the South, 1790–1915* (Chicago, 1990), 84–87.

90. Christ Church Record, Baptism and Marriages.

91. Saint Matthew's Parish Births and Baptisms, January 2, 1801–March 8, 1903, Department of Archives, Nassau, Bahamas.

92. Ibid.

93. C.O., 23/43/188.

94. Will of George Watkins, Sr., December 23, 1852, New Providence, Bahama Islands, Department of Archives, Nassau, Bahamas. The will was not probated until December, 1865 indicating that he lived for a long time after the will was made.

95. Christ Church Record, Baptism and Marriages.

96. C.O., 23/64/173A.

97. Blue Book of Statistics, 1829. C.O., 27/27/18.

98. Will of Timothy Cox (1856),dated 1835, Department of Archives, Nassau, Bahamas. book C, pages 232–34.

99. *Bahama Argus,* April 4, 1832.

100. Return number 1086, Bahamas, Register of Slaves, 1834, Department of Archives.

101. Bahamas Compensation Return, 1834, vol. 2, 779, Department of Archives.

102. Will of Stephen Rogers, 1832, New Providence, Bahama Islands, Department of Archives, Nassau, Bahamas; Christ Church Record, Baptisms and Marriages; *Royal Gazette and Bahama Advertiser,* April 3, 1832.

103. Will of Anthony Wallace, free Black Man, December 9, 1830, New Providence, Bahamas, return number 31, Bahamas, Register of Slaves, 1821, Department of Archives.

104. Christ Church Record, Baptisms and Marriages; Will of Anthony Wallace, free Black Man, December 9, 1830, New Providence, Bahama Islands, Department of Archives; C.O., 23/80/545; Christ Church, Anglican Diocese of Nassau, 1733–1805, Baptisms, Marriages, Burials, Department of Archives.

105. James Weldon Johnson, *Along This Way: The Autobiography of James Weldon Johnson* (New York, 1968), 3–4.

106. Will of Benebo Berry, 1852, New Providence, Bahama Islands, Department of Archives, Nassau, Bahamas return number 70, Bahamas, Register of Slaves, 1821, Department of Archives. This is the largest number of slaves that she owned.

107. Bahamas, Register of Slaves, 1834, Department of Archives.

108. Bahamas, Register of Slaves, 1821–1834, Department of Archives.

109. H. Johnson, *The Bahamas from Slavery to Servitude,* 66.

110. Timothy Cox, hired one of his slaves, but the slave did not always compensate his owner. H. Johnson, *The Bahamas in Slavery and Freedom,* 10.

111. Bahamas Compensation Return, vols. 2 and 3, Department of Archives.

112. C.O., 23/67/164; C.O., 23/67/166.

113. "Return of the Males who have been Manumitted in the Colony of the Bahamas during the last last Seven Years, given separately; and shewing the former and present mode in which these Persons were employed, For the Year 1827," C.O., 23/80/545; Bahamas, Register of Slaves, 1834, return Number 935, Department of Archives.

114. C.O., 23/88/93.

115. "Return of the Females who have been Manumitted in the Colony of the Bahamas during the last Seven Years, given separately; and shewing the former and present mode in which these Persons were employed, For the Year 1827," C.O., 23/80/541; "Return of the Males," C.O., 23/80/545.

116. *The Directory and Stranger's Guide for the City of Charleston . . . for the Year 1822* (Charleston, South Carolina, 1822); Chatham County Register of Free Persons of Color, 1817–1829, Georgia Department of Archives and History, Atlanta, Georgia; see also Whittington B. Johnson, *The Promising Years, 1750–1830: The Emergence of Black Labor and Business* (New York, 1993), 47–48; Whittington B. Johnson, "Free African-American Women in Savannah, 1800–1860," *Georgia Historical Quarterly,* 76, no. 2 (summer, 1992): 264.

117. C.O., 23/80/545.

118. See sources cited in note 101 for discussion of occupations in which free African-American males in Charleston and Savannah were employed.

119. C.O., 23/80/545.

120. C.O., 23/80/534.

121. James Carmichael Smyth to Lord Viscount Goderich, Government House Bahamas, November 3, 1832, C.O., 23/87/47.

122. Minutes of the Proceeding of the Board of Visitors of the King's School at Nassau, C.O., 23/87/49.

123. Ibid.

124. C.O., 23/88/146; Blue Book of Statistics, 1834, C.O., 27/32/70.

125. Christ Church Record, Baptism and Marriages; C.O., 23/87/89 "List of Persons Manumitted within the Bahamas between 1 January 1817 and 31 December 1830." Ann Watkins was manumitted by bequest.

126. C.O., 23/87/60; C.O., 23/88/146.

127. Will of Joseph G. Watkins, February 19, 1870, Hope Town, Little Guana Cay, Abaco, Bahama Islands, Department of Archives.

128. C.O., 23/81/54; C.O., 23/84/340.

129. *Bahama Argus,* November 3, 1831; Bahamas, Register of Slaves, 1825–34, Department of Archives.

130. Supreme Court Records: Land Grants: Grant of Land to Prince Clear (free black)—Grand Bahama, November 11, 1829, Department of Archives; C.O., 23/80/545.

CHAPTER V: BLACKS AND COLOREDS: THE WORLD IN WHICH THEY LIVED, 1816–1834

1. C.O., 23/72/32.

2. C.O., 23/72/31.

3. Bahamas Compensation Returns, 1834, Department of Archives, Nassau, Bahamas.

4. Higman, *Slave Populations of the British Caribbean,* 426.

5. C.O., 23/75/69.

6. Martin, *Statistics of the Colonies,* 7.

7. "Returns of Male and Female Slaves Manumitted by Bequest or Otherwise from the January 1, 1808 to November 1, 1822," C.O., 23/72/26.

8. "List of Persons Manumitted within the Bahamas Between 1 January 1817 and 31 December 1830," C.O., 23/87/89; Higman, *Slave Populations of the British Caribbean,* 385; Craton, *A History of the Bahamas,* 187.

9. Journal of the House of Assembly of the Bahamas, October 31, 1815, to January 27, 1817, 190–99, Department of Archives.

10. David E. Wood, "The Free People of Colour in Bahamian Society," *Journal of the Bahama Historical Society* 12, no. 1 (October, 1990): 21; Higman, *Slave Populations of the British Caribbean,* 380.

11. "Abstract of Returns Required by Despatch from Earl Barhurst dated 6 August 1822 . . .," C.O., 23/72/22.

12. Blue Book of Statistics, 1822, C.O., 27/19/77.

13. "A Return of the free black and Coloured Population January 1, 1823–January 1, 1825," C.O., 23/75/71.

14. Lewis Grant to Lord Viscount Goderich, Government House, Bahamas, August 12, 1827, C.O., 23/76/303.

15. C. R. Nesbitt to Samuel Nesbitt, Secretary's Office, Nassau, October 10, 1828, C.O., 23/78/346.

16. Higman, *Slave Populations of the British Caribbean,* 433.

17. Blue Book of Statistics, 1824, C.O., 27/21/114; ibid., 1825, C.O., 27/22/149; ibid., 1826, C.O., 27/23/105; ibid., 1827, C.O., 27/24/139.

18. Blue Book of Statistics, 1824, C.O., 27/21/114; ibid., 1825, C.O., 27/22/149; ibid., 1826, C.O., 27/23/105; ibid., 1827, C.O., 27/24/139.

19. Martin, *Statistics of the Colonies,* 105.

20. "A Return of the Number of Baptisms and Burial of Free Black and Coloured People, January 29, 1822–January 19, 1826 in the Parish of St. Thomas—Turks Island," C.O., 23/75/73.

21. "Questions Proposed by the Royal College of Physicians," London, 1829. C.O., 23/81/127.

22. C.O., 27/23/105; C.O., 27/24/139.

23. *A Relic of Slavery: Farquharson's Journal for 1831–1832,* 62, 83; D. G. Saunders, *Bahamian Loyalists,* 60.

24. Herbert Klein and Stanley L. Engerman, "Fertility Differentials between Slaves in the United States and the British West Indies: A Note on Lactation Practices and Their Possible Implications," *William and Mary Quarterly* 3rd ser., 35 (January, 1978): 368–69.

25. Blue Book of Statistics, 1825, C.O., 27/22/149.

26. *Bahama Herald,* August 6, 1856; *Nassau Times,* August 3, 1878. In the latter issue, the Youraba Societies announced the celebration of their 42nd anniversary, which indicates that they were not formally organized until 1836.

27. D. Gail Saunders, "Life in New Providence in the Early Nineteenth Century," *Journal of the Bahamas Historical Society* 11, no. 1 (October, 1989): 19. Howard Johnson says that the first Friendly Society was not established in the Bahamas until 1834; see Howard Johnson, "Friendly Societies in the Bahamas, 1834–1910,' *Slavery and Abolition* 12, no. 3 (December, 1991): 183–99.

28. *Royal Gazette and Bahama Advertiser,* March 17, 1832.

29. Johnson, *The Promising Years,* 67; Gary B. Nash, *Forging Freedoom: The Formation of Philadelphia's Black Community, 1720–1840* (Cambridge, Massachusetts, 1988), 218–19.

30. The Bienfaisance Society was "a lodge of freemasons" which collected contributions to bury foreign indigent people of color; see Heuman, *Between Black and White,* 36; see also Campbell, *The Dynamics of Change in a Slave Society,* 113.

31. "Return of the Number of White, Free Black, or Coloured Persons and Liberated Africans Apprentices Who May have been committed to any prison, cage, or other Public Place of Confinement, and Convicted, during the last Seven Years [1820–1827]," C.O., 23/80/539.

32. "Return of the Goals," Blue Book of Statistics, 1829,C.O., 27/27/168; C.O., 23/82/51.

33. Shirley C. Gordon, *A Century of West Indian Education* (London, 1963), 17–18.

34. Journal of the House of Assembly of the Bahamas, October 31, 1815, to January 27, 1817, 230, Department of Archives.

35. Boyd, *The Vision and Other Poems,* xi–xii.

36. John Stephen to William Parker, Nassau, New Providence, March 14, 1815.

37. William Hepworth to Samuel Wix, Nassau, New Providence, March 16, 1818, Letters of William Hepworth, 1818–1836, Bray/Bahamas Collection, F9, Rhodes House Library, Oxford University, Oxford, England.

38. Williams, *The Methodist Contribution to Education in the Bahamas,* 51–52; Blue Book of Statistics, 1828, C.O., 27/26/107. For a discussion of the monitorial system, see Curtis, *History of Education in Great Britain,* 206–7 and Howard C. Barnard, *A History of English Education from 1760* (London, 1961), 52–57.

39. Lewis Grant to Lord Bathurst, Government House, Bahamas, February 10, 1824, C.O., 23/73/15. The reference to William Turton does not appear in this document.

40. Lewis Grant to William Hukisson, Government House, Bahamas, March 29, 1828, C.O., 23/78/37.

41. Blue Book of Statistics, 1827, C.O., 27/25/12; ibid., 1828, C.O., 27/26/107.

42. Blue Book of Statistics, 1830, C.O., 27/28/62.

43. Ibid.

44. Blue Book of Statistics, 1831, C.O., 27/29/122.

45. Blue Book of Statistics, 1830, C.O., 27/28/62.

46. Blue Book of Statistics, 1832, C.O., 27/30/127.

47. James Carmichael Smyth to Lord Viscount Goderich, Government House Bahamas, November 3, 1832 C.O., 23/87/47.

48. C.O., 23/87/51. The information on the National Society of England was taken from Curtis, *History of Education in Great Britain,* 208.

49. James Carmichael Smyth to Lord Viscount Goderich, Government House, Bahamas, January 20, 1832, C.O., 23/84/14; James Carmichael Smyth to Lord Viscount Goderich, Goverment House, Bahamas, February 5, 1832, C.O., 23/86/36.

50. J. Stewart to Lord Viscount Howick, Treasury Chambers, London, May 13, 1831, C.O., 23/86/46.

51. C.O., 23/86/41(11).

52. Joseph G. Watkins to Charles R. Nesbitt, Nassau, September 25, 1830, C.O., 23/86/46.

53. C.O., 23/86/41 (11).

54. William Vesey Munnings to Sir George Murray, New Providence, Bahamas, February 24, 1829, C.O., 23/81/45.

55. Blue Book of Statistics, 1830, C.O., 27/28/49; ibid., C.O., 27/28/62.

56. Blue Book of Statistics, 1831, C.O., 27/29/76.

57. "Return of All Colleges and Schools of education within the Bahama Islands, with a list of the Professor or Masters Severally belonging to them, and also an account of the Respective salaries," C.O., 23/86/243.

58. H. Stebbin to Reuben Champion, Savannah, February 15, 1816. The Champion Family Papers, 1816–1869, Hargrett Rare Books and Manuscripts Library, University of Georgia, Atlanta.

59. Johnson, *Black Savannah,* 127–28; Johnson, *The Promising Years,* 14. For a dis-

cussion of black education, see Carter G. Woodson, *Education of the Negro Prior to 1861* (New York, 1915) and Henry Allen Bullock, *A History of Negro Education in the South from 1619 to the Present* (Cambridge, Massachusetts, 1967).

60. C.O., 23/66/75.

61. C.O., 23/68/183.

62. Irish E. Finlayson, *A History of St. Matthew's Anglican Church* (Nassau, Bahamas, n.d.), 9.

63. Lewis Grant to Lord Bathurst, Government House, Bahamas, September 1, 1821, C.O., 23/70/60.

64. *An Official Letter from the Commissioners of Correspondence of the Bahama Islands to George Chalmers Concerning the Proposed Abolition of Slavery in the West Indies* (Nassau, Bahamas, 1823), 45–46.

65. Lewis Grant to Lord Bathurst, February 10, 1824.

66. Lewis Grant to William Vesey Munnings, HMS *Barham,* December 23, 1828, C.O., 23/78/172.

67. William Vesey Munnings to Sir George Murray, New Providence, Bahamas, February 24, 1829, C.O., 23/81/45.

68. William Hepworth to Horace Twiss, Botesdale, Suffolk, March 3, 1830, C.O., 23/83/169.

69. B. T. Balfour to Lord Viscount Goderich, Goverment House Bahamas, August 3, 1833, C.O., 23/89/4.

70. Blue Book of Statistics, 1827, C.O., 27/24/68.

71. James Carmichael Smyth to Lord Viscount Goderich, Government House, Bahamas, February 5, 1832, C.O., 23/86/26.

72. Nash, *Forging Freedom,* 68, 127–28; Julie Winch, *Philadelphia's Black Elite: Activism, Accommodation, and the Struggle for Autonomy, 1787–1848* (Philadelphia, 1988), 9–11.

73. Harold T. Lewis, *Yet with a Steady Beat: The African American Struggle for Recognition in the Episcopal Church* (Valley Forge, Pennsylvania, 1996), 32.

74. Blue Book of Statistics, 1827, C.O., 27/25/11; ibid., 1831, C.O., 27/29/119.

75. Blue Book of Statistics, 1827, C.O., 27/25/11; ibid., 1830, C.O., 27/28/50; ibid., 1831, C.O., 27/29/119.

76. C.O., 23/89/27.

77. C.O., 23/6/155; Peggs, *A Mission to the West India Islands,* 110; "List of Chapels Belonging to the Wesleyan Methodist Society in the Bahama Islands," Blue Book of Statistics, 1831, C.O., 27/29/120; ibid., 1832, C.O., 27/30/133.

78. Peggs, *A Mission to the West India Islands,* 97–98; Symonette and Canzoneri, *Baptists in the Bahamas,* 13.

79. William Vesey Munnings to Lord Bathurst, Nassau, New Providence, December 31, 1818, C.O., 23/67/171.

80. Christ Church Cathedral, Marriage Register, 1791–1828, Department of Archives. Margaret Wilson (a black woman), the bride, made her mark *X* on the register, indicating that she could not write. Prince Williams was literate. The marriage was performed by the rector of Christ Church because Sambo Scriven, preacher of the Baptist Society to which the bride and groom belonged, was not authorized to perform weddings.

81. C.O., 23/81/316.

82. C.O., 23/81/315.

83. Symonette and Canzoneri, *Baptists in the Bahamas,* 18.

84. C.O., 23/78/152.

85. "Petition of Prince Williams," C.O., 23/81/320.

86. Ibid.

87. Symonette and Canzoneri, *Baptists in the Bahamas,* 11.

88. D. G. Saunders, *Bahamian Loyalists,* 63–64; Symonette and Canzoneri, *Baptists in the Bahamas,* 18.

89. Blue Book of Statistics, 1832, C.O., 27/30/133.

90. Symonette and Canzoneri, *Baptists in the Bahamas,* 1–2.

91. Ibid., 11.

92. C.O., 23/84/340.

93. Symonette and Canzoneri, *Baptists in the Bahamas,* 12–13.

CHAPTER VI: RACE RELATIONS, 1816–1834: A TIME OF PROMISE

1. For a discussion of the change of fortune in the United States, see Johnson, "Prologue," in *The Promising Years,* 1–20. See also T. Stephen Whitman, *The Price of Freedom: Slavery and Manumission in Baltimore and National Maryland* (Lexington, Kentucky, 1997).

2. C.O., 23/80/325; D. Gail Saunders, "The Slave Population of the Bahamas, 1783–1834" (masters thesis, University of the West Indies, Nassau Branch, 1978), 118; Lewis Grant to George Murray, Government House, Bahamas, November 11, 1828, C.O., 23/78/134; J. Carmichael Smyth to Lord Viscount Goderich, Government House, August 2, 1823, C.O., 23/86/273.

3. Lewis Grant to Lord Viscount Goderich, Government House, August 12, 1827, C.O., 23/76/303.

4. *Aspects of Slavery,* 2:24.

5. C.O., 23/78/134.

6. Charles Poitier to Lord Bathurst, Nassau, New Providence, February 8, 1825, C.O., 23/74/185; Charles Poitier to Lewis Grant, Nassau, New Providence, May 5, 1825, C.O., 23/75/25.

7. J. Carmichael Smyth to Lord Viscount Goderich, Government House Bahamas, February 5, 1832, C.O., 23/86/36.

8. C.O., 23/81/54.

9. C.O., 23/84/56.

10. James Stewart to Lord Howick, Treasury Chamber, December 9, 1830, C.O., 23/83/125; C.O., 23/81/263; William Vesey Munnings to George Murray, March 9, 1829, C.O., 23/81/84; J. Walker to C. R. Nesbitt, Customs House, Nassau, March 16, 1831, C.O., 23/84/103.

11. J. Carmichael Smyth to Lord Viscount Goderich, March 15, 1831, C.O., 23/84/56.

12. Santiago Pasos to James Carmichael Smyth, April 9, 1831, C.O., 23/84/154.

13. C.R.Nesbitt to Santiago Pasos, April 11, 1831, C.O., 23/84/156; Governor

Smyth supported Nesbitt and may have instructed him to make the remarks. See J. Carmichael Smyth to Lord Viscount Goderich, May 5, 1831, C.O., 23/84/150.

14. Lucille Mathurin, *The Rebel Woman in the British West Indies during Slavery* (Kingston, Jamaica, 1975), 25.

15. C.O., 23/63/322.

16. C.O., 23/63/312.

17. C.O., 23/63/249.

18. Charles Cameron to Lord Bathurst, June 23, 1817, C.O., 23/64/198.

19. Lewis Grant to Lord Viscount Goderich, September 28, 1827, C.O., 23/76/312.

20. William Vesey Munnings to George Murray, September 29, 1829, C.O., 23/81/139.

21. "A Return of the New Providence Militia, 1824," Blue Book of Statistics, 1824, C.O., 27/21/22; ibid., 1826, C.O., 27/23/11.

22. "A Return of the New Providence Regiment Militia," Blue Book of Statistics, 1828, C.O., 27/26/42.

23. "A Return of the New Providence Regiment Militia," Blue Book of Statistics, 1831, C.O., 27/29/45.

24. C.O., 23/86/41(11).

25. "Memoranda," Government House, Bahamas, April 30, 1833, C.O., 23/88/138. James Carmichael Smyth left this memo to his successor.

26. Handler, *The Unappropriated People,* 85; J. Harry Bennett Jr., *Bondsmen and Bishops* (Berkeley, 1958), 106.

27. Higman, *Slave Populations of the British Caribbean,* 393; J. Carmichael Smyth to Lord Viscount Goderich, Government House, Bahamas, May 4, 1832, C.O., 23/86/166. Governor Smyth mentioned the Jamaica disturbance in this dispatch.

28. Green, *British Slave Emancipation,* 112.

29. James Farquharson's mother was Kitty Davies, or Dixon, a free woman of color and Charles Farquharson's longtime common-law wife. See Craton and Saunders, *Islanders in the Stream,* 1:335–37; *Bahama Argus,* May 9, 1832.

30. C.O., 23/81/189; *Aspects of Slavery,* 2: 27–29; *A Relic of Slavery: Farquharson's Journal for 1831–32,* xiv, 50–51.

31. Higman, *Slave Populations of the British Caribbean,* 393.

32. Peggs, *Dowson's Journal,* 83.

33. C.O., 23/63/216.

34. William Wylly to Charles Cameron, Nassau, January 26, 1814, C.O., 23/63/218.

35. John Stephen to Charles Cameron, Nassau, January 28, 1814, C.O., 23/63/219.

36. William Wylly to Charles Cameron, Nassau, June 15, 1816, C.O., 23/63/232.

37. William Martin to Charles Cameron, Nassau, July 4, 1816, C.O., 23/63/233.

38. John Stephen to Charles Cameron, Nassau, July 8, 1816, C.O., 23/63/234.

39. Lord Bathurst to Charles Cameron, Downing Street, November 30, 1816, C.O., 23/64/154.

40. William Wylly to Charles Cameron, New Providence, March 10, 1817, C.O., 23/64/141.

41. William Wylly to Charles Cameron, New Providence, July 14, 1817, C.O., 23/64/201.

42. William Martin to Charles Cameron, July 12, 1817, C.O., 23/64/202.

43. Mathieson, *British Slavery and Its Abolition,* 164.

44. *Hints of the Propriety of Establishing by Law the Civil Right of the Free People of Color in the British West India Islands* (New Castle upon Tyne, 1824), 7; David Brion Davis, *The Problem of Slavery in Western Culture* (New York, 1966), 287.

45. Lewis Grant to William Hukisson, Government House, Bahamas, June 20, 1828, C.O., 23/78/54.

46. Lewis Grant to William Vesey Munnings, HMS *Barham,* December 23, 1828, C.O., 23/78/172.

47. Laws of the Bahamas, January 13, 1823, to December 29, 1834, Department of Archives, Nassau, Bahamas.

48. C.O., 23/82/142.

49. J. Carmichael Smyth to George Murray, Government House, Bahamas, April 29, 1830, C.O., 23/82/138; Laws of the Bahamas, January 9, 1826, to February 11, 1831, Department of Archives.

50. E. Cox, *Free Coloreds in the Slave Societies of St. Kitts and Grenada,* 101–3; Paul Knaplund, *James Stephen and the British Colonial System, 1813–1847* (Madison, 1953), 117.

51. Handler, *The Unappropriated People,* 102–3.

52. C.O., 23/84/148.

53. *Laws of the Bahamas, 1823–1834,* Department of Archives.

54. Samuel Nesbitt to William Vesey Munnings, Nassau, January 18, 1832, C.O., 23/86/22.

55. Ibid.

56. *Royal Gazette and Bahama Advertiser,* November 17, 1832.

57. *Royal Gazette and Bahama Advertiser,* December 8, 1832.

58. Minutes of the General Court from July 20, 1832, to April 20, 1836, Department of Archives.

59. *Royal Gazette and Bahama Advertiser,* November 17, 1832; ibid., December 8, 1832. The names of the free black and colored males who were added to the juries appeared in the later issue of the newspaper.

60. *Royal Gazette and Bahama Advertiser,* April 21, 1832.

61. *Bahama Argus,* April 4, 1832.

62. *Royal Gazette and Bahama Advertiser,* September 27, 1826. This is just one of the many advertisements that he placed in the newspaper. For a short biography on Dillet, see Johnson, *Along This Way,* 3–4.

63. *Royal Gazette and Bahama Advertiser,* July 24, 1824; ibid., January 16, 1833.

64. C.O., 23/84/146. The petition was addressed to the chief justice and assistant justices of the general court of the Bahama Islands.

65. C.O., 23/86/34.

66. Minutes of the General Court, 1832–1836, Department of the Archives.

67. *Royal Gazette and Bahama Advertiser,* June 16, 1832.

68. C.O., 23/86/18.

69. Ibid.

70. B.T. Balfour to William Hepworth, Government House, Bahamas, June 7, 1833, C.O., 23/88/235.

71. C.O., 23/88/194.

72. Craton and Saunders, *Islanders in the Stream,* 1: 232.

73. Laws of the Bahamas, March 23, 1823–December 23, 1834, Department of Archives; Blue Book of Statistics, 1833, C.O., 27/31/54.

74. Edward G. Stanley to B. T. Balfour, Downing Street, January 30, 1834, Secretary of State Correspondence, Gov. 15/1, 1800–1879, Department of Archives.

75. Blue Book of Statistics, 1833, C.O., 27/31/3.

76. Blue Book of Statistics, 1834, C.O., 27/32/60; Boyd, *The Vision and Other Poems,* iv. This information is in C. R. Nesbitt's introduction of the work. See also Wood, "Attainment of Civil Rights and Liberties," 19; D. Gail Saunders, "Life in New Providencee in the Early Nineteenth Century," *Journal of The Bahamas Historical Society* 11 (October, 1989): 20; Hartley Cecil Saunders, *The Other Bahamas* (Nassau, 1991), 31. This work erroneously listed Samuel Minns of Andros Island among the first nonwhite assemblymen.

77. Heuman, *Between Black and White,* 58; Cox, *Free Coloreds in the Slave Societies of St. Kitts and Grenada,* 108; Handler, *The Unappropriated People,* 104 n. 76.

78. Lord Viscount Goderich to J. Carmichael Smyth, February 11, 1833, C.O., 23/88/133.

79. *Royal Gazette and Bahama Advertiser,* May 11, 1833.

80. C.O., 23/88/235.

CHAPTER VII: RACE RELATIONS, 1816–1834: EMANCIPATION, THE HIDDEN AGENDA

1. Mathieson, *British Slavery and Its Abolition,* 227; Paul Knaplund, *James Stephen and the British Colonial System, 1813–1847* (Madison, 1953), 96–100; Albury, *The Story of the Bahamas,* 127.

2. C.O., 23/64/14.

3. C.O., 23/63/46.

4. C.O., 23/64/22.

5. C.O., 23/65/83; C.O., 23/66/75.

6. "An Act to Establish a Triennial Registration of Slaves in the Bahamas Islands," Laws of the Bahamas, December 22, 1814, to January 23, 1822, Department of Archives.

7. Lord Bathurst to Lewis Grant, Downing Street, December 22, 1824, Secretary of State Correspondence, Department of Archives.

8. "An Act to Establish a Triennial Registration of Slaves (1827)," Laws of the Bahamas, January 9, 1826, to February 11, 1831, Department of Archives; Lord Goderich to James Carmichael Smyth, Downing Street, December 16, 1830, Secretary of State Correspondence, Department of Archives.

9. Simpson, *The Debate on Abolition of Slavery,* 37; William A. Green, *British Slave Emancipation: The Sugar Colonies and the Great Experiment, 1830–1865* (London, 1976), 102–3, 106; Parry and Sherlock, *A Short History of the West Indies,* 182–83; Ward, *British West Indian Slavery,* 273.

10. Green, *British Slave Emancipation,* 101–2.

11. C.O., 23/72/10.

12. Peter Kolchin, *American Slavery, 1619–1877* (New York, 1993), 118–20, 133.

13. Laws of the Bahamas, January 13, 1823 to December 29, 1824. Much of the discussion on the amelioration perod is taken from my article entitled, "The Amelioration Acts in the Bahamas, 1823–1833: A Middle Ground between Freedom and

Antebellum Slave Codes," *Journal of the Bahamas Historical Society 18* (October, 1996): 21–32. Subsequent citations of the other acts in the trilogy will be referred to simply as the Consolidated Act and give the year it was passed. I used the name Amelioration Act in the article mentioned above when referring to the same acts.

14. Consolidated Slave Act (1824).

15. Ibid.

16. Consolidated Slave Act (1826), Laws of the Bahamas, 9 January 1826 to 11 February 1831.

17. For a discussion of negativisms which Englishmen harbored toward Africans see Jordan, *White over Black,* 3–8.

18. Saunders, *Slavery in the Bahamas,* 88.

19. Consolidated Slave Act (1826).

20. Ibid.

21. Ibid.

22. Ibid.

23. William Huskisson to Lewis Grant, Downing Street, March 5, 182?, Secretary of State Correspondence, Department of Archives.

24. Consolidated Slave Act (1826).

25. Consolidated Slave Act (1830), Laws of the Bahamas, January 9, 1826, to February 11, 1831, Department of Archives; James Carmichael Smyth to George Murray, Government House, Bahamas, April 29, 1830, C.O., 23/82/138.

26. Ward, *British West Indian Slavery,* 275; Mathurin, *The Rebel Woman in the British West Indies,* 15; Bennett, *Bondsmen and Bishops,* 114.

27. Knaplund, *James Stephen and the British Colonial System,* 105.

28. Ward, *British West Indian Slavery,* 272–73.

29. Higman, *Slave Populations of the British Caribbean,* 48.

30. Sheridan, *Doctors and Slaves,* 171; Bennett, *Bondsmen and Bishops,* 22.

31. Simpson, *The Debate on Abolition of Slavery,* 39. In this speech, Wilberforce deplored decreases in the slave population of theWest Indies when elsewhere "the negro race [was] found to have greatly inceased its numbered."

32. *An Official Letter from the Commissioners of Correspondence of the Bahama Islands to George Chalmers Concerning the Proposed Abolition of Slavery in the West Indies* (Nassau, 1823), 41–42. Interestingly, the letter was published in 1823, but the title alludes to "the proposed abolition of slavery."

33. C.O., 23/82/138.

34. James Carmichael Smyth to Lord Goderich, Government House, Bahamas, June 27, 1831, C.O., 23/84/229.

35. Lord Goderich to James Carmichael Smyth, (no date visible), C.O., 23/84/232.

36. C.O., 23/88/46.

37. Consolidated Slave Act (1824); Consolidated Slave Act (1826).

38. "Instructions for William McVicar, Esquire . . . From James Carmichael Smyth," February 1833, C.O., 23/88/51.

39. William Huskisson to Lewis Grant, March 5, 182?

40. Knaplund, *James Stephen and the British Colonial System,* 98.

41. Ward, *British West Indian Slavery,* 3.

42. See note # 32 for the name of this pamphlet.

43. Wilmot Horton to William Huskisson, Downing Street, November 6, 1827, Huskisson Papers, vol. 19, Correspondence, November–December 19, 1827, British Museum, London, England.

44. William Huskisson to Wilmot Horton, Earlham, November 7, 1827, Huskisson Papers, vol. 19.

45. Lord Howick to T. F. Buxton, Downing Street, April 7, 1831, Frank C. Stuart, "A Critical Edition of the Correspondence of Sir Thomas Fowell Buxton, with an Account of His Career to 1823" (master's thesis, University of London, 1957), 2: 198–200.

46. Ibid.

47. Knaplund, *James Stephen and the British Colonial System,* 98.

48. Green, *British Slave Emancipation,* 118–19; Williams, *From Columbus to Castro: The History of the Caribbean, 1492–1969,* 198–99.

49. Michael Craton, *Sinews of Empire: A Short History of British Slavery* (Garden City, New York, 1974), 175.

50. Priscilla Buxton to Sarah Maria Buxton, Devonshire Street, May 16, 1833, in "Correspondence of Sir Thomas Fowell Buxton," by Stuart, 2:253–54.

51. Green, *British Slave Emancipation,* 122.

52. Knaplund, *James Stephen and the British Colonial System,* 110. In Bermuda, slaves were emancipated unconditionally beginning August 1, 1834, Terry Tucker, *Bermuda Today and Yesterday, 1503–1980s* (London, 1983), 115.

53. Green, *British Slave Emacipation,* 105.

54. Parry and Sherlock, *A Short History of the West Indies,* 183.

55. Ibid.; Williams, *From Columbus to Castro,* 284–85; Green, *British Slave Emancipation,* 35; David Brion Davis, *The Problem of Slavery in Western Culture* (Ithaca, New York, 1966), 55. Davis believes the decline did not come as quickly as Williams and the others state.

56. "Address to the Slave Population of the Bahama Islands," C.O., 23/89/19.

57. Peggs, *A Short History of the Bahamas,* 21–22.

58. Humble Address of the Legislative Council, C.O., 23/91/115.

59. "An Act Auxiliary to an act of the Imperial Parliament, entitled, 'An act for the Abolition of Slavery throughout the British Colonies . . .' [February 15, 1834]," Laws of the Bahamas, March 23, 1832–December 23, 1834, Department of Archives.

60. Bahamas Compensation Return, 1834, 3 vols., Department of Archives. Because of the fragile state of the first volume, I was only allowed to peruse its first page, which contains a summary of the information in that volume.

61. Craton, *A History of the Bahamas,* 203–4.

62. *Bahama Argus,* June 27, 1834.

63. Blue Book of Statistics, 1834, C.O., 27/32/4.

64. Craton and Saunders, *Islanders in the Stream,* 1:392–93.

65. Bethell, *The Early Settlers of the Bahamas,* 116–17.

EPILOGUE

1. Boyd, *The Vision and Other Poems,* vi–vii.

2. *Bahama Argus,* February 18, 1832.

Bibliography

PRIMARY SOURCES

Manuscripts

Bahama Islands

Department of Archives, Nassau

Church Records

Christ Church Anglican Diocese of Nassau, Baptisms, Marriages, Burials. 1733–1805, Carmichael to Adelaide.

Christ Church Cathedral Marriage Register. 1791–1828.

Christ Church Record of Baptisms and Marriages. 1753–October 21, 1805, and 1733–1843.

Saint Matthew's Parish Births and Baptisms. January 2, 1801–March 8, 1903.

Government Documents

Bahamas Compensation Return. 3 vols. 1834.

Bahamas Register of Slaves. 1821–1834.

Colonial Office Papers. 1723–1834. C.O., 23/10–91. Microfilm.

Journal of the House of Assembly of the Bahamas. October 31, 1815, to January 27, 1817.

Laws of the Bahamas. December 11, 1795, to November 23, 1798. Ms. duplicate.

Laws of the Bahamas. December 22, 1814, to January 23, 1822. Ms. duplicate.

Laws of the Bahamas. January 13, 1823, to December 29, 1824. Ms. duplicate.

Laws of the Bahamas. January 9, 11826, to February 11, 1831. Ms.duplicate.
Laws of the Bahamas. March 23, 1832, to December 23, 1834. Ms. duplicate.
Minutes of the General Court. July 20, 1832–April 20, 1836.
Plan of the Town of Nassau Virons, Island of New Providence. 1788.
Records Relating to the Bahamas. U.S.P.G. Anglican Church, 1726–1822.
Register of Freed Slaves. Eighteenth and nineteenth century.
Secretary of State Correspondence. Gov. 15/1 1800–1879. Loose papers.
Supreme Court Records: Land Grants.

Wills

Will of Benebo Berry. 1852.
Will of Timothy Cox. 1856.
Will of Stephen Rogers. 1832.
Will of John Simms, a Black man. 1809.
Will of Anthony Wallace, Free Black man. 1830.
Will of Betty Watkins. 1803.
Will of George Watkins Sr. 1852.
Will of Joseph G. Watkins. 1870.
Will of John Williams. 1818.

Great Britain

British Library, London

Correspondence of George Chalmers. Vol. 1. 1787–1798. Ms. 22900.
Huskisson Papers. Vol. 19. Correspondence, November–December 19, 1827. Additional Ms. 38752.
Liverpool Papers. Vol. 201. Additional Ms. 38390.

Public Record Office, Kew

Bahama Blue Book of Statistics. 1822–1834. C.O., 27/19–32.
Colonial Office Papers. C.O., 318/77.

Rhodes House Library, Oxford University, Oxford

Bray/Bahamas Collection

United States of America

Duke University Library, Durham, North Carolina

Mrs. ——— Smith's Journal. March 17, 1793.

Georgia Department of Archives and History, Atlanta, Georgia

Chatham County Register of Free Persons of Color. 1817–1829.

Hargrett Rare Books and Manuscripts Library, University of Georgia, Atlanta, Georgia

Champion Family Papers. 1816–1869.

Books

Asplund, John, ed. *The Universal Register of the Baptist Denomination in North America for the Years 1790, 1791, 1792, 1793, and Part of 1794.* Boston: John W. Folson, 1794.

———. *The Universal Register of the Baptist Denomination in North America for the Years 1794 and 1795.* Hanover, N.H.: Dunham and True, 1796.

Bahama Agriculture Society. *Rules of the Bahama Agriculture Society.* Nassau: Printed by Eve and Owen, 1801. Society was established in 1801.

———. *Different Subjects Addressed to the Bahama Agriculture Society.* Nassau: Printed by Joseph Eve, n.d.

Boyd, John. *The Vision and Other Poems in Blank Verse.* London: Longman and Company, 1834. Prefaced by some preliminary observations by C. R. Nesbitt.

[Bruce, Peter]. *Bahamian Interlude, Being an Account of Life at Nassau in the Bahama Islands in the Eighteenth Century.* London, 1782. Reprinted from the memoir of Peter Bruce, Esq.

Coke, Thomas. *An Account of the Rise, Progress, and Present State of the Methodist Missions.* London: T. George Story, 1804.

———. *A History of the West Indies Containing the Natural, Civil, and Ecclesiastical History of Each Island.* 3 vols. London: T. Blanshard, 1811.

[Commissioners of Correspondence], *An Official Letter from the Commissioners of Correspondence of the Bahama Islands to George Chalmers Concerning the Proposed Abolition of Slavery in the West Indies.* Nassau: Royal Gazette, 1823.

The Directory and Stranger's Guide for the City of Charleston . . . for the Year 1822. Charleston, S.C., 1822.

Edwards, Bryan. *The History Civil and Commercial of the British Colonies of the West Indies.* 3 vols. London: Printed for John Stockdale, 1793.

[Farquharson, Charles]. *A Relic of Slavery: Farquharson's Journal for 1831–1832; Copied from the Original by Ormond J. McDonald.* 1903. Reprint, Nassau: Deans Peggs Research Fund, 1957.

Forbes, Rosita. *A Unicorn in the Bahamas.* New York: E. P. Dutton, 1940.

Garstin, Crosbie, ed. *Samuel Kelly: An Eighteenth Century Seaman.* New York: Frederick A. Stokes Company, 1925.

Hints on the Propriety of Establishing by Law the Civil Rights of the Free People of Colour in the British West India Islands. New Castle upon Tyne: R. T. Edgar, 1824.

Instructions for Missionaries to the West India Islands. London: Printed at the Philanthropic Reform, 1795.

The Interference of the British Legislature in the Internal Concerns of the West Indies Respecting Their Slaves Deprecated. London: J. Mawman, 1816.

Letters from the Bahama Islands Written in 1823–4. Philadelphia: H. C. Carey and I. Lea, 1827.

Lockey, Joseph Byrne, ed. *East Florida, 1783–1785: A File of Documents Assembled, and Many of Them Translated.* Berkeley and Los Angeles: University of California Press, 1949.

Martin, Robert Montgomery. *Statistics of the Colonies of the British Empire.* London: William H. Allen and Company, 1839.

McKinnen, Daniel. *A Tour through the British West Indies in the Years 1802 and 1803, Giving a Particular Account of the Bahama Islands.* London: Printed for J. White by R. Taylor, 1804.

Peggs, Deans, ed. *A Mission to the West India Islands: Dowson's Journal for 1819–1817.* Nassau: Deans Peggs Research Fund, 1960.

Rippon, John, ed. *The Baptist Annual Register, 1790–1793.* London, n.d.

Schoepf, Johann David. *Travels in the Confederation, 1783–1784.* 2 vols. Translated and edited by Alfred J. Morrison, Baltimore: Lord Baltimore Press, 1911.

A Short Journey in the West Indies in Which Are Interspered Curious Anecdotes and Characters. 2 vols. London: J. Murray and J. Forbes, 1790.

Simpson, D. H., ed. *The Debate on Abolition of Slavery, 1823.* London: Dawson's Pall Mall, 1968.

Stephen, James. *The Slavery of the British West India Colonies Delineated.* 2 vols. London: J. Butterworth and Son, 1824–30.

Urofsky, Melvin I. *Documents of American Constitution and Legal History.* 2 vols. New York: Alfred A. Knopf, 1989.

West Indian Slave-holders' Lust of Cruelty, the Same Now as Ever. Extracted from the *Dublin Morning Post,* July 28, 1830. This work is found in the British Library, London, call number 1879c.5.(14).

Wylly, William. *A Short Account of the Bahama Islands.* London, 1789.

Newspapers

Bahama Argus (Nassau), 1831–1834.

Bahama Gazette (Nassau), 1784–1819.

Bahama Herald (Nassau), 1856.

Lucayan Royal Herald and Weekly Advertiser (Nassau), 1789.

Nassau Times, 1878.

Royal Gazette and Bahama Advertiser (Nassau), 1819–1833.

SECONDARY SOURCES

Books

Albury, Paul. *The Story of the Bahamas.* London: MacMillan Education, Limited, 1975.

Anderson, James Stuart Murray. *The History of the Church of England in the Colonies and Foreign Dependencies.* 3 vols. London: Francis and John Rivington, 1845–56.

Barnard, Howard Clive. *A History of English Education from 1760.* London: Universtiy of London Press, Limited, 1961.

Bennett, J. Harry, Jr. *Bondsmen and Bishops: Slavery and Apprenticeship on the Codrington Plantations of Barbados, 1710–1838:* Berkeley: University of California Press, 1958.

Bethell, Arnold Talbot. *The Early Settlers of the Bahamas and Colonists of North America.* 3rd ed. Norfolk, England: Rounce and Wortley, 1937.

Brathwaite, Edward. *The Development of Creole Society in Jamaica, 1770–1820.* London: Oxford University Press, 1971.

Buckley, Roger Norman. *Slaves in Red Coats: The British West India Regiment, 1795–1815*. New Haven: Yale University Press, 1979.
Bullock, Henry Allen. *A History of Negro Education in the South from 1619 to the Present*. Cambridge, Mass.: Harvard University Press, 1967.
Burn, William L. *Emancipation and Apprenticeship in the British West Indies*. London: Jonathan Cape, Limited, 1937.
Campbell, Mavis Christine. *The Dynamics of Change in a Slave Society: A Sociopolitical History of the Free Coloreds of Jamaica, 1800–1865*. Rutherford, N.J.: Fairleigh Dickinson University Press, 1976.
Commonwealth of the Bahamas. *Aspects of Slavery*. 2 vols. Nassau: Government Printing Department, 1974–84.
Cox, Edward L. *Free Coloreds in the Slave Societies of St. Kitts and Grenada, 1763–1833*. Knoxville: University of Tennessee Press, 1984.
Cox, F. A. *History of the Baptist Missionary Society from 1792 to 1842*. 2 vols. London, 1842.
Craton, Michael. *A History of the Bahamas*. London: Collins, 1962.
———. *Sinews of Empire: A Short History of British Slavery*. Garden City, N.Y.: Doubleday, 1974.
Craton, Michael, and Gail Saunders. *Islanders in the Stream: A History of the Bahamian People*. 2 vols. Athens: University of Georgia Press, 1992–98.
Cremin, Lawrence A. *American Education: The National Experience, 1783–1876*. New York: Harper and Row Publishers, 1980.
Curtis, Stanley James. *History of Education in Great Britain*. 4th ed. London: University Tutorial Press, Limited, 1961.
Davis, David Brion. *The Problem of Slavery in Western Culture*. Ithaca, N.Y.: Cornell University Press, 1966.
———. *The Problem of Slavery in the Age of Revolution, 1770–1823*. Ithaca, N.Y.: Cornell University Press, 1975.
Finlayson, Iris E. *A History of St. Matthew's Anglican Church*. Nassau, n.d.
Frey, Sylvia, and Betty Wood. *Come Shouting to Zion: African American Protestantism in the American South and British Caribbean to 1830*. Chapel Hill: University of North Carolina Press, 1998.
Gordon, Shirley C. *A History of West Indian Education*. London: Green and Company, 1963.
Green, William. *British Slave Emancipation: The Sugar Colonies and the Great Experiment, 1830–1865*. London: Oxford University Press, 1976.
Handler, Jerome S. *The Unappropriated People: Freedmen in the Slave Society of Barbados*. Baltimore: The Johns Hopkins University Press, 1974.
Hausman, Gerald, and Kelvin Rodriques. *African-American Alphabet: A Celebration of African-American and West Indian Culture, Custom, Myth, and Symbol*. New York: St. Martin's Press, 1996.
Heuman, Gad J. *Between Black and White: Race, Politics, and the Free Coloreds in Jamaica, 1792–1865*. Westport, Conn.: Greenwood Press, 1981.
Higman, B. W. *Slave Populations of the British Caribbean, 1807–1834*. Baltimore: The Johns Hopkins University Press, 1984.
Johnson, Howard. *The Bahamas in Slavery and Freedom*. Kingston, Jamaica: James Currey Publishers, 1991.

———. *The Bahamas from Slavery to Servitude, 1783–1933.* Gainesville: University of Florida Press, 1996.

Johnson, James Weldon. *Along This Way: The Autobiography of James Weldon Johnson.* 1933. Reprint, New York: Viking Press, 1968.

Johnson, Samuel, and O. Johnson. *The History of the Yorubas: From the Earliest Times to the Beginning of the British Protectorate.* 1920. Reprint, Westport, Conn.: Negro Universities Press, 1970.

Johnson, Whittington B. *The Promising Years, 1750–1830: The Emergence of Black Labor and Business.* New York: Garland Publishing, 1993.

———. *Black Savannah, 1788–1864.* Fayetteville: University of Arkansas Press, 1996.

Jordan, Winthrop. *White over Black: American Attitudes toward the Negro, 1550–1812.* New York: W. W. Norton, 1968.

Knaplund, Paul. *James Stephen and the British Colonial System, 1813–1847.* Madison: University of Wisconsin Press, 1953.

Kolchin, Peter. *American Slavery , 1619–1877.* New York: Hill and Wang, 1993.

Lewis, Harold T. *Yet with a Steady Beat: The African American Struggle for Recognition in the Episcopal Church.* Valley Forge: Trinity Press International, 1996.

Manning, Frank E. *Black Clubs in Bermuda:Ethnography of a Play World.* Ithaca, N.Y.: Cornell University Press, 1973.

Mathieson, William L. *British Slavey and Its Abolition, 1823–1838.* London: Longman, Green, and Company, Limited, 1926.

Mathurin, Lucille. *The Rebel Woman in the British West Indies during Slavery.* Kingston, Jamaica: The Herald, Limited, 1975.

McKenzie-Grieve, Averil. *The Last Years of the English Slave Trade: Liverpool, 1750–1807.* London: Frank Cass and Company, Limited, 1968.

Methodist Church, Jamaican District. *For Ever Beginning: Two Hundred Years of Methodism in the Western Area.* Kingston, Jamaica: United Printers, Limited, 1960.

Miller, Randall M., and John David Smith, eds. *Dictionary of Afro-American Slavery.* Westport, Conn.: Greenwood Press, 1988.

Nash, Gary B. *Forging Freedom: The Formation of Philadelphia's Black Community, 1820–1840.* Cambridge, Mass.: Harvard University Press, 1988.

Northrup, David. *The Atlantic Slave Trade.* Lexington, Mass.: D. C. Heath Company, 1994.

Parry, John H., and Philip M. Sherlock. *A Short History of the West Indies.* 2nd ed. New York: St. Martin's Press, 1968.

Pascoe, C. F. *Two Hundred Years of the S.P.G.: An Historical Account of the Society for the Propagation of the Gospel in Foreign Parts, 1701–1900.* London: Published at the Society's Office, 1901.

Peggs, A. Deans. *A Short History of the Bahamas.* Nassau: Deans Peggs Fund, 1959.

Porter, Dale H. *The Aboliton of the Slave Trade in England, 1784–1807.* Hamden, Conn., Archon Books, 1970.

Raboteau, Albert J. *Slave Religion: The "Invisible Institution" in the Antebellum South.* New York: Oxford University Press, 1978.

Ragatz, Lowell Joseph. *The Fall of the Planter Class in the British Caribbean, 1763–1833.* New York: Century Company, 1928.

Richardson, Bonham C. *Caribbean Migrants: Environment and Human Survival on St. Kitts and Nevis.* Knoxville: University of Tennessee Press, 1983.

Riley, Sandra. *Homeward Bound: A History of the Bahama Islands to 1850, with a Definitive Study of Abaco in the American Loyalist Plantation Period.* Miami, Fla.: Island Research, 1983.

Ros, Martin. *Night of Fire: The Black Napoleon and the Battle for Haiti.* Translated by Karin Ford-Treep. New York: Sarpedon, 1994.

Saunders, D. Gail. *Bahamian Loyalists and Their Slaves.* London: MacMillan Caribbean, 1983.

———. *Slavery in the Bahamas, 1648–1838.* Nassau: Nassau Guardian, 1985.

Saunders, Hartley C. *The Other Bahamas.* Nassau: Bodab Publishers, 1991.

Schweninger, Loren. *Black Property Owners in the South, 1790–1815.* Chicago: University of Illinois Press, 1990.

Sheridan, Richard B. *Doctors and Slaves: A Medical and Demographical History of Slavery in the British West Indies, 1680–1834.* New York: Cambridge University Press, 1985.

Stark, James H. *Stark's History and Guide to the Bahama Islands.* Boston: Photo Electrotype Company, Publishers, 1891.

Symonette, Michael C., and Antonina Canzoneri. *Baptists in the Bahamas: An Historical Review.* El Paso, Tex.: Baptist Spanish Publishing House, 1977.

Thompson, Anthony. *An Economic History of the Bahamas.* Nassau: Commonwealth Publications, 1979.

Tucker, Terry. *Bermuda Today and Yesterday, 1503–1980s.* London: Robert Hale Limited, 1983.

Ward, J. R. *British West Indian Slavery, 1750–1834.* Oxford: Clarendon Press, 1988.

Whitman, T. Stephen. *The Price of Freedom: Slavery and Manumission in Baltimore and Early National Maryland.* Lexington: University of Kentucky Press, 1997.

Wilkinson, Henry Campbell. *Bermuda from Sail to Steam: The History of the Island from 1784 to 1901.* 2 vols. London: Oxford University Press, 1973.

Williams, Colbert. *The Methodist Contribution to Education in the Bahamas.* Glouster, England: Alan Sutton Publishing, Limited, 1982.

Williams, Eric Eustall. *From Columbus to Castro: The History of the Caribbean, 1492–1969.* New York: Harper Row Publishers, 1969.

Williamson, Joel. *New People: Miscegenation and Mulattoes in the United States.* New York: The Free Press, 1980.

Winch, Julie. *Philadelphia's Black Elite: Activism, Accommodation, and the Struggle for Autonomy, 1787–1848.* Philadelphia: Temple University Press, 1988.

Woodson, Carter G. *Education of the Negro Prior to 1861.* New York: G. P. Putnam's Sons, 1915.

Other Published Secondary Sources

Bethel, Edward Clement. "Music in the Bahamas: Its Roots, Development, and Personality." Masters thesis, Universtiy of California, Los Angeles, 1978.

Ellis, David. "The Traffic in Slaves between the British West Indian Colonies, 1807–1833." *Economic History Review,* 2nd ser., 25 (1972): 55–64.

Farnsworth, Paul. "Archaeological Excavations at Promised Plantation in New Providence." *Journal of the Bahamas Historical Society* 16 (October 1994): 21–29.

Gatewood, Willard B., Jr. "Aristocrats of Color: South and North, the Black Elite, 1880–1920." *Journal of Southern History* 54 (February 1988): 3–20.

Johnson, Howard. "Friendly Societies in the Bahamas, 1834–1910," *Slavery and Abolition* 12, no.3 (December 1991): 183–99.

Johnson, Whittington B. "Free African-American Women in Savannah, 1800–1860." *Georgia Historical Quarterly* 76 (summer 1992): 260–83.

———. "The Amelioration Acts in the Bahamas, 1823–1833: A Middle Ground between Freedom and Antebellum Slave Codes." *Journal of the Bahamas Historical Society* 18 (October 1996): 21–32.

Jordan, Winthrop D. "American Chiaroscuro:The Status and Definition of Mulattoes in the British Colonies." *William and Mary Quarterly,* 3rd ser., 19 (April 1962): 183–200.

Klein, Herbert, and Stanley L. Engerman. "Fertility Differentials between Slaves in the United States and the British West Indies: A Note on Lactation Practices and Their Possible Implications." *William and Mary Quarterly,* 3rd ser., 35 (1978): 356–74.

Kruger, Patricia E. Interview. Charleston, South Carolina, May 21, 1997.

Norton, Mary Beth. "The Fate of Some Black Loyalists of the American Revolution." *Journal of Negro History* 58 (October 1973) : 402–26.

Peters, Thelma. "The Loyalists Migration from East Florida to the Bahama Islands." *Florida Historical Quarterly* 40 (October 1961): 123–41.

———. "The American Loyalists in the Bahama Islands: Who They Were." *Florida Historical Quarterly* 40 (January 1962): 226–40.

Saunders, D. Gail. "The Slave Population of the Bahamas, 1783–1834." Masters thesis, University of the West Indies, Nassau Branch, 1978.

———. "Life in New Providence in the Early Nineteenth Century." *Journal of the Bahamas Historical Society* 11 (October 1989): 16–21.

Siebert, Wilbert H. "The Legacy of the American Revolution to the British West Indies and Bahamas." *Ohio State University Bulletin* 17 (April 1913): 3–50.

Stuart, Frank C. "A Critical Edition of the Correspondence of Sir Thomas Fowell Buxton, Bart., with an Account of His Career to 1823." Part 2, "The Buxton Correspondence." Masters thesis, University of London, 1957.

U.S. Bureau of the Census, *Preliminary Report of the Eighth Census of the United States, 1860.* Washington, D.C., 1862.

Wesley, Charles H. "The Emancipation of the Free Coloured Population in the British Empire." *Journal of Negro History* 19 (April 1934): 137–70.

Wilkie, Laurie A. "Continuities in African Naming Practices among Slaves of Wade's Green Plantation, North Caico." *Journal of the Bahamas Historical Society* 15 (October 1993): 32–37.

Wisdom, Keith Gordon. "Bahamian Junkanoo: An Act in Modern Social Drama." Ph.D. diss., University of Georgia, 1985.

Wood, David E. "The Attainment of Civil Rights and Liberties by Free Persons of Colour in the Bahamas during the 19th Century." *Journal of the Bahamas Historical Society* 8 (October 1986): 19–21.

———. "The Free People of Colour in Bahamian Society." *Journal of the Bahamas Historical Society* 12 (October 1990): 20–24.

Wright, James M. "History of the Bahama Islands, with a Special Study of the Abolition of Slavery in the Colony." In *The Bahama Islands,* edited by George Burbank. Baltimore: The Johns Hopkins University Press, 1905.

Index